P9-APK-175

An Investigator Book

Our Troubled Schools

Investigator Books
Advisory Editor S. Encel

Economic Policy in Australia
Bruce McFarlane

Our Troubled Schools
John McLaren

Laws and Men
K. E. Enderby

John McLaren

Our Troubled Schools

F. W. Cheshire Melbourne Canberra Sydney

Library of Congress Catalog
Card Number 68-23235
National Library of Australia
Registry Number Aus 68-458

First published 1968
Printed in Australia for
F. W. Cheshire Publishing Pty Ltd
380 Bourke Street, Melbourne
Garema Place, Canberra
142 Victoria Road, Marrickville, NSW
by Wilke & Co. Ltd.
Registered in Australia
for transmission by post as a book

To my wife

Contents

Preface

The idea of a crisis in education has become a part of the mythology of our time, to such an extent that we are in danger of forgetting that a crisis is a turning point or a moment of dramatic resolution, whereas the situation in our schools can only be one of continuing change and difficulty. The problems our children face will not be solved by bricks and mortar alone, for they represent a central aspect of the problem of our time. This problem includes the expansion of knowledge and of population, an increase in human expectations and an increase in human misery. Education is both a victim of these problems and a means by which we may make some progress towards solving them. It is in this conviction that this book is written. However, in emphasizing that the problem is intellectual and moral rather than material, I do not wish to appear to be giving substance to the platitudes of politicians who wish to disclaim all responsibility for providing the conditions within which education can take place. An education to meet the needs of the modern world will be an expensive one, but I believe we will have a greater chance of obtaining the material pre-requisites for such an education as more people come to understand the dimensions of the problem.

I have not attempted here to present an academic or scholarly thesis. Education impinges on and arises from the whole of life, and only a renaissance polymath could hope to have the expertize in sufficient fields to attempt to cover the whole subject authoritatively. However, I hope that there is value in putting forth ideas even in fields to which I can lay no claims or expertize, and I trust that those who have the specialist knowledge will find some of these ideas provocative, if only of criticism, and will be helped to an understanding of other fields from the other parts of the book.

The only authority which I claim for these pages is that they are the fruit of a number of years of experience, broadened by reading, discussion and thought. The list of further reading at the back is in no way a list of sources, but merely an indication of books and articles which I happen to be acquainted with, and which provide evidence, discussion or analysis relevant to some of my themes.

Every man is a product of his environment, both as he assimilates it and as he rejects it. Accordingly, I would like to pay tribute to some of those people who share the responsibility, although not the blame, for the development of the ideas in these pages. Dr Stephen Murray-Smith has consistently guided, prompted and urged me into expressing my ideas. Professor Sol Encel, the editor of this series, has given invaluable advice and recommendations. My publishers have shown incredible patience. Mr D. R. Driscoll and Mr G. R. Allinson, of the Secondary Teachers' College, Melbourne, gave me valuable assistance by reading parts of the manuscript and discussing it with me.

Finally, and more generally, I wish to express my thanks to my parents, for their vision and understanding, to my wife, for her wisdom, and to those of my colleagues through the years who, by their practice, have made real the meaning and possibility of education.

J. McL.
Melbourne, 1968

1 Aims and Origins

Australia does not have a system of education. It merely has a number of systems of schools. Yet, although they cannot be said to constitute any single school system, there is a depressing uniformity of outlook and methods within these schools. This uniformity is a product of neglect rather than of intent, for the systems are based on administrative, not educational, convenience. The sad truth behind all the official statements is that the education a child receives from the day he steps into an Australian classroom is the product, not of any system designed with his needs and personality in mind, but of the chance contacts he makes with sympathetic teachers and with appropriate materials at times when he needs them.

Many people would argue that this haphazard quality is a necessary characteristic of any form of universal education, but the most superficial glance at other countries will show that this is not so. Rightly or wrongly, American schools have been deliberately planned to produce loyal citizens for a democracy. The faults of their system seem to rest more on their conception of democratic citizenship than on any failure to plan a rational system for attaining their ends; and these faults should not be allowed to blind us to the magnitude of the achievement of American schools in helping to create a homogeneous society from so many diverse strands.

In Sweden, a different conception of democracy has led to a system of schooling which recognizes both universal rights and different abilities, and seeks to accommodate both. The American system tends to pay attention to individual differences among the pupils only to the extent that it allows different children to take different courses towards a common goal of conformity, ironically termed 'socialization' by the psychologists. But Swedish schools are designed to allow the individual to develop his peculiar abilities in a common atmosphere.

In France and Germany the most prized quality is intelligence, and consequently their schools are ruthlessly organized to promote the competitive development of individual academic talents. There is a similar emphasis in English schools, but here the ideal of excellence tends to be confused with that of the scholarly gentleman, and so games and social accomplishments are allowed their place in the school curriculum.

Now, it cannot be said that any of these countries achieves its ideal, nor even that these ideals remain static. America, in particular, is asserting the importance of new aims, and its schools are being changed to accommodate them. But the fact is that in each of these countries a relatively clear aim has shaped, and is continuing to shape, its educational system, whereas in Australia we have a form of organization which is merely the product of historical circumstances, which lacks any commonly agreed ideals, and which in consequence lacks any clear standard of judgement apart from the ubiquitous external examinations.

However, just as the professed aims of English schools have been modified by the inherent values of a strongly class-conscious community, so the practice of Australian schools has been heavily influenced by the values of a society which likes to imagine that it is egalitarian. But the conscious values of this society have largely been moulded by the proletariat, whereas teachers are strongly attracted to the middle classes. The result is that, although our schools are a product of our society, they are not firmly rooted in any part of it. Such orientation as they do possess is towards examination success, a goal readily valued by teachers who are themselves striving upward in society, and whose own progress is so much dependent on how well they themselves succeed in promotion examinations. Moreover, public examinations yield tangible rewards in the form of marketable qualifications, while their competitive form is itself a tribute to the urban zeal to outdo one's neighbours. On the other hand, earlier Australian traditions leave their mark on the schools in a distrust of individual excellence, except in the approved form of piling up marks, an aversion towards heterodox behaviour, and a disliking for any intellectual enthusiasm. Finally, this depressing jelly of philistinism is set in its mould by moral overtones of loyalty to queen and country, worship of the flag, and reverence for the pioneers, the diggers and the sportsmen.

That these conditions continue is only partly a consequence of financial stringency, large classes, rigid departmental control over teachers and lack of proper teacher-training. These conditions themselves are only symptoms of our society's lack of interest in education, which stems both from its practical and hard-working past and from its affluent present. The lack of clear goals has been a characteristic of Australian education since the collapse of the great sectarian debates of the last century. It may be that the renewal of this debate in recent years will lead to a similar renewal of interest in the purpose of our schools, and perhaps ultimately to a resolve to direct our school system towards the realization of ends which have importance in contemporary society.

The earliest schools established in Australia had a clearly moral aim. They were intended to cultivate the principles of good religion, industry, and thrift, and so turn the wastrel children of convicts into sober and reliable citizens. It seems that reading and writing were prized more for their disciplinary value than for any intellectual advantage they might confer on their students. Certainly, the early governors who patted the heads of orphans and bestowed prizes on the diligent had no intention of educating a proletariat to share in the government of the country.

On the other hand, the prosperous citizenry had every intention that their offspring should play the full part for which nature had so obviously destined them, and consequently the early secondary schools were intended to instil the principles of gentlemanly behaviour and prepare their scholars to occupy positions of leadership in society. Then, as now, the affluent were fully prepared to pay for these privileges, although this did not inhibit their demands for state aid, but nevertheless practically all these early foundations eventually foundered on the rock of economic circumstance.

It was against this background that the bases of our present systems of education were laid down. Successive governors and governments wrestled with intransigent clergymen while the bulk of the population laboured under every conceivable disadvantage in obtaining any sort of education for their children. Rival schools' boards competed for funds, while the parents took advantage of whatever facility was available. There was little significant difference between either the denominational composition or the religious instruction of secular and of spiritual institutions, and both shared a similarly low quality of schoolmaster. The typical occupant of this post was either a person who had failed in all else, or one who was merely waiting to find a more congenial and profitable position. It was in this period that Australian attitudes to both education and educationists were formed.

Inevitably the sole practicable aim of educational administration in these circumstances was efficiency. Such early officials as Rusden and Wilkins, lacking both adequate funds and suitable teachers, could only endeavour to establish as many schools as possible and to see that minimum standards were observed in them. They had at hand as an instrument the monitorial systems of Bell and Lancaster, which were equally applicable to educational and to penal institutions. By combining this device with centralized authority and rigidly pre-determined standards these early educationists were able eventually to provide minimum standards of education in at least the settled and relatively prosperous areas. When eventually the dual system collapsed under its own manifest inefficiency, it left as its legacy this stern deference to outside standards and to superior authority which has cursed Australian schools ever since.

At first the main concern of the state was to provide the elements of reading, writing and counting to the lower orders. Naturally, instruction in these skills was to be combined with the same kind of moral exhortation and example which had been hoped for from the earlier schools, but by the end of the nineteenth century a wider definition of morality was accepted by our civic fathers. They did, of course, hold firmly to such doctrines as the sanctity of the sabbath and the evil of strong drink, but they were also belated children of the enlightenment in their belief in the wholesome value of learning for its own sake and as a useful vehicle on the road of economic advancement. The advantages of learning were believed to be so obvious that once a man was given the elements it was felt that he could well be trusted to his own efforts to complete the task. Those who did not persevere were self-evident failures, not to be heeded in that best of all possible worlds which was being built in the Antipodes. As well as the period which saw the spread of universal elementary education, this was the great age of self-education, the age of mechanics' institutes and of the first technical colleges.

Meanwhile, the bourgeois were not prepared to allow nature to complete unaided the education of their own offspring. While the colonial governments were establishing primary schools, the churches, particularly in the gold colony of Victoria, were busily founding and strengthening the colleges and grammar schools which were to ensure their students' welfare in this world and the next. Although from necessity most of these institutions were forced to rely on day pupils for most of their support, they were modelled as closely as a raw new society would allow on the pattern established by Dr Arnold at Rugby. It is both the pride and the folly of these 'Public Schools' that they have departed little from that model to this day.

The essential purpose of the independent or church school, now as then, is to train Christian gentlemen to act as leaders to the rest of the community. It is no fault of the schools themselves if these aims are often distorted by parents who regard social prestige and material advantages as the most important signs of such leadership, or if many of their ex-students show a greater concern for exacting Christian duties from others than for performing Christian service themselves. The guest list of any charity ball will reveal the zeal with which the public school set renders its annual mite to the deserving, a zeal which easily excuses some absence of mind concerning the suggestion that charity be not a matter for public display. Similarly, a stroll down the old-school-tie end of Melbourne's Collins Street, Sydney's Macquarie Place or Adelaide's North Terrace will show the success with which these people obtain positions of responsibility and leadership.

The aims of the independent schools are not achieved so much through overt teaching as through pervasive atmosphere. In externals, certainly, they have moved far from the standards of Thomas Arnold, while at the same time their natural conservatism has preserved many of the better features of nineteenth-century England which elsewhere have been swept aside in the tide of progress. The parent who would have his child educated in the classics has little option but send him to one of the independent schools, while his neighbour, who sets a greater stock on science and mathematics, can be similarly secure in choosing the same institution. For the flexibility conferred by wealth and prestige has enabled these schools to march with the van of curricular innovation while still fighting successfully in the rearguard of tradition. They have the oldest honour-boards and the newest science laboratories, the biggest libraries and the widest playing fields. Now they have pulled off the greatest coup of all, for they have obtained the state finance which the nineteenth century denominationalists demanded without at the same time ceding the independence which the secularists of the old debates had demanded should be surrenderd.

Yet beneath their varied and progressive surface, the independent schools remain depressingly uniform and conformist. Their independence is a quality which they prize most highly, more highly in some cases than their church connection, yet they have done remarkably little with this independence. Certainly, they have a far broader curriculum and a much wider range of extra-curricular activities than most state schools can afford, but we find in them no experiments with true collegiate control, with tertiary or adult education, or with community integration. Their experiments have so far been confined to such matters as teaching Asian languages or operating rural appendages. Only two major schools, Friends' School in Hobart, and Mt. Scopus College, in Melbourne, have so far taken the revolutionary step of becoming co-educational, while the one which tried to escape from the strait-jacket of traditional classroom teaching and control, Melbourne Church of England Girls' Grammar School, reverted to form upon the change of head mistresses.

Proud, aloof and privileged, the independent schools remain a series of communities for the status-seekers rather than a part of the overall system of education. In Sydney, where they have admitted the senior high school to their ranks, they have conferred upon themselves the title of 'Greater'; in Melbourne, they have not deigned to enter into any form of formal association with the state schools. For the landed aristocracy, Geelong Grammar, which has never claimed academic distinction, and King's School, Sydney, remain the ultimate, with Oxford or Cambridge a more fitting locale for tertiary education than one of Australia's provincial redbricks. Victoria's Scotch College and Melbourne Boys' Grammar are the meccas for the commercial and professional elite, while St Peter's in Adelaide confers the special accolade of the South Australian establishment.

The very uniform of a big independent school is itself a status symbol in an affluent society, and the buildings and surroundings within which the student moves add to his sense of belonging to a select band of brothers. The best of the masters are selected for their excellence from the cream of state-school teachers, while the worst, who would be unlikely to get a job elsewhere, are of no importance, for they are not entrusted with the education of those students with any ability. At the head of the hierarchy the principal combines the attributes of European god-professor, English milord and American tycoon, while somewhere on the fringes a chaplain operates the spiritual dispensary which, like the best metropolitan hotels, combines the most elegant of traditions with the slickest of service.

It is loyalty to this community which is the secret of the independent school's success. The mystique of the sportsfield, the fanaticism of school and house spirit, the camaraderie of tuckshop or dormitory, the indiscipline of the classroom—all foster the spirit of corporate identity which enshrines the school's ultimate values. It is this loyalty, extended upwards, which draws the public-school boys to the call of the flag and the mess in time of war, the board-room and the club in easier days. This loyalty can be relied on to open cheque-books during building appeals and office-doors whenever an old school mate is in need of a job, always provided he has not let down the side by having unworthy thoughts, criminal convictions or unkempt clothes. The same noisy loyalty can be heard at football matches and boatraces, at summer beach resorts and in winter ski lodges, in cosy night clubs and opulent passenger-liner lounges. It is the price paid for the best of educations, and the fact that its dominant characteristic is perpetual adolescence is no disadvantage in a country whose leaders show no dissatisfaction with that period of life.

This is not to say that the independent school succeeds in turning all its products into the same mould. The academic advantages of an independent school are so obvious, particularly in a time of depression in the state schools, that many able students are attracted to them for purely educational reasons. Some of these succumb to the virus, but many react violently against it, some joining the

Communist or Labor parties, others withdrawing into academic isolation, and some even becoming long-haired stage satirists. These rebels draw the greatest of advantages from their public school background, for they have the ultimate satisfaction of kicking the beast while knowing they are part of it, and are thus able to maintain a comfortable sense of superiority to the rest of the community.

Yet the mysticism of school spirit is not confined to the independent schools. The earliest state secondary schools had to struggle for acceptance, both in the eyes of the public who believed they were charity schools for the second rate, and in the eyes of the 'Public School' headmasters who feared that state high schools represented the first nail in the coffin of the independent school. Amid this general suspicion, the quickest path to success was to ape the externals of the 'Public Schools', and so they adopted the full insignia of uniform, prefects, house competitions, school songs, cadet corps and the rest. Such was their success that today Sydney Boys' High School is a member of the Greater Public Schools Association, and Melbourne Boys' and University High Schools are considered, in the colder Victorian climate, to be nearly as good as the Associated Public Schools of that state.

Officially, Victoria has no selective schools, and so the two major high schools allegedly take all comers. In fact, they draw from a number of central schools in select areas, and from outside these areas those students who wish to take subjects not provided in their local schools and those students whose parents attended the school. Land values alter as the Education Department changes the boundaries which determine residential qualification, and the demand for admission on other grounds is so great that the schools can afford to pick and choose.

These schools have been able to establish the same element of continuity which characterizes the 'Public Schools'. Staff are in many cases willing to forgo opportunities of promotion in order to remain at the school of their choice, and thriving ex-students' associations maintain the link with the traditions of the past. The prestige of the schools is great enough to attract some of the best departmental teachers. However, the Victorian schools have still not been able to establish complete equality with the 'Public Schools', who have a more liberal staffing schedule, better equipment and grounds, and a generally broader outlook. The examination complex is even stronger in the High Schools, and they obtain great success in pushing large numbers through at pass level, but the 'Public Schools' still manage to carry off the greatest number of top honours and exhibitions with depressing regularity. Nevertheless, these schools, with their constant emphasis on their own virtues, do give their students the same kind of confidence arising from a certainty of their own superiority which characterizes the products of the 'Public Schools'. So the student whose parents can afford 'Public School' education looks down on those who go only to the smaller independent schools, and these look down on the better high schools, whose students look down on those attending ordinary high schools, who in turn look down on the unfortunates attending poorer high schools in beaten-up or run-down areas, who are still able to scorn those at the very bottom of the ladder, the junior technical school students, who attend an institution which has either been abandoned or is being abandoned in every state except Victoria.

Yet the fact is that a school does need confidence in itself if it is to succeed as an institution. There is nothing more depressing than teaching in a school which is regarded by many parents as merely a preparatory school for another institution. Victoria's junior technical schools are depressed not because their staff or equipment is inferior or their courses less demanding, but because they have a reputation as a dumping ground for the social and intellectual rubbish. On the other hand, the 'Public Schools' and the older high schools do give their students a code of behavior, however inadequate, to match the self-confidence which is their other major gift.

If Australia were starting to build an education system from the beginning, there is no doubt that it would be better to avoid the evils of both the academic-technical and the state-independent divisions. However, these schools have now served the community well for many years, and it would be of little service to anybody to scrap them overnight. There is a degree of truth in the doctrine that loyalty to mankind as a whole, or even to a particular society of mankind, is too abstract a concept to be readily understood, and that the individual can only develop social responsibility through loyalty to a steadily widening succession of small, familiar institutions. So his loyalty grows from family to neighbourhood to school to profession or institution to political party to nation to mankind. Beyond the school, there may be a number of different chains leading to the same end, but if one of the earlier links is broken the ultimate development of a man's proper relationships to his society is jeopardized. However faulty they may be, the schools with established traditions do help their students to find this bridge to society, and to eliminate them from our educational system would be to deny to the community a number of separate elements of commitment and competences which at present enrich its variety.

The fault of these schools is not that they have a tradition, but that the tradition can become exclusive and introverted, so that instead of leading students into society it herds them into self-contained little groups which remain separate within society. One reason for this may well be the very continuity which these schools have maintained. Headmasters, housemasters, staff stay so long that the school becomes an end in itself, and they fail to see beyond it to the larger community of which it should be a part. If one of the most pressing needs of the state schools is a greater continuity of staff, there is an equally urgent need in the independent schools for a freer exchange of staff, not only among themselves, but with the state system as well. While teachers should be able to stay in a position long enough to complete a job, they should never be allowed to stay until the job has taken them over. It is unfortunate that in many cases the people who do so stay on are those who use the school to cover their own personality defects, and who consequently cannot contemplate facing the outside world, and thus play their part in preventing their schools fulfilling their bridge functions. On the other hand, the teachers who remain for years in the one school while still maintaining a whole variety of outside activities bring a strength and stability which rests on the very fact that they are themselves complete members of the community in which the school is located, and so they help to multiply the links between the school and society.

If the staff of a school is turned out to the community, then the students will tend to look outwards for their own commitment. Such a tendency may weaken old boys' clubs, but as such bodies usually represent the most conservative element in a school's life this would be no bad thing. Those adults who still need to look back to their schooldays for their justification and confidence are no good advertisement for the school's educational success, and it would be better off without them. A more serious consequence of persuading the staff to get away from the school and into the community would be to weaken the traditional strength of the independent schools in games and other activities outside the normal class routine. At present, a teacher employed in an independent school is expected to be freely available after school and at weekends. One headmaster has said that his reason for providing comfortable staff rooms is to discourage his staff from seeking the consolation of their families too early. This attitude gives the school organizational strength, but only at the cost of divorcing the school from the wider society and of stunting the personal growth of its staff.

This attitude points to the further weakness of the 'Public Schools', that because they belong to no community themselves they must try to be all things to all their men. Their students are drawn from the whole metropolitan area and beyond, and thus there is a definite division between home and neighbourhood on the one hand and school on the other. This has led to trouble even within the churches which nourish the independent schools, for a conflict arises between a student's parish duties and the school's religious obligations. The temptation is for the school chapel to become his parish church, but such a development is strongly resisted by the local clergy. On the other hand, as his life is necessarily centred at the school, his parish connections become tenuous and its religious services meaningless. It may be that in this conflict lies the explanation of the failure of the 'Public Schools' to fulfil the religious expectations of their founders.

Similarly, the school attempts to provide its students with complete facilities for sports, drama, music, clubs and social activities. But the very richness of the school life in these respects takes students and staff away from their own communities and nourishes that restricted loyalty which is their greatest curse. On the other hand, the notorious poverty of many state secondary schools in extra-curricular activities can be an indication of their success in integrating their life with that of their local community. It may be better for the students to play football for the local club, and for the staff to support the local drama society, provided that the school is encouraged to get behind these activities, than for it to try to conduct its own activities in emulation. It is in this respect that a free interchange of staff between state and private institutions could have its greatest benefits. On the one hand, the private school teachers could bring to the state schools their dedication to the wider aspects of school life. On the other, the state school teachers could give to the independent schools a stake in the community at large, instead of in one narrow segment of it.

If one of the by-products of a less exclusive concern with the interests of a particular school was a less obsessive worship of sport, this would be an incidental dividend of no mean worth. On the other hand, it may well be that a greater degree of attention to sporting activities would be the first step towards giving some of our poorer state schools that self-esteem which is a necessary pre-requisite of any educational success. The trouble with sport in the 'Public Schools' is that it has been allowed to develop so far beyond this original function that it can usurp the attention which should be given to more important matters.

However, whatever we may do to lessen the difference of esteem between state and 'Public' schools, their present existence faces many parents with an intolerable dilemma. They may not believe in the principle of being able to buy a superior education, but by sending their child to a state school, they condemn him willy-nilly to at least the possibility of an inferior education, and the certainty of a narrower range of choice, thus leaving the advantages of independent education to those who least merit them because they most believe in them. On the other hand, should they decide to pay the fees for an independent school they are not only risking their child becoming tarred with the worst of brushes, but are also helping to perpetuate a pernicious system.

For there can be no doubt that the existence of dual system of education acts to the disadvantage of the state schools. If on the one hand, the two systems were in genuine competition to provide the same services, like our two state-supported airways, or if, on the other, the two systems were designed to offer alternative forms of education, the existence of each would act as a stimulus to the other. If Catholic schools were to be maintained by the state they might just possibly have this effect. However, the position at the moment among non-Catholics is that those who are able to pay for an independent school education do so, and the rest take pot luck with what the state provides. Since most members of the political Establishment are able to afford to pay for education for their children and grandchildren, even if they have not been given an independent schooling themselves, there is naturally no great anxiety to improve the standard of state schools. Moreover, those members of the Establishment who have enjoyed 'Public School' education are inclined to attribute their success to superior talents rather than to superior advantages, and are consequently disinclined to admit that the state schools are in any way inferior. The inferiority of their products is just another indication of the inherent disabilities of the lower classes.

The material advantages of the independent schools, together with the wilful blindness of most authorities to this fact, leads to some amusing consequences. On the one hand, we have the spectacle of high school headmasters leaping at the chance to be associated with public school principals in disclaiming any difference of standard between the two types of institution. On the other, we have 'Public School' principals proclaiming the theory that any encroachment on their independence would rob their schools of all their best qualities—qualities which, by definition, cannot be enjoyed by state schools. Again, we have the spectacle of the public schools denying that they skim the cream from the high schools, or that they are seats of privilege, at the same time that they advertize scholarship examinations which will enable children privileged in ability to join those privileged in wealth or their choice of parents. But the proof of the pudding is in the eating. In Victoria, where the dual system has reached its most absurd development, only Melbourne High School can compare with the public schools in the number of Commonwealth secondary and tertiary scholarships, and the number of matriculation honours and exhibitions, gained by its students each year.

The independent school system, then, has developed as an institution for maintaining the privileges and recruiting to the numbers of the more affluent professional, managerial and rural classes. Barristers, medical specialists, diplomats and business directors, particularly in Victoria, come disproportionately from the 'Public Schools', and almost without exception send their children to them. The people who buy this education are accustomed to insisting on value for money, and they ensure that the schools they support provide it. The value is measured in terms of university places gained, social ease and business connections. In fulfilling these objectives, the schools have largely subordinated their ostensible religious aims until they have become merely a kind of genuflection in the direction of well-bred decency, a code in which loyalty to the sovereign rates well ahead of any unbecoming concern with the ways of the Almighty.

The 'Public School' system does not, however, flourish with equal vitality in every state. Although the atmosphere of the Greater Public Schools in Sydney is every bit as dignified and stuffy as that of the Associated Public Schools of Melbourne, they do not in fact enjoy the same social prestige as their southern counterparts. Many leading New South Wales businessmen and politicians, including Liberal Party leaders, have not only come from state high schools themselves, but are content to send their children to the same institutions. On the contrary, in Victoria even successful Labor politicians send their children to Associated Public Schools, and those few Liberals who did not enjoy this advantage themselves are quite determined that their children will. Yet a great deal of the fault for this can be put on the state school system itself, which, as we have seen, has preferred to ape its independent rivals rather than exploit its own peculiar advantages and opportunities. Unfortunately, the explanation of this phenomenon is probably that the community which, directly or indirectly, pays for education likes the kind of education which is provided in the 'Public Schools'. What is more, this education does, at its best, produce just those qualities of conscientious leadership which the community needs. Until the state schools can demonstrate their ability to develop similar qualities of confidence and dedication among their students, without merely copying the most obvious features of the 'Public Schools', they will remain second-rate copies dedicated mainly to promoting upward social mobility by means of examination success.

The state school system has, of course, been forced to widen its function from its original conception of providing universal elementary literacy. The first impetus towards this extension in scope was given by the need to provide teachers for the increasing number of state schools. Parliaments, which could not see that secondary education for the masses was any concern of theirs, were forced by circumstances to provide post-primary education for potential teachers. At first this was done through the pupil-teacher system, then at teachers' colleges, and then by providing continuation schools to bridge the gap between school and college. Eventually these last became fully-fledged high schools, and the states were committed to secondary education.

The legacies of this haphazard growth are still with us. As secondary education was originally conceived as a preparatory course for higher education, it acquired no rationale of its own. It was governed by the requirements of public examinations, and as these were ultimately determined by the qualifications demanded for university entrance, the universities obtained an undue influence over a field of education which was not properly theirs. Only in New South Wales was any effective barrier erected against this encroachment of authority. In all states, however, secondary education had to be fitted into an administrative mould which had been designed for the needs of primary schooling. Secondary schooling has been provided at various times and places in classes tacked on to primary schools, in junior high schools, in selective and special purpose schools, and in comprehensive high schools. In some states co-education has been normal, in others schools are still segregated. Decisions on these matters have been taken not for reasons of principle but because of administrative convenience or prejudice.

Only since the second world war has secondary education for all been recognized as a legitimate demand, and the material problems of providing sufficient facilities have prevented much attention being given to formulating a philosophy for such an education. As yet there is not even general agreement on its proper duration or most suitable entrance level. No state has given any attention to the proposition that the whole concept of primary and secondary education may be outdated, and that three stages of four years each may in fact be the best way of organizing universal education.

Until the nineteen-forties state secondary schools, and most Catholic secondary schools, served mainly as recruiting grounds for the lower levels of the administrative and professional classes, particularly banking, teaching and the public service. The other pupils left school at fourteen, having achieved in most cases a certificate which indicated a high degree of general knowledge and a low standard of education. This was a sufficient pre-requisite for most trades and clerical occupations. Today, most students stay until the age of fifteen or sixteen, and most salaried occupations require a fourth-year certificate which denotes a low standard of education and is irrelevant as an indicator of technical skill or knowledge.

A major reason for the expanding proportion of students seeking secondary education in the last twenty years has been snobbery. White collar employers, such as banks and insurance companies, want to increase the prestige of the jobs they offer, so they raise the standard of the qualifications they demand. Similarly, the various fringe professions wish to improve their status, so they raise their entrance standards. At the same time, better wages and security of employment enable parents to keep their children longer at school and give them a better chance than they ever had, by which they mean getting a higher certificate than they ever had.

On the receiving end, teachers and administrators stand amazed.

At first they anxiously assured each other that the crisis was temporary and occupied themselves shoring up the worst gaps in their defences. Now that they have realized that this is no flash flood but a permanent change in the climate, much of their energy is dissipated in mutual recriminations as teachers gloomily predict that the only time worse than the present is the imminent future, and the administrators reply by pointing to the flood itself as evidence that things have never been so good. So far, the administrators, acting as both judge and advocate, have had the best of the argument; the teachers have had the worst of the job, and the students the worst of the deal.

The reaction of teachers to the crisis has been to fall back on the defence line of examination standards. As more students crowd into the starting stalls, and as less and less able, trained or experienced teachers are available for their early secondary years, the battle of the standards wages fiercer and hotter.

On the one hand, there are those who claim that there is no reason to assume that students today are in any way different in ability from their predecessors. If they come from different backgrounds and display different interests, we must respect these qualities and adapt our standards accordingly. Teaching is of students, not subjects, and anyone who works diligently and displays reasonable ability should be granted a pass. If we need to develop some particular skill for vocational purposes, this can be done later, in the employer's time and preferably at his expense, but the job of the school is education, not training. Examinations are suspect, anyway, as a measure of ability, so the only reliable standard is the students themselves.

On the other hand stand the traditionalists, who maintain the absolute purity and eternal sanctity of subject standards. Teachers, they believe, are too closely involved with their students, too human, too soft intellectually to assess their students. Standards are measured by formal examinations in which the student is required to demonstrate unambiguously his command of factual knowledge and technical skill. The ideal examination is set and marked externally, for this prevents irrelevant factors of personality or prejudice intruding. Moreover, the external examination gives the teacher a standard by which to measure his own performance, and so prevents that creeping intellectual flabbiness which can overtake the most conscientious teacher when he is isolated from contact with his peers and his subject by the more immediate demands of the classroom and its correction. Finally, such an examination gives the employer and the community at large an accurate and worthwhile guide to the performance and abilities of any individual in whom they may be interested.

Unfortunately, few adherents of this philosophy are prepared to follow it to its logical conclusion, which is to abandon teaching altogether so that such chance factors as the ability of the instructor will not interfere with the reliability of the assessment. Instead, they tend to prune the syllabus of all such extraneous elements as might promote interest in or understanding of the subject and concentrate instead on those parts of the course which are most easily examinable. For while the greatest fool may be able to ask a question which the wisest man is unable to answer, the cleverest examiner has yet to devise a question which the dullest crammer cannot prepare for. The syllabuses devised for such examinations form a bleak mass of fact and technique, often quite irrelevant to any real understanding of the subject. Many private coaches have grown fat on the profits of such unappetising intellectual diets.

Within the state schools, the usual result of this conflict has been a dull sort of compromise. Most teachers attempt to devise a syllabus which will do justice to both their students and their subject, but the pressure of external examinations and a lack of confidence in themselves gradually distorts this syllabus to emphasize the examinable portions and atrophy the less tangible elements of the course. Students from quite a different background from those for whom these courses were originally devised, and far worse taught in their preparatory years, could, in the hands of the most capable teachers, both enjoy the subject and acquire an apparent understanding of it. But the exigencies of the timetable and of the school organization force them to tread an identical path to all their fellows, and the size of the classes prevents them from receiving more than a minimum of personal attention, so that the appearance rarely corresponds to any reality. They pass examinations which are as difficult as any their predecessors were required to attempt, but whether the passing can today be said to indicate anything about the student is doubtful. The gap between the students and the school is too great to be crossed by anything more than the paper bridge of examination certificates.

The one state which has made a determined attempt to devise a philosophy and a course of studies to meet the new situation is New South Wales. The scheme is based on the report of a committee led by the Director-General, Dr H. S. Wyndham, who has provided the inspiration needed to carry out his ideas in the face of suspicion and hostility from many teachers and parents. The idea is the quite simple one that each child should be able to study those subjects in which he is most interested at a standard which will suit his own ability. This does not mean that the less able students should follow a watered-down course. Dr Wyndham likes to quote the example of the surgeon whose hobby is home carpentry, a subject to which he is probably unable to give any time from his early years in secondary school until many years after he has completed his university and hospital training. This situation would be changed under the new scheme, for each student would be given time, apart from that which is needed for his major academic studies, to follow up a general or cultural interest, not for examination purposes, but purely for the satisfaction afforded by the subject itself.

To give this principle practical effect, New South Wales high schools will offer each subject at three levels for each year of the secondary course. The advanced level will be followed by those students with particular aptitude in a certain direction, the ordinary level by the average student, and the lowest level by those with less time or ability for a particular field. As well as offering a range of levels for each subject, the schools will offer their students a wide choice of courses, so that each student can, in theory, pursue a course individually tailored to his actual needs. In a pilot study made before the introduction of the new scheme, some schools were able to offer as many as two hundred different courses. All of these courses are, however, built about a common core of basic studies, including English, with increasing specialization as the student moves up through the school.

This scheme is in contrast to the traditional method of coping with differences in ability by providing separate streams in which all subjects would be taught at different levels. Those students in the A-stream would study mathematics, perhaps two languages, history, geography, science and any general subjects which could be fitted into their time-table. On the other hand, the students in the C-stream would study no languages, but take far more practical subjects, such as woodwork and art. The assumption was that as they were no good with their brains they had to learn to use their hands. Meanwhile, they would be given no additional time to cope with such academic studies as they did pursue, and would at the end of the year either sit for, and fail at, a common examination with the A-stream, or be given a pass in their own special examination, which neither they nor their teachers for a moment imagined to be comparable in standard to that normally expected of their form.

New South Wales, in particular, took this system to an extreme with selective high schools for the most able students. There was much heart-burning among parents when these were eliminated, and dark mutterings about education for mediocrity. Certainly, there are great apparent advantages to be gained from separating the brightest pupils for special teaching, not least of all for their teachers who find their burden so much reduced. The company of their peers provides that element of competition needed to stimulate the better students to produce their best work, there is no tail to the class to hold back the progress of the brightest, the general ability of the class enables the course to be rich and rewarding. Furthermore, there should be a commensurate advantage for the duller pupils, who can be given work and taken at a pace suitable to their more limited abilities.

Yet the answer is not as simple in practice as it might appear in theory. For a start, it is quite impossible to grade human beings like sheep into bright, average and dull. Nor will a grading in one field correspond even approximately to that in another. Nor can we even be sure that gradings made on a test given at one time will correspond with those made as the result of a test given six months, one year, or four years later. If we do in fact grade our students on any one of these bases we limit the opportunities which will be open to them in the future. For the one thing we can be certain of in a streamed school is that we will teach the members of the lowest stream that they are in fact dull. Thus our prophecies ensure their own fulfilment.

Before we consider why this should be so, we must clearly distinguish between streamed classes and remedial teaching. In the former case, students are graded into separate streams according to some assessment of their ability. Each stream follows a course which differs both in standard and in content. In remedial teaching, however, smaller groups of students suffering from various handicaps, such as language difficulty, inadequate earlier education, or mental retardation, are placed in small classes where special teachers, preferably with specialist training, assist them to cope with their difficulties. They may spend their whole time in these classes, they may go to them at various times during the day, or they may attend the classes for short but intensive crash course to bring them up to normal standard in particular subjects.

In the streamed school all classes are taught by the general teaching staff. Many teachers dislike taking the slower streams, which they find less interesting and less stimulating. Others cannot be spared for them because they are required to concentrate on the higher examination forms. Still others, because of the nature of their subjects, are unavailable. Consequently, the slower streams are likely to have more than their share of incompetent, inexperienced, untrained or resentful teachers. Even one year of such teaching can be sufficient to retard a class so far that few of its members will ever again be able to cope with the work they are officially required to undertake.

The evidence that streaming retards the lower forms is indisputable. On the other hand, there is very little evidence that it assists the brighter students. The brighter student needs, like anyone else, not so much a form of his equals, as two or three others of similar interests and abilities with whom he can share his zeal.

This can be provided as well by grouping within the unstreamed class as by segregating him into a special stream. Furthermore, the variety of abilities, interests and experiences in the unstreamed class can offer a stimulating challenge to both teacher and students. The range of possible activities, and the number of opportunities for different individuals exercising leadership or displaying their talents is so much greater that it is possible to create an environment which will be a microcosm of the community and within which every individual can be encouraged to develop his own abilities to their maximum. In fact, in some recent experiments[1] schools are abandoning even the rigidity of the graded structure where every student enters at form one and progresses by yearly stages through to the top. Instead, the students are organized in small groups, each of which works at its own pace on work suited to its abilities.

In the New South Wales scheme, however, these advantages have yet to be realized. The first hindrance to the successful implementation of the Wyndham scheme was the speed of its initial introduction. For political reasons, the decision was made at the end of 1961 that it would commence in 1962. There was no time for the program of teacher training and preparation which is essential if any such revolutionary change is to be imposed on schools from above. There was not even time for syllabus committees to give adequate thought to the new course. One such committee devoted its first meeting to elucidating some of the basic assumptions of the course. At its second meeting the members of the committee were informed that they had just over a month to prepare the final syllabus. In this time there was only opportunity to divide the work among the members of the committee so that they could individually prepare rough drafts and bring them back to the third, and final, meeting to be gummed together as the final syllabus. Even so, the delays in getting the various courses of study into the schools, and the further delays in obtaining the necessary textbooks, led to a haphazard and

[1] Melbourne High School in Florida, U.S.A., is the best-known school to be organized on these principles. Maryvale High School, Victoria, is trying out similar ideas.

makeshift start from which the scheme has never entirely recovered.

The second hindrance to the scheme was the centralized and rigid framework within which its flexible provisions were expected to operate. It shared some of the disadvantages of streaming in that, once a student had embarked on a given level of study in a particular subject, there was little opportunity for him to shift to a higher level if his interests changed later. Consequently, teachers advised their better students to undertake all their academic studies at the highest level, thus recreating the old A-streams under the new system, together with all the old pressures and restrictions inherent in the older form of organization. Furthermore, the central control of courses and examinations inhibited the freedom of the individual teacher to devise courses based on local needs and interests.

The final, and perhaps most serious, blow to the scheme was the refusal of the major universities to accept its principles as a basis for their entrance requirements. Instead, they required students to take at least three subjects at advanced level to be considred for admission. This flung the emphasis back onto high-pressure formal studies from the earliest level, and highlighted a major unresolved conflict in the aims of secondary education. For although only about 12 per cent of students who enter the lowest form of a secondary school will eventually seek university entrance,[2] their needs tend to dominate the whole school course.

It is impossible to decide at form-one who will eventually prove capable of proceeding to a university, so it is necessary to leave all options open for as many students as possible. But universities base their entrance requirements on the assumption that students have completed a five or six year secondary course in their major studies, so that even the form-one course must be seen as the first rung up the ladder towards the academic heaven. If it does not serve as such, however well suited it may be to the requirements of form-one children, it must be eliminated. Thus the whole

[2] Martin Report, Vol. 1, p. 37. Predictions for 1975 suggest that one-sixth of a male student generation and one-twelfth of a female student generation, or 9 per cent of all 17-22 year olds, will be at a university.

student community is forced into a mould suited to about one-eighth of its members.

New South Wales has attempted to overcome this problem by instituting a barrier at the fourth year level. The first four years are regarded as years of general education, the last two as specific preparation for university entrance. However, entrance to these two years presupposes a certain standard, and studies at advanced level in the final years require studies at advanced level in the same fields during the earlier years, so the barrier is not entirely effective.

The problem of general education at the lower secondary levels has been with us for at least twenty years without apparently coming any closer to a solution. Now we are meeting the same problem in the senior forms as more students stay the full six years without any intention of proceeding to a university, or for that matter to any tertiary institution. Victoria has been particularly prolific with suggestions for some alternative certificate, course, or institution to meet the needs of such students, but no suggestion so far has avoided the implication that it is just a way of providing a second-rate substitute for the real thing.

The first step towards overcoming the problem would seem to be a recognition that secondary education is an integral part of the educational system, as entitled to scholarly esteem and academic independence as any other. Such recognition will have to be earned rather than granted, and will not come while teachers lean on others to preserve their standards, nor while there is no restriction on the qualifications of the people allowed to undertake the responsibility of teaching. However, once the teaching profession can obtain and accept the responsibility of conducting its own affairs, it will be well on the way to breaking the academic stranglehold. The next move will be to break the lock-step system of promotions by which every child moves up through the school a year at a time in every subject. It should be possible for some students to complete six years' work in four in their best subjects while covering, perhaps, only three years' work in others. Then, if their ambitions change at a later stage of their school career, they should be able to devote additional time to those subjects in which they have a leeway to make up. Thus, a student entering fifth-year with only, say, third year standard in physics could devote twice the time to this subject and finish at fifth year standard in all his science subjects. On the other hand, the student who passes six out of eight subjects in third year should not have to face the present alternatives of repeating the entire year, dropping the subjects he has failed in, or carrying them on at fourth-year level despite the fact that he knows he has not reached this standard. Instead, he should be able to proceed to fourth year in the subjects he has reached this standard in, and keep working at the others until he does reach the required standard. This need not, of course, take a full year.

Finally, the universities will have to be taught to make their entrance standards much more specific in terms of their needs rather than of assumed standards of competency. For example, a study at the Australian National University in Canberra has shown that, of a number of students who had passed university entrance standard English, almost one-third showed gross deficiencies in a test designed to reveal their capacity to deal with English at the standard required at a university.[3] It would seem that universities would be wise to define the standard and directions of ability they require of students entering their various courses, and then design tests of developed ability to select those students who meet these standards. Tests of this kind have already been designed for Commonwealth Secondary Scholarships, and can be administered regardless of the details of the course the students have followed, for they measure understanding rather than knowledge. That is, they test teaching and learning rather than cramming and memorization. Their use would enable universities to select by whatever criteria they found important without restricting the freedom of the schools to teach as they thought best.

However, such a system is far removed from the realities of Australian schools today. In the meantime, New South Wales' Wyndham scheme is the best we have. But we still have to consider one major objection to it. Its critics maintain that it is edu-

[3] W. S. Ramson and K. S. Inglis—'Remedial English at the Australian National University', *Vestes*, IX, 4 December 1966.

cation for adjustment rather than for excellence, by which they suggest that it is based on psychological rather than academic principles. If this were true it would not be surprising, for academics have not, generally speaking, concerned themselves with secondary or primary education until recent years, and the field has been left by default to the psychologists. According to this school of thought, the prime purpose of schooling is to foster the processes of maturation in order to achieve the ultimate objective of complete socialization, by which is understood total conformity to the normative mores of the community. Once we add the word democratic we have here a complete formula for state education, and one which, moreover, is so vague in its concepts that no critic can measure any perceptible failure of the system to meet its objectives. After all, it is of little importance that our teachers are themselves uneducated if they are teaching not subjects but children, not mathematics but cognitive realization, not English but group adjustment, not woodwork but manipulative facility.

It is not, however, fair to characterize the Wyndham scheme as a product of this mentality, which is not confined to any one state, and is more common in institutions of teacher-training than in either the classroom or the administrator's office. Certainly, the Wyndham committee was concerned, as is every competent teacher, with the physical and psychological needs of the students, and with facilitating their adjustment to the demands of adult life in their community. There is nothing new in such an idea, which merely enunciates what has been a central concern of education in all societies since long before there were any formal institutions for the young. What is new is the ignorant assumption by academics that they are above such matters, and by educationalists that subject matter is irrelevant. It is not proper to accuse Wyndham of either of these assumptions.

The assumption behind the Wyndham scheme is that each child will master as many subjects as he can at advanced level, and at the same time acquire some understanding of a number of others. It is better for him to explore one subject fully than to fail in an attempt to obtain a smattering of a large number. But it is still organized around subjects, and there is no reason to suppose that students at the top end of the academic range will not receive just as thorough and intensive an academic education as they received under any older scheme. There is a hope, if the universities allow it to survive, that such students will also leave their secondary schools with a wider range of knowledge than their predecessors, without any sacrifice of depth, and that at the same time some less able students may enjoy the experience of studying a small field in depth as a part of their general education. Certainly, no examination of the syllabuses prescribed for the two higher levels for matriculation purposes leaves any doubt that the highest standards of traditional academic study are being required. A more legitimate criticism would be that tradition is being emphasized to such an extent that any relevance to the present has been lost.

The traditional organization of courses into separate academic subjects is not, of course, sacrosanct. Most secondary schools prefer to divide their students' time into neat compartments for the separate subjects. In each of fields they are given a specialist teacher, who may or may not be an expert. The subjects themselves are chosen because they represent that body of knowledge which the authorities believe an educated man should possess. As the theory of democracy demands that all citizens should be educated, we tend to provide broad courses for students up to the statutory leaving age, and then to allow increasing specialization. At the latter stage, the content of the subjects is so organized as to offer a preparation for later studies, although this is also an important characteristic of courses in the junior forms in such key areas as mathematics and languages, in which a failure at first form can determine a man's lifetime career. However, the more important determinant of course content at this junior level is the determination to take every student on a quick trot around the whole field of human knowledge.

The assumption behind this form of education is that we use a child's schooldays to cram him full of all that knowledge which he may be called upon to use during his adult life. Childhood and adolescence are valued not for themselves but merely as a preparation for adulthood. As the society in which our schools operate has so changed its values that these stages of life now dominate our mental horizons, the school organization appears increasingly irrelevant to the youngster for whom it has supposedly been designed. Much of the concentration in our schools upon the trivialities of examinations and certificates can be explained by the fact that they have no confidence in the intrinsic value of their goods and so they concentrate on the externalities of job-oriented packaging. The less relevant any particular subject appears to contemporary life, the more cunningly it has to be sold in terms of its value in broadening the mind, strengthening mental discipline, or otherwise cultivating the skills which will be required in a toughly competitive modern world.

An alternative approach to the problem of determining the content of school courses is based on the principles of the American educationist Dewey, who, firmly grounded in the pragmatism of a nation which had succeeded to the extent that it had escaped the inhibitions of its European traditions, taught that the present is the most important tense in a schoolchild's experience, and that the immediate concern of this eternal moment should be the determining factor in what he studies. So, if he sees an earthworm, you let him learn enough biology to satisfy his curiosity. If he is interested in growing lettuces, you allow him to garden, and so allow him to develop an understanding of the whole field of ecology by studying it in miniature. From these ideas have developed such concepts as the activity curriculum, or learning by doing, and the core curriculum, or learning by studying a succession of immediate human problems.

The objection to the traditional subject curriculum is that it disguises a concentration on the past as a concern with the future. It is apparently designed to prepare the students for a future adulthood, but it assumes that every student will need the same body of knowledge which men have had in the past. It demands that the individual master this tradition before his own initiative and judgment can be trusted. It tries to make him responsible by denying him responsibility. Furthermore, by splitting knowledge into separate compartments it destroys the essential unity of human understanding and obscures the relevance of what has been learnt in one class to what is being studied in another.

The pragmatic answer is, however, equally confused in its use of tenses and its definition of relevance. Its concern with the present is merely a disguised utopian belief in a future which can be determined by the free operation of the human intelligence in the practical sphere. Its denial of any intrinsic importance to the past is a denial of the relevance of human experience. Its destruction of the traditional subject boundaries leaves the way open for every kind of fashionable quackery which has no other criterion than that it works according to the standards of its practitioners, which are usually merely the unexamined assumptions of modern society. While it is true that the fact that a particular subject has been studied in the past is no sufficient reason for it continuing to be studied in the future, and that the practitioners of every discipline should be constantly called upon to re-establish its relevance and importance in the present, it is equally true that new subjects and new forms of curriculum organization should be thoroughly tested not only for relevance but also for acceptable criteria of judgment before being admitted to the schools.

It is unfortunate that so much of the defence of the traditional subject organization in our schools has been undertaken from a reactionary position which obliges the defenders to join equally in support of formal examinations, chalk and talk methods, the birch, the whip and the gallows as the ultimate sanctions of society. The traditional academic subjects are best understood not as arbitrary chunks of subject-matter but as separate disciplines by which man has learned to comprehend his environment. They are not separate and interchangeable estates of learning, but instruments, and the function of these instruments is to enable their possessors to do precisely what the psychologists require, that is, operate efficiently within their natural and social environment. But no individual can expect to possess fully more than one instrument, so one of the aims of any modern system of education should be to ensure that we are preparing experts in the use of each of as many different instruments of learning as possible.

The five basic disciplines which man has evolved to handle

his environment are mathematics and philosophy, language and literature, the arts, the sciences, and theology. The social sciences may now also be emerging as a new discipline separate from the humanities on the one hand and the sciences on the other. But once we understand that all these disciplines are instruments for use rather than data for learning our concept of education must undergo a radical change. For a start, the most elementary instruction in any one of these fields should be entrusted only to a person who understands the fundamental principles. Any relics of the old pupil-teacher system, which kept the teacher one step ahead of his students, must be abandoned, together with the notion that if you can teach anything you can teach everything. Secondly, we must realize that the function of these instruments is to help us discover the truth, and that a measure of the success of our educational system will be the dissent it promotes rather than the conformity it induces. There is place for neither loyalty to accepted ideas nor indoctrination of received truths in any school which is worthy of its name. Nor is there any room for fear of discussion and controversy.

Yet at present these are the features most sternly shunned by state systems of education in Australia. Teachers are subject to public service acts designed to inhibit their freedom of public comment, let alone their freedom to pursue their academic discipline to its limits. The official excuse for this is the need to guarantee parents that their children will not be subjected to any baleful indoctrination while they are at school. The legislatures which prepared these inhibitory acts were not concerned with niceties of distinction or definition, and had no scruples about adding various loyalty tests to the statute book, but officially to this day the teacher in a state school is prohibited from discussing any matter of religious or political import. The economics teacher may teach the history of the Commonwealth Bank, but he must allow no comment to escape him on the virtues of public enterprise. The history teacher can be required to teach the intricacies of the Reformation, but he must allow no comment on religious questions to escape his lips. The teacher of literature can read patriotic tales of the Anzacs, but he must never mention the existence of either the R.S.L. or the Republican Party, except of course when he sells red poppies on Remembrance Day.

The dilemma of the state systems of education is that the logical consequences of what they teach would horrify those who support them. However, except for odd occasions in the narrower country districts, this has little effect on the actual practice of teachers who either ignore the regulations or are oblivious to the implications of their teaching. Whether parents can afford to be complacent is another matter. They need have little fear of indoctrination, for no subject has any agreed doctrine, and what is said by one teacher will be unsaid by another. What they should fear is the refusal to push facts to their logical conclusion, which is the only possible result of legislative refusal to trust teachers to go about their own business. Unfortunately, the average parent is all too ready to leap at the throat of the teacher if his offspring betrays any mind of his own, instead of writing to his local member if he does not.

We have so far said little of the Catholic system of education. This is because, in many respects, it merely duplicates the systems we have already looked at. The wealthier Catholic schools are a part of the Public School system, and need no special attention, except perhaps to point out that they take their religious functions more seriously than any Protestant schools other than those run by the Lutherans and by some of the fundamentalist sects like the Adventists. The poorer church schools, on the other hand, approximate to the state system, except that they work under even greater financial and physical handicaps in many cases. With classes of over sixty quite common, it is only the dedication of their staffs which enables them to continue. Yet, ironically, when one of our daily newspapers pointed this out, it was subjected to an organized campaign of abuse and boycott, although this simple fact constitutes the greatest single argument in favour of government aid for church education.

The problem facing the Catholic Church is that, while it finds the state system of education unsatisfactory for its youth, it can no longer afford to support an alternative and competing system of its own. Other denominations faced this situation when the state withdrew support from church schools in the 1870's and set about providing a universal system for all who wished to use it. The more scattered congregations of the smaller churches, and the lesser zeal of adherents to the larger, made it apparent that they could not hope to provide schools for all their people. In these circumstances they were content to provide schools for those who could afford them while their poorer members were flung on the state and left to keep their faith as best they could. Now the Catholic Church is faced with following a similar course, but the greater importance it places on both religious training and on education within a religious environment makes the decision much more difficult to take.

There have been voices raised within the Catholic Church which suggest that schools are not an essential part of the Church's mission, and that an excessive concern for their maintenance may in fact be distracting the church from more important tasks. These thinkers would in some cases be content with a Church smaller in numbers but greater in faith, whose members belonged through deep thought and conviction rather than through habit and upbringing. Certainly, the implication that the Church would be seriously weakened if it were to lose the exclusive supervision of its children's upbringing does, to the outsider, suggest a lack of faith in the persuasive power of its doctrine. On the other hand, the Catholic parent who does not provide every possible facility for his children's instruction may well believe that he is jeopardizing their eternal welfare, and the democrat must ask himself whether this is a burden any citizen should be asked to carry.

The problem for the state, however, is that, once it subsidizes independent schools for some of its citizens, the rest have the right to demand similar treatment. Catholic spokesmen have dodged this question by concentrating their attention on existing schools, and on the undeniable fact that the church is, at present, saving the state a considerable amount of money. The issue has been highlighted, however, by the action of the Anglican Synod in Sydney, which has demanded that any aid to church schools should be allotted on the basis of the total number of adherents to each denomination, and not on the number of children at present in church schools. If such aid were to be given in sufficient amounts to be effective, it could well lead to a denominational fragmentation of state education which would reproduce more disastrously the circumstances which led to the state making its original decision to withdraw from the field of religious education. So far, Australian governments have avoided the problem by granting sufficient tokens of aid to satisfy the denominationalists and shore up the present system without affecting any of the basic structure.

The ramifications of the question of state aid lie outside the scope of this book, but the existence of separate systems of schooling is of fundamental importance in the pattern of Australian education. The Catholic school system offers the one example in our community of schools organized with a clear aim and philosophy of education. This purpose is not only the indoctrination of the students with a particular religious dogma, but also their initiation into full membership of a community in which each member has a clearly defined place and obligations, and which gives meaning to every part of his life. This philosophy presents a clear challenge to the vague liberalism of the founders of the state school, and the equally undefined social utilitarianism which has succeeded it.

The success of Catholic schools in promulgating their doctrines is another matter. Recent studies based on the responses of ex-students have proved inconclusive, but the behaviour of members of the Catholic community suggests that its members have both a better understanding of the Church's teaching and a greater sense of obligation to perform their religious duties than do the members of the larger Protestant churches. On the other hand, critics may suggest that these characteristics indicate that a greater importance is placed on the externals of behaviour than on the essentials of faith. What is certain, however, is that behind a great deal of the opposition to any extension of state aid is the Protestant fear that Catholic education is quite efficient enough to take over the whole community if it is once given full state support.

Quite apart, however, from the overtly religious aspects of their organization, Catholic schools do differ from others in a pervasive authoritarian element in their ethos. This stems in part from the authoritarian element of a religion which teaches that a human institution has divine guidance, and that it is consequently a duty of the faithful to believe absolutely the pronouncements of the spokesmen for this institution. This element of the faith has not, however, been enough to discourage many Catholic theologians and philosophers from pursuing their speculations with a freedom which would shame many of their Protestant and agnostic or rationalist colleagues. A more important source of this characteristic is possibly the nature of the religious bodies which conduct the schools, whose members have taken vows of obedience which will influence their attitude to their students. But ultimately the reason probably lies in the physical conditions which we have already noted, which leave little option for anything other than the most authoritarian methods of discipline and instruction. On the other hand, many Catholic schools deliberately avoid awkward areas in their teaching of controversial subjects, and the habits of thought so promoted are unlikely to lead to free enquiry at a later stage.

It is difficult to ascertain the consequences of this influence on the community at large. Certainly, the Catholic Church has become one of the last refuges of puritanism, and Catholic Leagues of Decency play a major role in support of the rigid censorship which is a characteristic manifestation of Australian culture. Public debate in the community can be inhibited when any expression of intellectual disagreement is liable to be interpreted as an outburst of sectarian rancor. The stubborn solidarity of Protestant alliances is maintained partly at least by fear of a disciplined Catholic vote.

These consequences are, however, comparatively minor. More important has been the acceptance of authoritarian attitudes as a part of the Australian way of life. While this cannot by any means be attributed solely to the Catholic element in the population, it has probably been reinforced by the role of the Catholic schools in preparing candidates for the various public services. This has not been due to some machiavellian plot to take over our free white democracy, although there have been influential minorities in the Catholic Church who have thought this way from time to time. Rather, it is due to the simple fact that most Catholics were of working class origin, and so they had neither an established business nor the possibility of a university course when they completed their schooling. Moreover, until recently sectarian prejudice prevented the employment of Catholics in a number of large private enterprises. The avenues left for them were teaching and the public service, whither they took the authoritarian attitudes established at school, and here they played their part in propagating the Australian myth that authority is something to be suspected but not questioned.

One of the interesting questions in Australia today is what will happen to these older attitudes as the Catholic community spreads over the whole range of social classes. Already the political changes can be seen in the rise of the Democratic Labor Party, which gives middle class Catholics the opportunity of preserving their traditions by voting Labor and their interest by electing the conservatives. We may expect changes of similar magnitude to occur in the schools as both the Catholic community and the church to which it subscribes change in their composition, outlook and teaching.

This, then, is the pattern of Australian schools today. On the one hand, they are divided horizontally according to the wealth of their supporters. On the other, they are divided vertically by denomination, and geographically by states. Yet, beneath this apparent division, there is a depressing uniformity of practice and confusion of aims. Only in the Catholic segment is there still a clear purpose, and it is doubtful whether even this is, in practice, wide enough to embrace all the function of the school in a modern society. This modern society is making increasing demands of the schools, but is not yet prepared either to involve itself with them or to give them the facilities they need. Fashion, administrative convenience and political expediency are greater arbiters of change than thought or planning. Teachers are restive, pupils bored, parents apprehensive. To understand why, we must now look more closely at what happens within the classroom, and then we can turn to some of the changes that will be needed if Australian schools are ever to be dragged into the twentieth century.

2 The Child

One of the factors commonly ignored in considering the aims and organization of schooling is the child. We tend to think instead of such problems as illiteracy, shortage of skilled labour, immorality or juvenile delinquency, or of such large abstractions as supply and demand, growth potential and economic capability. Our education system comes to reflect the resources available for its construction or the most pressing requirements of the community rather than the needs of the people for whom it is supposedly designed—the children who sit at the desks and benches and worktables their elders provide for them. But while the most notable feature of the systems we provide is their uniformity, the most important characteristic of the children is their diversity. Yet although this obvious fact is an educational commonplace, its implications are rarely considered by those responsible for our schools.

The pressures, in fact, tend to be in the reverse direction. People required by their employment to move interstate complain that their children lose a year's schooling. Employers complain that every state has a different set of examinations and qualifications. Teachers' organizations protest that other states have better pay and conditions. Newspapers editorialize about the need for Commonwealth control and co-ordination. On a more domestic plane, parents complain when little Willy is unable to use his older brother's carefully preserved textbooks, and students object that Mr Smith is not giving them the same notes that Miss Brown used the year before. It would seem that most people are able to hold simultaneously the twin beliefs that they are each unique and each entitled to identical treatment with everyone else.

The paradox of education is that equal treatment of everybody will produce inequality. There are those who argue that inequality is the very business of education. If our aim is individual excellence, then we must recognize that few will achieve this standard in anything, and no two in the same things. The business of the state is to give every person an equal opportunity to prove himself, and allow natural ability to do the rest. In this way everyone will be educated to the limit of his capacities, and the country will obtain its necessary supply of engineers and scientists and managers while still having plenty of people available to sweep the streets and collect the garbage.

One of the weaknesses of this argument is contained in its own premises, for if our standard of education is to determine the opportunities available to us we have every right to object to a state which is allowing its resources to be used to give a few people access to privilege and power while the rest of us are left to perform their menial duties. Meritocracy in this form would be as objectionable as, and no more fluid than, the older form of social division based on birth or wealth. The long duration of aristocracy, moreover, and its ability to adapt to changing circumstances, provides indisputable proof that ability is no necessary pre-requisite for power. If a country is to be controlled by the few it is probably better to allow them to be thrown up by chance than to have them selected and trained like Plato's guardians.

A further objection to any deliberate attempt to educate for inequality is that there is no satisfactory method by which ability, either developed or potential, can be determined. We can certainly assess whether a particular person has particular ability at a given time, and this assessment can be a useful means of making a selection when a number of candidates present for a single job. Tests of specific ability can be even more usefully applied to determine what particular course of education an individual should follow at the moment, or what type of occupation he should follow in the immediate future, but when they are used, as in the case of the Commonwealth secondary scholarship scheme, to select those people who will be entitled to further training (at the expense of the rest of the community), and therefore, eventually, to higher pay, such use should be questioned.

Our present education system operates chiefly, if unintentionally, to promote inequality. The degree of success it obtains in this remarkably undemocratic direction is partly obscured by the social mobility which accompanies the process. The system of free state schooling does allow the gifted son of a poor man to rise to the Supreme Court bench, although we should not forget that the independent school system may also allow the stupid son of the rich man to get just as far. Nor is such success necessarily the product of the contacts he has made at his school, or the clubs to which its tie has admitted him. Close cultivation of poor soil can produce as heavy a crop as meagre sowing of the richest acres.

The course of schooling we provide today is like a hurdle race over a series of successively higher obstacles. The strongest athletes will reach the prizes at the end, but so will those who are well-coached, those who can afford to have a second run at some of the trickier barriers, and those who possess the best running-spikes. But this is no Saturday-afternoon sports meet, for from each barrier leads off an avenue bordered by walls which can be breached only by the greatest skill and luck or in times of national cataclysm.

The barriers in this course are the annual examinations to which we are as a nation so passionately addicted. These examinations are designed as a test of the candidates' success in coping with a given body of studies, but in fact they determine the classes into which students will be graded the following year, and hence the course they can take and their chances of success in future examinations, their chances of remaining at school, their opportunity of continuing to university, and eventually the range of the vocations to which they may aspire. Nor is the importance of examinations lessening, for as the scale of our society and its enterprises increases so the lines of advancement within it become more formal, more restricted, and more dependent on school achievement.

Yet the whole idea of rationing the amount of education a student is enabled to receive according to the ability he is supposed to possess is as ridiculous as a scheme to provide hospitals only for those in perfect health. Although teachers will still talk of a student having reached the limit of his ability, this notion has no more scientific validity than the now exploded theory of athlete's heart. The truth behind this statement is that the school is no longer able to educate the person concerned, but this is a reflection on the institution rather than on the scholar. The success which athletics coaches have had in recent years in improving man's physical performance indicates the possibilities which might lie ahead of similar efforts in the field of mental development, but our schools are neither equipped nor prepared to undertake such a project. However, there is no direct analogy between mind and muscle, and the cultivation of the former is a far more complex and expensive task than is the development of physical prowess.

Yet none of these objections suggests the fundamental error in our acceptance of education for inequality. Men are not so much unequal as different, and it should certainly be a major task of education to develop these differences. However, the ability which a man develops in any sphere is due at least as much to his environment as to his natural endowment, or rather it depends on the interaction of these two factors, not on their addition. However fortunate an individual's natural endowment, he will not develop even the power of speech unless he receives external prompting. Similarly, a person who never learns to read is, in a modern community, deprived of one of the most important sources of stimulation. He will spend his schooldays sitting uselessly in a desk, and as an adult will be considered, and will in fact be, sub-normal, unless he has at some stage had the good fortune to develop compensating abilities in, for example, manual skills. Long before a person reaches adulthood, it is impossible to distinguish the parts played in his development by heredity and by environment.

Yet in our schools we provide a common environment for all, or nearly all. The schools in wealthier districts will be far better equipped, and far more pleasant to work in, than those in poorer neighbourhoods. But these differences between areas are probably not as significant as the differences in the family backgrounds of the children who come to the individual schools, except to the extent that the poorer neighbourhood is likely to provide a generally less satisfactory environment for the children who grow up within it. The first step towards providing education for greater equality would be to ensure that the school compensates for the general environment of its students. This would mean providing the best schools in the poorest areas. But the more important step would be to provide within each school a different education for each individual student. For only by recognizing differences can true equality be promoted.

Let us consider a few of the more obvious differences which children bring to the school as a result of their home environment alone. First there is Andrew, from Sydney's North Shore. Andrew lives in a medium-sized house on a large garden block in a quiet street. He has few companions, but they are well-chosen, quietly-behaved and softly-spoken. He also has some less favoured friends with whom he exchanges insults over a neighbour's back fence, but his parents are unaware of this. He is the oldest of four, and sees little of his father, who is busy at the office and the club during Andrew's waking hours, nor of his mother, who is kept busy and distraught with looking after a succession of babies, coping with the domestic help, and keeping herself and the house clean and fresh for her husband's social life. On the other hand, by the time he starts school Andrew has had two years at one of the best private kindergartens, and from his birth he has been surrounded by expensive books and toys. His manipulative skill is well developed and he has a good background of experience to fit him for the task of formal learning. However, his lack of attention from his mother has made him quiet, and he is not used to putting his experiences into words. This disadvantage, however, may be overcome by the sense of innate superiority which he has already had instilled. As he grows older, his school experience, and that of his sisters, will be supplemented by music and piano lessons, tennis coaching, interstate holidays and frequent visits to theatres and cinemas.

Our next example is Cheryl, whose mother is a former primary school teacher married to a dairy farmer. Cheryl's early years are rich and busy, but she lacks much company from children of her own age, whom she sees only when her parents exchange visits. She has, however, a reasonable supply of books and toys, and she is almost constantly in the company of one or other of her parents. Not only is she familiar with the natural processes of life, from the large scale of the milking shed to the small scale of the ants on the back lawn, but she is used to chattering about them, and has a well-developed vocabulary and sense of speech structure. This wide background will not necessarily continue throughout her school life. Although she is well ahead of her urban contemporaries at the age of five, by fifteen her life and experience may seem narrow in comparison. Her classmates will have few, and identical, interests, her understanding of values will be determined by the code of the local town, her knowledge of careers will be limited to teaching, nursing and the female glamour trades. Her greatest hero will be the local football captain, her greatest thrill the day she joined a crowd to welcome a visiting pop star, and her greatest ambition to marry a farmer like her father and settle down to produce a family like her mother's. Having achieved this ambition, she will no doubt continue to display her interest in matters of the mind by joining the C.W.A. younger set and entering her crochet work in the art section of the local show.

Then we have Larry, of 15 Rennison Street, Oakville, a government housing commission estate in one of the desert suburbs of our expanding metropoles. Larry is fourth in a family of six, quick with his wits and polite to his elders. He is already the best cricketer among the mob who play in the road by his front door, where it takes strength of arm and loudness of voice to obtain or retain the bat. Like his companions, Larry is thrust outside to play as soon as breakfast is over, and returns only for a few minutes at lunchtime to gulp down a sandwich and a cup of tea before returning to the game. If his father arrives home before dark Larry will be given two bob to go down to the corner shop and buy himself an icecream and some lollies. He does most of his mother's daily shopping, a job which will be taken over by his younger brother when he goes to school next year. He knows the streets for a mile around, but his conversation is limited to monosyllables, and outside the realm of games he is almost completely inarticulate. He receives generous gifts of toys at Christmas time, but they are soon broken or lost. After tea at night he watches television until he starts to drop off to sleep, when he takes himself to bed.

None of these children has abnormal problems. They are all well fed and clothed, have stable homes and affectionate parents. Yet their readiness for school is quite different, apart from the different emotional problems they will have in adjusting to a new environment. Already it is possible to predict their school careers. Barring a miracle, Andrew will complete at least a full course of secondary schooling, and possibly university, Cheryl will leave at the end of fourth or fifth year of secondary school, and Larry will leave from one of the lower streams as soon as he reaches statutory leaving age, if an attractive job is available. This prediction assumes, of course, that these three students have similar innate ability. If it happens that Andrew is exceptionally stupid, or Larry particularly intelligent, their places could be reversed, but these occasional exceptions do not alter the general picture.

Outside this normal range live the fringe-dwellers, the children whose emotional or parental background causes them difficulties which only exceptional luck and ability can overcome. I am not speaking here of the mentally and physically handicapped, whose neglect by the state constitutes a national disgrace which is not lessened by the hard work of those charitable organizations which attempt to bear a responsibility which should not be theirs. Rather am I thinking of those children who occupy desks in state schools which have neither the facilities nor the organization to provide for their special needs. With special and imaginative attention to their problems, they could fit happily and profitably into the school community, but as it is they are wasting their own time and that of their teachers. They include the children from aboriginal settlements, whose personal and cultural background is so different from that of their fellows, and of their teachers, that they have great difficulty in benefiting from a conventional school education. There are the migrant children, whose language difficulties provide a barrier of understanding, the malnourished, whose physical stamina is inadequate for the demands of a school day, and those who are overwhelmed by the mental and emotional problems of their homes. Few of these children need treatment in special institutions, and some states have made a gesture towards solving the problems by providing remedial teachers and student counsellors to deal with particular cases. But solution of the problem will mean giving every school immediate access to a full range of remedial, counselling, psychiatric and health services, as well as giving each school the opportunity to devise its own programme to meet the needs of the community it serves. This cannot be done only by the administrative act of granting authority to the headteacher to act as he sees fit, but will require special studies and facilities for schools with special problems.

One step towards providing at least an initially equal opportunity would be to make kindergarten and pre-school education universal. In extending it towards this goal, priority should be given to those areas with the greatest need. At present, most kindergartens are provided in response to public demand, and thus are placed in those areas where parents have already demonstrated their interest in education, and therefore can presumably be trusted to give their children the intellectual, if not the social, benefits of kindergarten training at home. The system of subsidizing kindergartens is the most inequitable which could be imagined. The whole community is taxed, but those who choose to pay kindergarten fees are given a concession. They are then given a further handout, paid for by the taxes extracted from the rest of the population, to make sure that their kindergarten is adequate. As a direct consequence of this community generosity, these same children are then given a start over their fellows in the sterner race of primary schooling.

The objection to our present practices is not only one of social morality but also one of economic practice. Some years ago a survey conducted by Melbourne University[1] revealed that approximately half of the students of demonstrated university capacity left school before reaching matriculation. The proportion continuing to sixth form has improved since then, but this would be more than offset by the numbers who have never been educated to the standard where they can show university potential. The latest estimate is that of the 25 per cent in the relevant age group who are capable of benefiting from university and equivalent education, 13 per cent are receiving it.[2] If half of the best students in our schools are being undereducated, then it is reasonable to suppose that the proportion among the less obviously able is no less. Consequently, we must assume that we are wasting at least

[1] E. R. Wyeth, University of Melbourne. Unpublished paper.

[2] Schonell, Presidential Address, ANZAAS Conference, 1967. Unpublished.

part of the potential ability of not less than half of our community, a waste which we can scarcely afford if we are to keep our place as a developing nation in an increasingly complex world. Those who fear that an extension of education of the magnitude needed to overcome this wastage would rob us of our menial labourers should reflect that a properly educated society could be trusted to cope with this problem when it met it.

It is no argument against an extension of educational opportunities to point to those members of older generations who have lived full and successful lives despite a paucity of formal schooling. As society grows more complex, so do its organizations grow larger. This does not only lead to an increasingly private and public bureaucracy, with correspondingly fewer opportunities for personal advancement for individuals lacking the approved qualifications. It also means that the tasks within these organizations grow more complex, more demanding of such technical and managerial skills as can be developed by formal education. Furthermore, the growth of large business means a reduction in the opportunities for the man on the make unless he can compete with the managers on their own terms. So both within and without the large organizations those men who lack formal educational qualifications, and the skills which these should indicate, are finding their opportunities becoming increasingly limited.

The pace of technological change is a further handicap to those who have failed to continue their education as far as possible. Automation is just one of the developments, if the most dramatic of them, which are changing the pattern of employment as well as of daily living. The white-collar worker who once enjoyed a sure salary with annual increments and an eventual pension is now sharing the insecurity of employment which he had previously thought a monopoly of his blue-collared brother. The older a man is the more difficult it is for him to acquire the skills of a new job, but this difficulty is minimized by adequate formal education, education which is designed to develop flexibility of mind rather than merely induce a knowledge of facts. Unfortunately, Australian schools cannot claim to provide such an education before their final years, at the best.

But none of these economic or social arguments suggests the most important reason for expanding the educational opportunities available to every individual. The crucial argument is that every human being is entitled as of right to an education which will enable him to develop his talents to the utmost and take his place as a full member of the community in which he lives. More primitive societies provide this education, for the community is its own medium of schooling, and the least fortunately endowed individual is able to play his part to the full. The community itself may be limiting, although even this proposition is doubtful, but within it all are given equal opportunity to be themselves. In a modern society, however, final responsibility for education rests neither with society as a whole nor with the families which together constitute it, but with a formal and specialized institution set up for the purpose. To the extent that this institution fails any individual, it fails in its duty to society as a whole.

It could well be argued that we have our priorities exactly reversed. The more ability a student displays, the more education we give him, while the child who fails to cope happily with school is thrown out to cope unaided with the world as soon as we feel decently able to get rid of him. Yet the child who does best at school is precisely the one who least needs it. He can be trusted to complete his own education, possibly better than his teachers can, while we expect the child who fails in form four to take full responsibility for his education from that time forth.

The need to improve the general standard of education in Australia cannot be doubted by anyone who cares to look about him. The standard of popular television programs, the low level of public debate, the quality of the popular press are all indications of an abysmally low level of general taste and intellect and of the absence of any sizeable minority committed to maintaining higher standards. After nearly twenty years of unparalleled prosperity, we are still unable to run our own businesses, care for our poor, or develop our own designs. Our performing artists have to travel overseas before we notice them, our writers have to work at other trades to keep alive. While we have in our universities thinkers and scholars of world stature, their influence on the community at large is negligible. No other country in the world is so enamoured of mediocrity and few lavish such admiration on public figures distinguished only for their lack of any talent other than sycophancy. These characteristics are both a result and a cause of our educational backwardness.

To make such criticisms is to risk being accused of intellectual arrogance and the ambition to become a cultural commissar, deciding what standards must be observed and what kinds of entertainment are suitable for public consumption. Yet a person is free to choose only what he knows, and if the main result of a century of public education is two million readers of the Sunday papers, it is more reasonable to look for deficiencies in the quality of education than for unsuspected merit in the pages of the newspapers. Not the least betrayal of contemporary society by its secular clerisy has been their acceptance of the doctrine that their principles have no application outside the charmed circle of a small academic elite. The whole history of popular culture proves that the ordinary man is able to both understand and enjoy work of the greatest subtlety and profundity, and it is intolerable irony that the era which has given the power of the ballot to the common man has at the same time reduced him to the status of a single grain in a mass, without the capacity or the opportunity to choose for himself what he will read, what he will hear, what he will see. Herein lies the greatest challenge to contemporary education, and here lies the task of the educated minority, not to impose its own prejudices, but to see that all men are given the same opportunity to develop the powers of discrimination which the few have always enjoyed.

It is the great illusion of our century that the common man has become the arbiter of taste, when the reverse is in fact the case. The man in the street does not write the newspapers, direct the films, or promote the pop songs which constitute his cultural environment. Nor does a modern society even provide a community structure within which public opinion can be said in any meaningful sense to be formed. The economics of scale dictate that the channels of communication are controlled by an increasingly small number of people. At the same time, the numbers who have the opportunity to make effective decisions are becoming fewer while the consequences flowing from these decisions are becoming greater. At the very time when man has the technical capacity to control his environment he has lost the capacity to control himself. The effect of this is twofold.

In the short run, more power is given to the arbiters of society. Their economic power is so great that the individual is unable to understand it, or to challenge the way in which it is used even if he does feel that he has some concept of the issues involved. But in the longer term, the few experts are more seriously limited by the lack of comprehension by the ordinary people, for such serious questions as the planning of cities, or the preservation and utilization of the natural environment, require the co-operative efforts of experts, managers and ordinary people. Yet the decisions which need to be taken in these areas appear to conflict with individual liberties, and the issues are too abstract and too remote from their immediate experience to be comprehended.

The solution to this dilemma lies outside the province of the schools, but they have their part to play in it. This is not an aspect of education where we can look overseas for guidance, for none of the countries comparable to our own has obtained any success in it so far. But our smaller population, with its egalitarian traditions, active migrant communities, freedom from archaic customs and still relatively undeveloped natural environment has at the moment a possibly unique opportunity to pioneer in this direction. But if the spoliation of the countryside, the sprawl of the cities, the aping of anything which happens to be American, continues for only a few more years without any attempt being made to do something different, the chance may be gone for ever.

The concept of equality in education depends on the recognition that everyone has both a common stake in the community and a unique contribution to make to it. The scientist and the farmer must work together to utilize the wealth of the land without destroying its potential for future generations. Politicians, economists, manufacturers, workers and consumers are all involved in decisions about which industries should be given priority and where they should be located. The crucial issue of human satisfaction cannot be decided by experts, but neither can it be achieved without them. It must be the task of the schools to educate their students so that their special talents are developed for the benefit of the community, but also so that they themselves are fitted to play their full part as individuals in the life and decisions of the community.

There should be no suggestion that the schools should seek to achieve this end by the deliberate promotion of any particular scale of values. It is doubtful whether a school does effectively transmit values at any rate. A study[3] carried out in an English grammar school showed that both teachers and students held very clear views about the important values in education, but that these views scarcely coincided. The highest value believed to be propagated by the staff was the practice of honesty and truthfulness, followed by the belief that there is more to life than material gratification and the exercise of tolerance. The pupils, more realistically, gave the highest rating to being able to use one's special abilities. Yet if this aim alone were achieved, there would be no reason to worry about the others, for each individual could be trusted to take care of them for himself.

The failure of schools to transmit their consciously held values is, however, a symptom of a more deep-seated malaise. Although the most successful student of a school is probably the one who dissents most strongly and intelligently from community values, the typical student in contemporary Australian schools is perfectly satisfied with the standards of society but regards the values of the school as perverse or irrelevant. This dissent is not based on any reasoned objection, and is expressed not so often by rebellion as by a determination to get all the possible material advantages from the school without subscribing to any of the ideals we might imagine as being implicit in the very nature of study. Among few students is there any respect for truth and reason as being worthwhile in themselves, but only a concern to complete the minimum amount of work necessary in order to pass an examination. Even the minority of students with an ambition to excel too often interpret excellence purely in terms of examination marks, and

[3] *New Society*—See Further Reading list.

see little connection between the work of the classroom and life outside. This is partly a result of teaching which is too narrowly conceived, but it is more the product of a social and cultural environment which is actively hostile to education and to learning, and which pays no respect to endeavour but only to material success. A school is an intellectual supermarket where the customer pays his price and picks up the instant education that has taken his eye, and just as in the commercial supermarket, the product is valued by its label rather than its contents. It is this situation that explains the otherwise incredible phenomenon of the student who, after giving at school every indication of appreciating the human understanding of Rembrandt or Shakespeare, can of his own choice spend his leisure hours among tawdry ornaments, shoddy comics and the trashiest of television entertainment, and yet not perceive the incongruity of his two worlds.

The explanation for the instant appetites and the absence of any regard for sheer effort possibly goes beyond the immediate commercial environment and lies in the sentimental cult of childhood which has afflicted the twentieth century. Based on a compound of a half-understood idea of Freud about infancy being the formative period of a human life and a tenuous survival of the older conception of it as the age of innocence, this modern doctrine elevates the child into supreme arbiter of the universe. The parents' only function is to care for their offspring, whose slightest whim must be obeyed. The family home, the holidays, the entertainments are all planned for the delectation of little Johnny. To him the parents sacrifice even their own personality, so that by the time he grows out of leading strings they have no longer any worthwhile character from which to offer him companionship. So a spoilt childhood is succeeded by a moody and fractious adolescence, whose incipient but undirected rebellion is quickly exploited by commercial interests ready to pander to their audience with the mindless distractions of constant sensation. At this stage adults react either with the exaggerated horror of outraged innocence or with the resigned apathy of those who have accepted the sad inevitability that boys must always be boys. Either approach leaves the adolescent alone as no previous age has ever left him, and this loneliness is easily exploited by the commercial manipulators who, by imposing on him a ready-made culture, ensure that this year's rebel becomes next year's adult conformist.

The sad thing is that so few of the parents who sacrifice themselves to their children in this way are prepared to make any real effort to understand what their children in fact need. Having no personality of their own, they cannot enjoy observing it grow in another, and instead smother it in a welter of lavish gifts. Their children are not encouraged to make or find out things for themselves, but instead are surrounded with glossy artefacts which come without effort and disappear again without regret. This 'boredom of perpetual novelty' brings them to the threshold of adolescence with regard for nothing except their own immediate gratification and with no stable interests or talents to serve as a basis for the development of their own personality. When they are confronted with the demands of the school, they have no option except either to dismiss them altogether or to put them into a neat compartment of their lives as something which must be endured for a short time for the sake of lasting affluence to come.

The lavishness of childhood indulgence varies according to the wealth and wisdom of the parent, but it is found to some extent in all levels and parts of society. It exists where the parents mortgage their future to buy an education for their children at one of the 'best' and most expensive schools, and it is found in homes where there is no money to buy school uniforms but the children always have plenty of pocket money to spend on lollies and pictures. In every case it marks the substitution of the ease of spending for the effort of understanding. It is both a reason for current concern about education and the greatest enemy of any proper education. If the schools are ever to do their job for all their students they must succeed in convincing each one that, while there is a course available especially suited to his particular talents, there is also a price of effort which he himself must pay for it.

The essential fault of the contemporary outlook is that it regards childhood, or adolescence, as a separate period of being rather than as a part of the ongoing process of life. Beneath the lavish façade the child is too often left alone and neglected. It is allowed no part in an adult life which itself loses something of its meaning by its failure to meaningfully include the child. The closest approach we have left to the natural upbringing of a child is probably still to be found on those farms where from the earliest age the child is required to assume its share of adult responsibility. Its place in the scheme of things is subordinate, but real. Unfortunately, these children seldom find a similar responsibility or meaning in the life they are offered at school, a fact which both wastes some of their potential and contributes to the separation of the farming community from the rest of society. Yet it is probably in rural communities, with their close-knit ties both between individuals and with the essentials of life, and with their more responsible family upbringing of children, that there is the greatest hope of evolving an education suitable to the needs of the individual in a modern society.

3 Science and Mathematics

The most fashionable area in education is that of the sciences and mathematics. Our concern can be traced back to the launching of the first Sputnik, an event which sent Americans of all ranks into orbit and whose echoes are still reverberating through Australian academies today. Yet, like many other fashions, this one has been responsible for distorting our patterns of demand, in this instance to the detriment of the less fashionable sciences as well as of other fields of endeavor.

Many boys who hope to proceed to higher education have a romantic vision of becoming nuclear or astro-physicists, computer scientists or electronic engineers. In order to achieve this ambition, they embark on a specialized study of mathematics, physics and chemistry as soon as they are allowed, normally at fourth form level. But a failure in any one of these subjects can in practice disqualify them from the possibility of undertaking any science course, and as they have probably dropped the language which is still regarded as a desirable pre-requisite for an arts course, they must either turn to economics and commerce or start earning a living in the business world. Unfortunately, there is little incentive for them to turn to an apprenticeship at this stage, and the senior technical courses require much the same subjects as do the universities.

The effects of this are twofold. In the first place, the non-scientific studies come to be regarded as a second-best alternative, good enough for girls and for those who have failed in more demanding areas. The reaction to this of the dedicated humanists is far too often a defensive contempt for all things scientific, with a consequent increase in mutual misunderstanding which is grossly detrimental to all concerned. But equally seriously, the all or nothing approach of the faculties of science adds to the shortage of trained scientists, technologists, and technicians, as well as narrowing the education of those who do qualify in their profession.

A more satisfactory approach to the problems of selecting candidates for admission to university faculties of science could be to demand evidence of the ability to think in a scientific field, but to teach each subject at first-year level on the assumption that many of the students will have not studied any of it previously. Such a change would not only free the schools to teach science in terms of the students' interests rather than with both eyes fixed on university requirements, but would defer the date at which a student has to choose a specialty, allow university science faculties to select students from a wider field, and allow prospective scientists, if they wished, to benefit from a broader secondary education than is now available to them. Alternative means to the same end would be a special pre-science course for those who matriculate without the pre-requisites necessary for the subjects they wish to study, or a reduction of the numbers of mathematics and science subjects available at matriculation. The present specialities could perhaps be combined into Natural Philosophy and General Mathematics. This change would both lead prospective scientists to undertake some studies in the humanities or social sciences, and allow prospective humanists to gain some understanding of scientific thought.

There is some disagreement about the reasons for the failure to train greater numbers in the scientific disciplines. On the one hand, the present science faculties are fully extended, and could take no more students even if they were available. But this is a problem they share with practically all other faculties, and two attempts to create universities devoted predominantly to the sciences, at the University of New South Wales and at Monash University in Victoria, have largely failed, mainly because the demand for additional facilities in other fields has been at least as great. In fact, the prevalence of scientific ambition among schoolboys is a phenomenon matched only by the failure of a similar demand at university entrance level. The myth that scientific education is the one field of pressing need is one that dies hard.

The practice among examination authorities of passing a predetermined proportion of candidates in each subject may well make science subjects more difficult than others. Once they acquire the reputation of difficulty the less able candidates will be warned off into ostensibly soft options, and the task of the able student in passing will become correspondingly more difficult. Furthermore, the fact that they must pass in all key subjects, though not necessarily at one sitting, gives them a further handicap compared with their colleagues in the humanities, who can afford a failure in any single subject without affecting their chances of continuing with studies in their chosen field. The cumulative effect of these factors is indicated by evidence that students who complete university science courses do in fact have a higher level of general ability than those who have taken or commence arts.[1] Yet examiners in the sciences assert that the general standard of examinees has declined in recent years. This claim is used to support the thesis that more means worse, that an increase in the total number of students means an inevitable decline in their average quality, but it may equally well be used to demonstrate the extent to which our teaching standards have failed to keep pace with the increased demands being made on them.

The desirability of improving the standard of science teaching is the one element in the catastrophic condition of Australian education which is coming to be acknowledged by the public mind. Although the Commonwealth government refused for years to take official cognisance of the existence of primary and secondary schools, political expediency finally compelled it, in 1963, to promise special financial grants for scientific and technical education. When, in 1967, it finally appointed a full-time minister to supervize education, it coupled science with his portfolio, thus indicating the priorities which it expected him to observe. At the same time, Melbourne University made a practical gesture towards the cause by instituting a special degree course for science teachers, to be jointly conducted by the Faculties of Science and Education, with the co-operation and facilities of the Secondary Teachers' College. The implications of this course could have profound effects on the whole profession of teaching, but its immediate significance is that the step was taken to relieve a desperate situation in science teaching.

The sad thing, however, about this apparent increase in public activity to remedy the deficiencies of science teaching is that these

[1] University of Melbourne, Bachelor of Education—First Year—Educational Psychology—Data from testing of first year students (in Education), March 1967. Supplied by courtesy of Mr G. Bradshaw, School of Education, University of Melbourne.

deficiencies have nowhere been officially defined so that remedial action can have some logic. The Commonwealth science grants are split three ways, between state schools, Catholic schools, and the others. The criterion for the division is the total number of students in each kind of school, and superficially this would seem to be just. However, such rough justice ignores the differences in need between different schools, and the fact that the majority of students, far from receiving their fair share of the benefit from the available funds, will obtain no significant benefits for years, if ever. Moreover, the method which allows the money to be used for either buildings or equipment has led to many schools receiving equipment which is either irrelevant to their particular courses or useless because they lack the room to put it to use. So every Victorian high school has received a refrigerator, although in most cases it is used only to store a couple of rats for two or three months a year. Similarly, expensive incubators and telescopes moulder uselessly in schools which lack room to organize practical classes, or teachers qualified to take them.

A more useful way of distributing the money would have been to have established a proper minimum standard of accommodation and equipment for science teaching. All schools could then have been rated in order of priority, regardless of whether they were state or private, and each could then in order of need have been brought to this standard. But such a method would not have had the simplicity and political appeal of the present one, and so has not been considered. Instead, we find the Commonwealth Minister of Education and Science announcing that he expects the grants to have served their purpose in another three years, and so anticipating a similar scheme in some other field of education. But what the purpose is, and what measures will be used to ascertain that it has been achieved, have not been announced.

The most important reason for public concern about science teaching is presumably our need for scientists and technologists in defence, industry and agriculture. This need appears so obvious that it is rarely demonstrated, except for pointing out the lack of scientists in these fields and our consequent dependence on overseas research. The need, however, is at least equally great for men trained to apply the results of research as for those interested in carrying it out themselves. The growing field of computers is just one case where this particular demand will become increasingly urgent. In fact, except for agriculture, where a unique natural environment produces unique problems, there seems no necessary economic justification for carrying out very much research locally at all. The economics of scale prevent us from making a significant contribution in those fields which demand large teams of workers and tremendously expensive facilities. The best we can hope for here is such projects as Woomera, where an international venture has brought the necessary facilities to our shores. However, it is not clear that this has brought any immediate economic advantage to Australia, apart from the creation of a new town in the middle of a desert, and the growth of an aura of glamour which has led to the over-production of physicists and a shortage of biologists and chemists.

Defence projects on a smaller scale but no less demanding in terms of scientific expertize could prove far more rewarding in terms of national independence. The example of Sweden shows that it is not beyond the resources of a relatively small nation to support its own aircraft industry, but it is unlikely that we have at present sufficient appropriately trained experts to support such an enterprise. A greater supply of science graduates would also enable our Defence Laboratories to expand sufficiently to stand on their own rather than remain as a complement to overseas establishments. These possibilities are however of little relevance at a time when the problem of defence scientists is one of under rather than over employment.

In the manufacturing industries the true value of local research would be in the effects it might have on the climate of thinking rather than on any immediate discoveries which might be made. Industrial management in Australia is still suffering from the code of the amateur gentleman, on to which has been grafted an hypnotic enchantment with American efficiency. The result is that most Australian enterprises are content either to continue in their age-old ways, to become second-rate copies of overseas originals, or to entrust their affairs to foreign experts. The life offices would be the classic example of the first approach, the retailers of the second, and the oil concerns and motor manufacturers of the third, although the overseas ownership of this last group has at times given them sufficient self-confidence to trust the initiative of the local men.

The extension of research and development activities in local industry would provide a body of expert opinion which could stand up to overseas competitors, partners and proprietors. It was the lack of such a body which handicapped the Australian purchasers in their negotiations with foreign combines over the supply of natural gas. Further, the local expert has the advantage of understanding local customs and conditions, which may invalidate the conclusions of overseas consultants. Efficiency in industry is not a purely scientific proposition, but involves consumer habits, social attitudes, employee relationships and industrial legislation. Any one of these factors can be of deciding importance in making a particular decision.

These requirements depend for their fulfilment on an increasing supply of trained scientists and technologists at all levels, but this is only the start of the school's task. A great part of the prestige which science enjoys in modern culture is dependent not on any real understanding of its nature but on a superstitious awe induced both by the magnitude of its practical achievements and by the incomprehensible language with which scientists work. But, although this situation may be flattering to the self-esteem of individual scientists, it does not provide the circumstances in which they can produce their most effective results. As with the arts, science is most likely to thrive in a community which understands and respects its function. Such a community will not only use the findings of science more efficiently, and liberate the individual scientist from demands for the dazzling tricks of the conjurer, but is also likely to produce more and better scientists. For this reason alone fundamental research is worth encouraging without thought of immediate practical advantages.

The problem of the two cultures, scientific and humanist, is no less real for having become a commonplace of polite discussion. It is not one which can be simply overcome by teaching all humanists the laws of thermodynamics, and all scientists the names of Shakespeare's major works, for one of its basic causes is the distrust by the expert for the dilettante, a distrust which is likely to be increased by forcing him to dabble in some foreign discipline. For these dabblings either will lead him to feel that this foreign subject is in fact pretty simple, and its practitioners unworthy of great respect, or will make him appreciate its difficulties so well that he will despair of learning anything from it, and abandon further interest. Moreover, as one common characteristic of the specialist is a devotion to his own field, he is likely to resent any time he is forced to give to work which appears irrelevant to his main interests, and which he knows he cannot carry far enough to be worthwhile in itself. The answer to the problem does not seem to lie in any attempts to force-feed a superficial polymathic culture as a pre-requisite of any higher studies, but rather in an attempt to recreate a community of learning which will be based on the mutual respect of specialized scholars. Such respect demands an understanding of each other's methods, and a willingness to question each other's basic assumptions, but not any necessary common core of factual knowledge.

The same community of interest which should exist between scholars in different fields is equally necessary between scholars and the community which supports them and makes use of their expertize. As universities and research institutions become more expensive and more complex, they become more dependent on governments and other non-scholarly bodies for finance. On the old principle of the payer, the piper and the tune, this makes them increasingly subject to the detailed direction of these outside bodies, whatever legal fictions of independence may be observed. This has gone to such lengths in America that some universities are now totally dependent on the defence establishment, on philanthropic foundations, and on private industry that their whole research program is directed from outside, and their staffing and teaching shaped in accordance with these demands. The corollary of this situation is that once a project is approved the scientists responsible for it have almost unlimited authority over expenditure on it, because the questions involved are beyond the comprehension of any mere administrator. The most striking examples of this process are the rocket research projects in both America and Australia.

But if it is in the interest of the scientist to have enlightened administrators, the interest of the layman goes further than being able to curb scientific extravagance. The implications of modern advances in biology, for example, are such that the whole community has a responsibility to understand them. The danger of the chemical devastation of our environment, the potential of biological pest controls, the desperate moral choices involved in the possibility of transplanting organs and prolonging some human lives indefinitely, are matters demanding the attention of all men, not only scientists.

The twofold function of the school, therefore, is to provide sufficient basic training to maintain an adequate number of professional scientists in all fields, and to induce a basic understanding of scientific method and potential in all students. As in most other spheres, present practice falls somewhere between these two stools.

The basis for scientific understanding is laid in the primary school, where syllabuses of science are replacing the older nature studies. In some ways this is a pity, for the older course was possibly one of the most successful taught in primary schools, and can possibly claim its share of the credit for such increased awareness of the need to preserve our natural heritage as has been manifested in recent years. The older course had the further advantage of utilizing the children's own knowledge, and of harnessing their natural interest in their surroundings to produce an overt awareness of the environment. Moreover, it was a course of unique educational value to teachers from the cities who found themselves in charge of rural schools where their students were experts in one part of the course. Not only did this experience of exchanged roles promote their understanding of the children beyond the rudiments of text-book psychology, but it also gave them a body of knowledge which they were able later to bring to their city appointments. We should not underestimate the part this element of teaching experience has played both in maintaining an element of social cohesiveness between town and country and in perpetuating that part of our national myth which sees us all as bushmen actual or manque.

It is to be hoped that the new techniques of primary science teaching will not displace this older and still valuable culture, but will be regarded as a complement to and extension of the older subject. For they, too, are intended to utilize the child's personal knowledge and gifts of observation to build up a body of experience which will enable him to understand the abstract concepts he will encounter at later stages in his schooling. Modern primary school science courses, ultimately based on principles developed in Switzerland by Piaget, and embodied in actual courses of study by the American Physical Sciences Study Committee (PSSC), differ from all older methods by the emphasis they place on the range of activities experienced rather than the body of knowledge covered. In theory, it would not matter if a child at the end of primary schooling had learnt nothing, in the sense of memorizing factual knowledge, provided he was ready to learn what the secondary school had to teach him. In practice, such an outcome of primary teaching would not be tolerated because the secondary schools are not geared to teach on this basis.

According to Piaget, children in their early years are concerned with exploring their immediate surroundings, and with gradually extending the range of their direct knowledge. They will be interested in rolling a beach ball against a wall and watching it bounce, but they are not yet ready to anticipate where the bounce will take it. Then, during the years roughly corresponding with primary school, they are concerned with concrete relationships. They can anticipate the bounce of the ball, play formal games, construct models of increasing complexity, design simple apparatus to achieve certain results. But they are not yet ready to codify their learning and to operate solely on the level of abstractions. This comes later, in their secondary school years.

This is the principle behind the new primary science teaching. Children are not taught about weight and mass and volume and momentum, but find these out for themselves. They heat cans of water and watch the tops blow off. They balance lead weights and bags of feathers, pour water into containers of various shapes and learn not to argue about who gets the tallest glass of cordial, knock draftsmen from the bottom of piles without disturbing the ones above them. To the child, each science period should be a fascinating experience, but for the teacher it is an exacting exercise. What is a mass of chaotic adventure for the children should be, for him, a carefully planned course which will cover all the basic scientific principles in the appropriate order, and which will repeat the encounters with different principles at intervals carefully designed to see that the second experience reinforces the first.

Nor does the teacher have the aids which once assisted him in the task. He should be able to curb the extravagances of juvenile high spirits without resorting to the time-honoured method of putting notes on the board for the pupils to copy down in their books. This has the further result that there is no clear record of completed work to be produced for the Inspector and learnt by the students. Yet not only must the work be properly ordered in a systematic program, but the students' experiences must be followed up by individual questioning to assist them to both understand and put into words what they have seen and done. This last step is possibly the most difficult, for it is so easy to omit it when pressed for time, or to short-circuit it by giving the children the answers instead of letting them find them themselves, and thus creating the illusion that something has been learnt instead of the reality. Finally, the questioning should force them to describe exactly what has happened, without prematurely demanding the abstract principles behind it. Yet the teacher should not restrict the child who can understand these principles.

For success, the courses for this style of teaching should be designed, not by experienced teachers who have picked up a smattering of science, but by first-rate scientists who are prepared to rely on the advice of teachers about what is practicable within the classroom. At the same time, the teacher needs a sufficiently advanced education in science to understand the aims and principles behind the classroom practices, and the opportunity for close and leisurely study of the particular course before he is required to implement it. The days when the primary teacher needed to be no more than sufficiently literate to read the handbook before he took the lesson have long since passed.

Yet neither of these conditions is met in Australian education. Some academic scientists have started to concern themselves with what happens in secondary schools, mainly because they are involved in teaching their products, but most of these would regard this interest as a hobby to be followed in the time they have to spare outside their main work. But the task of designing a primary school curriculum is as demanding as any other part of an academic discipline, and calls for the best brains available. There is some evidence that scientists are at their most productive and original in the earlier years of their careers, and thereafter give their most valuable service in positions of scientific leadership. It should therefore be possible to employ senior scientists as a matter of practice to act for limited periods with teachers and psychologists as teams to prepare and implement new school courses. A period of twelve months would be sufficient to acquaint themselves with the relevant findings of other disciplines, elaborate the principles of the task they are engaged on, prepare the syllabus, and train a nucleus of teachers to institute it. A further year would then be needed to work with these teachers on a pilot scheme and make the amendments to the syllabus which experience showed to be necessary. At the end of this time the experts could go back to their normal tasks and the teachers could gradually train others to put the scheme into practice throughout the country. Meanwhile, another team of experts could carry out an evaluation of the results of the course, and after some five or six years a new team could be appointed to commence work from the beginning again.

Such a scheme would both lead to the constant evaluation and revision of school courses and ensure that all the teachers conducting them had been fully trained. Certainly, it would mean that some schools would be a number of years ahead of others, but such a situation would be preferable to the present one where most schools are conducting outdated courses with maximum inefficiency. Furthermore, regular contact between the men on the frontiers of learning and the shock-troops in the field of ignorance could prove mutually refreshing and stimulating, giving the scientists the chance of gaining a broader view and the teachers the opportunity to obtain some depth of understanding. Finally, the scientists would be furthering their own interests both by promoting community understanding and by eventually producing a greater supply of scientific novitiates.

The task of teaching science in secondary schools is similar, although here a greater depth of understanding is aimed at. The steps of learning are from practical experience to understanding the immediate process to enunciating the general principle. But, just as in the primary school, the emphasis is ideally on understanding, not on knowledge, and the principles should not be learnt and memorized, but rather distilled by the students out of many individual experiences. The same principles of syllabus construction by experts which apply at the primary level should be applicable in secondary schools, except that at this stage the problem of implementation should be simpler because the teacher is an expert in a single field rather than a jack of all trades.

However, these simple principles are complicated by three factors—the demands made by universities, the standard achieved in the primary school, and the quality of secondary teaching. The influence of the universities, as we have seen, extends at least as far down the chain as the lowest forms of secondary schools, because the earliest courses must be sufficient to lead the students on to university entrance standard. As the volume of knowledge expands, more and more factual knowledge is being passed down the line to the schools. Work which was once covered for final honours examinations in the universities now appears in intermediate certificate courses. The most important subjects for university entrance are physics and chemistry, where knowledge tends to be cumulative, with an understanding of step two depending on a mastery of step one. Consequently, these facts, often dull in themselves, are packed into science courses right to the foot of the school, to the exclusion of many more interesting and educationally more valuable aspects of science.

It is this problem which is bringing about the revolution in teaching methods from knowledge to understanding. But to a great extent the success of this change depends on the foundations laid in the primary school. When Piaget's principles are translated into what is known as the spiral curriculum, the students entering secondary school will already have encountered during their primary schooling a range of concrete situations embodying the principles they are now to study in secondary school, and consequently should readily be able to develop their understanding to the level of theory. However, in the absence of sufficient primary teachers trained and experienced in these methods, the secondary teacher cannot assume any such background among his students. The situation is further complicated by the ignorance of primary schools which normally prevails among secondary teachers. The young teacher, in particular, is likely to be equally embarrassed by discovering that his class is completely ignorant of principles or techniques he had assumed them to possess and by finding that work he has carefully prepared himself to teach is already familiar to them from their primary classroom. Neither of these problems is likely to be as acute when the emphasis is firmly shifted from factual knowledge, but during the transitional period they can cause frustration and disillusion.

Finally, the implementation of any new approach to science teaching is gravely hindered by the serious shortage of qualified science teachers. It is difficult to discover accurate figures to show the actual state of affairs, as official statistics are designed to conceal rather than reveal. No reliance can, for example, be placed on figures dealing with the proportion of qualified teachers in the teaching service as a whole, as these figures do nothing to indicate how many of these teachers are being employed to teach subjects outside their professional competence. Not even figures showing the proportion of science classes being taken by qualified science teachers are particularly illuminating, as these classes tend to be concentrated at the top of the school, and leave the junior forms to the tender mercies of whatever staff the headmaster or staffing officer is able to scrape out of the pool. An adequate picture of the situation would require a survey of a cross-section of secondary schools over a number of years to show what proportion of students were taught by appropriately qualified teachers throughout their school life, as even one year with a total incompetent can do irreparable damage in any subject which depends on cumulative learning. This damage may not be evident at the time, but may only become apparent in later years when an imperfect understanding of fundamental principles leads to an inability to master more complicated operations. Such a failure of comprehension can be concealed in the earlier years by an ability to memorize appropriate formulae for repetition in the examinations, and may be so well concealed by the time its effects become noticeable that only the greatest good fortune can lead to an accurate diagnosis of the trouble. There can be little doubt that such weaknesses in the staffing of secondary schools are an important factor in later failures, but how widespread the trouble is we can, in the absence of complete figures, only speculate. However, a study carried out in Victorian secondary schools suggests some of the magnitude of the problem when it reveals that less than half the state's classes in junior science and mathematics are conducted by staff who are both trained as teachers and educated as scientists, even on the lowest definition of the latter. The situation in New South Wales appears to be better only because that state provides emergency and abbreviated courses of teacher training to obviate the need to employ the totally incompetent.

But beneath these structural deficiencies of science teaching lies a deeper uncertainty of purpose. This does not relate only to the conflict between teaching for understanding and for knowledge, but also, and more seriously, to the division of aims between laying the basis of a professional training in science and providing a general scientific education for the layman.

The fulfilment of the first of these objectives requires a rigorous and progressive course in the fundamentals of the natural sciences, a course which is conceived as part of a nine-year course towards the first degree in science. It will fit the needs of those who wish to continue to this level as well as of those who intend to branch off to some slightly different track, such as technology or medicine. For these students, the goal will make the effort seem worthwhile, even if they miss out on a certain amount of breadth on the way. But the more adequate the course is for this purpose, the less well it fits the student to understand science as a whole.

The trouble is that in the modern world there are no scientists—there are chemists, physicists, astronomers, biologists, geologists and so on. These are not necessarily completely unconnected disciplines, but their relationships exist most clearly at the highest levels of understanding. An attempt to integrate them at junior school level leads only to some mish-mash of 'General Science', which too often turns out to be a series of disconnected fragments of factual knowledge which have to be accumulated before the specialists are allowed to get on with their real studies and the others to drop the subject altogether.

Yet the ordinary student does need to be given some understanding of both how the scientist sees the world and how he is changing it. Science, properly taught, can combat the old myths of race. It can reveal something of the potential of our own bodies and of the world we live in. It can show the complex relationships which bind all living things and the earth from which they spring. It conveys a sense of the mystery of the infinitely large and the infinitely small. It offers to every man the chance of a partnership for his profit and pleasure, or of a hostility leading to his destruction or reduction to impotence. It is the responsibility of the school to show these things to all its students, and to give them some sense of involvement in the exciting new discoveries which are taking place around them in the realms of computers and electronics, biochemistry and immunology, physics and astronomy. It needs, also, to give some understanding of scientific method, of the need for objectivity and the constantly open mind, as well as of the impossibility of ever achieving these, of the place for hard work and the time for serendipity, of the need to respect facts and the necessity to use the imagination.

It is not only the layman who is entitled to this vision and understanding, but the future scientists and technicians also, for mere technical competence is inadequate unless it rests on the broadest understanding possible. The fortunate few who pursue their discipline to its frontiers will find this vision for themselves, but the rest of us need to be given it at school.

The most serious attempt to solve this conflict of purposes is that made by the Wyndham scheme in New South Wales. By providing science courses at three levels, it was intended that a student would have the choice of following a course of professional training, one of broad general interest, or one with something of each. The highest level would be followed by those destined for university science, the next by those intending to enter a branch of technology or to undertake an apprenticeship, and the last by those interested in the humanist, clerical or unskilled fields, who would, of course, also be following their particular interests at a high level. The scheme, however, provides only for transfer downwards between the levels, and so a second-year student who may just possibly decide in the long run to undertake a tertiary science course must already take the highest level. Consequently, the three levels of teaching tend to cater, not for different levels of interest, but, as in the old system, for different grades of ability, and the problem remains unresolved.

The same problems which confront the science teacher face the teacher of mathematics, and much of what I have said would apply equally well to him. But although mathematics is the language of science, it is not a science itself, it is not necessary to all the sciences, and an ability in one does not necessarily indicate an ability in the other.

Beneath all these attempts to make science teaching in the schools a bridge between the layman and the scientist as well as a preparation for the scientist of tomorrow lies a fundamental problem which is inherent in the very nature of our scientific knowledge. This contradiction is that science is not a matter of facts but of theories, but these theories arise from a study of facts. The problem of the teacher is how to acquaint the student with enough facts to understand the theories without misplacing the emphasis on the memorizing of facts. The facts cannot be properly understood unless they are presented within a theoretic framework, yet if such a framework is presented ahead of the facts it can only be presented as a formula resting on the authority of the teacher. This is in itself most unscientific, yet the error is worse when we consider that the teacher's knowledge itself is probably not derived from his own observation and judgement, but from the fruits of book learning. Yet it is difficult to avoid this intellectual dishonesty when students are being invited to theorize about what goes on at the molecular level, which is to them unobservable.

It can be argued that an understanding of mathematics is even more important in the modern world than an understanding of science, for mathematical methods are becoming the primary instruments of understanding in the social sciences, such as economics and sociology, market research and business management, and are even invading such apparently unrelated fields as history. It has, of course, long been indispensable for any study of modern philosophy. Moreover, quite apart from its instrumental value, mathematics is a study which, like language, can become a pursuit meriting the ultimate devotion of a man's life. Yet, like the sciences, mathematics has suffered in the schools from a reputation for difficulty which is probably similarly related to the shortage of competent mathematics teachers.

In the field of mathematics teaching we again observe the shift in emphasis from knowledge to understanding. The traditional school mathematics courses were concerned with learning means of manipulating numbers, starting with tables and finishing with the mysterious processes of the higher calculus. But the advent of cuisenaire has changed all this, and primary teachers now claim to be able to lead their students through processes which were once the exclusive possession of the sixth form. The difference is that today's students are not taught the principles and then set to apply them, but are presented with problems which lead them to discovering the principles for themselves. Nor are they limited to the single decimal digital system of numeration which their parents learned. The development of understanding through the use of the solid cuisenaire blocks in the primary school enables the secondary teacher to explore a whole range of mathematical concepts from the binary system to set theory. This is the approach which makes a modern mathematics textbook seem so strange to parents who accidentally happen to pick it up.

Another development within the field of mathematics has been the growing popularity of the inaptly named Mechanical or Technical or Instrumental drawing. Formal geometry has largely disappeared from the official mathematics syllabus, but it is creeping back in this new guise. Unimaginatively taught, this subject can be nothing but a series of disciplinary exercises of doubtful vocational value. But, in the hands of a teacher who understands its possibilities, it conveys through immediate and practical experience that sense of spatial relationships which is basic to geometry, to architecture, to engineering, even to mathematics itself.

However, just as science teaching is made ineffective by the people teaching science, so is mathematics teaching made ineffective by the teachers of mathematics. A year's ineffective teaching in mathematics is, however, more serious in its effects than in any other subject except perhaps foreign languages. In other subjects misconceptions can be corrected later, if they become apparent, but by its nature mathematics is such that failure to grasp a particular principle, or a misunderstanding of it, can break the chain of learning forever. When the principles are misunderstood by the teacher himself, as they must be unless he is fully versed in the discipline, the practices become rigid formulae to be learnt, and their purpose is lost. Unfortunately, the damage done by such methods of teaching is often concealed for years, as the pat memorized formulae will give the student an apparent command of the subject until he reaches the more demanding levels of senior years, when his failure to cope will be attributed to a lack of native ability rather than to the incompetent teaching which is actually responsible. Until the community is able and prepared to provide sufficient mathematics teachers, it will neither have sufficient expert mathematicians for its other needs, nor sufficient understanding of mathematics to utilize it effectively where it would be appropriate. Nor can it expect to supply this deficiency cheaply by training the same teachers to take both mathematics and science, for, although the fields are related, each is more than sufficiently complex to require an individual's complete devotion if he is ever to understand it sufficiently to teach it to others. Until we have sufficient teachers so qualified, it would be preferable to omit the teaching of mathematics entirely in some forms rather than entrust it to incompetents whose employment serves only to give parents a completely unjustified confidence that their children are being educated in this important subject.

A further deficiency in mathematics education is a lack of sufficient courses at a senior level for non-mathematicians. Where there are courses in General Mathematics, they can be taught only in those schools which have already provided facilities for the pure and applied studies required of those going on to specialize in the sciences or in mathematics. Because of the general shortage of mathematics teachers, it is only the biggest schools which can supply all these courses, and so most of the students who will go on to the humanities or into business are denied any acquaintance with this field of knowledge after their junior secondary years. Because mathematics is so dependent on its own language, this is not a deficiency which they can overcome by general reading in later life, and yet it is a deficiency which will also exclude them from a proper understanding of great tracts of the physical and social sciences.

A subject of uncertain classification in the schools is geography. This subject would once have been placed unhesitatingly with the humanities, although practical geographers have always been at least technologists, if not scientists. It is still often to be found in the Arts faculty of a university, but increasingly its methods are becoming less descriptive and more scientific. Within the school, it offers perhaps unique possibilities for showing the bond which links together all human activities with their natural and physical foundation.

In geography once again we find the conflict between the old methods of factual teaching and the new methods of cultivating understanding. Where once the atlas of maps was the basic aid of the geography teacher, modern geographers are prepared to dispense with it altogether. The traditional geography course required an extensive knowledge of countries, rivers, cities and towns. This study was organized to proceed from a survey of the immediate locality to a study of the state, the Commonwealth, and finally all the countries of the world. After the political and topographic features were learnt, some attention could be paid to economic matters, such as the major products of various countries, and the commercial activities of particular areas. At the same time, a certain amount of physical geography would be learned, from the disposition of the solar system to the factors controlling climate. Finally, in the senior forms, these various aspects of learning could be brought together to reveal some pattern of human activities. The courses always appeared arbitrary and disorganized, leaping with no apparent reason from a detailed study of the countries of South America to a study of the patterns of world-wide vegetation regions, and from an analysis of subsistence farming to an investigation of soil profiles and a summary of desert land forms. Yet the subject has always had the essential virtue of being finally concerned with human activities.

The new approach is different, relevant and exciting. The local area is no longer used as merely a starting point for an otherwise random survey of the world, but as a laboratory wherein the various geographical processes can be observed and studied. Sample studies are made of various areas ranging in size from a square yard of soil to a whole farm or suburban block, and the interrelation of the various natural factors and of men's attempt to utilize them is noted. This knowledge is then used as a basis of comparison with similar data taken from various areas at home and abroad. Meanwhile, the student learns from practical experience the various skills of the practical geographer, including mapping, soil surveys, botanical recording and weather observation. At the end of his course, he may not know where London or Paris is located, but if he should ever visit them he will be able to understand what has brought them into existence, what makes them different, and what keeps them alive. More importantly, he will understand better than their own inhabitants the importance of their links with their natural environment.

There are certain obvious dangers in this approach. In the first place, a certain amount of purely factual knowledge is necessary in order to appreciate many of the events in the modern world. The post-war troubles in Azerbaijan could not be explained by any knowledge of the ecology of that interesting piece of territory, but only through an understanding of the history of Russia's territorial ambitions and a knowledge of the geographical layout of the Middle East. Yet such a knowledge was unlikely to have been obtained from school days, or if it had been, would have long since been forgotten. It could, however, be obtained by the simple means of opening an atlas, a step which would occur to anyone who had an understanding of the role of geography in shaping international relations.

The more serious dangers to the new approach to geography lie in the conservatism of the old guard, which will no doubt be healed by the passing of time, and from the lack of a properly trained new guard who both understand the new principles and have the opportunity to carry them out. In this last respect geography is worse off than most other subjects, for the proper application of the new principles demands that the geography teacher, or at least the teacher in charge of geography in each school, have a detailed knowledge of his immediate locality. Such a knowledge will be built up over a number of years, but by this time the teacher will probably be ready for promotion and transfer to another school. Yet neither he in his new position nor his successor in his old is likely to find a headmaster who will, or can, give him three months off to make the local survey which should precede any attempt to teach his subject. The alternative, of course, is that he should regard his students as colleagues with him in the task of making such a survey. This would be the ideal method of teaching, but would require facilities and time far beyond that available in the normal school. In the absence of either of these opportunities, the best that the teacher can usually make of his job is to exploit the patience of the local community, the existing knowledge of his students, and his own ingenuity to construct an uneasy compromise. If he is successful, only he will know how far short of the ideal this compromise is. In this respect, he will be at one with his colleagues not only in the sciences but in all other fields of teaching. Fortunately for the administrators, the various public service acts prevent them from informing the community of what it is losing by its own parsimony.

If geography is moving from the field of the humanities to that of the physical sciences, the social sciences are steadily establishing their claims to a field of their own. This claim can be disputed on the grounds that they differ from the physical sciences not in their methods but only in their subject matter, but it can also be argued that their use of a model of enquiry derived from the physical sciences was only a necessary prop for the earlier stages of their development, and that they have now reached the stage where such a model is more likely to inhibit than to assist further growth.

Whatever argument there may be about the place of the social sciences in the spectrum of human understanding, there is no doubt about its place in our schools—it does not yet exist. Certainly, we have the vaguely inter-disciplinary subject of 'Social Studies', which tends to be descriptive rather than inquisitive, and economics has now been accepted as a respectable study at senior levels. We also have in several states various forms of education in health which draw their content from the work of psychologists, but as these studies are admonitory rather than educative they will be considered with religion rather than with the sciences. Our concern at the moment will be limited to the potential for primary and secondary education of a study drawing on psychology, sociology, anthropology, political science and related disciplines not for its content but for its methods and principles.

The usual argument offered for the inclusion of these subjects in school courses is that they deal with the central problems of choice which will face our students when they become adult citizens in a democracy. Through an understanding of such matters as poverty, old age, mass media, communications and social statistics, the individual will have a better understanding of the way in which his community works, the measure of control which can be exercised over it, and the causes of discord within it, and consequently will be able to make more reasoned choices in his personal and political activities and thus collectively ensure a responsible parliament and bureaucracy.

This argument is, however, dangerously close to the point of view from which the function of the school is seen as being to furnish its students with all the knowledge they may be eventually called upon to use during their adult life. The aim of school should rather be to initiate the development of those mental concepts which are needed to handle the different fields of human endeavour. In most cases, the period of secondary schooling is not long enough to develop any of these concepts to be of practical value, and a smattering of knowledge can be more dangerous than complete ignorance by giving an illusion of competence. What, however, can and should be done during the years of secondary schooling is to give the students an acquaintance with the methods of all the major disciplines so that they can develop their understanding subsequently through their own efforts, and in the meanwhile will appreciate both their own limitations and the accomplishments of the experts in fields in which they themselves can claim no mastery. One of the fields in which they should have such a seminal understanding is certainly the social sciences. Such an understanding will enable them in later life to use the work of the experts instead of being mesmerized by witch-doctory into either an admiring servitude or a fearful rejection. It will also create a climate in which the social scientists themselves will be able to work more effectively, and in which more candidates will be likely to come forward for professional studies in these fields.

If the social sciences are to be introduced to the schools, the first requirement will be a proper training program for future teachers. This might most valuably take the form of a seminar form of study for practising teachers who are already able to show some evidence of interest and competence in this field. The leaders of these courses should be professional social scientists seconded specifically for this purpose, rather than crash-trained departmental teachers. Out of the course should come not only the trained teachers, but also a course of studies designed to encourage the students to look out at their community with the same attitude of objective enquiry which is expected of physical scientists. The model for such a course might well be found in the new junior biology course, which takes as its basic subject matter the living environment in which the student finds himself. The course in social sciences would similarly take the social environment, and encourage the students to discover for themselves the rules governing its behaviour. The least that could be expected of such a course would be an understanding of the complexity of a modern society, and a rejection of the more simplistic myths explaining human behaviour. The best result that could be hoped for would be a recognition that man can obtain a similar degree of control over his social environment as he already exercises over his physical.

In all the sciences and mathematics, there needs to be a rigorous and constant re-examination of courses and methods in the light of the aims of the individual subjects, conceived in the widest possible terms. The sciences are not a self-contained field, but share with all parts of education the aim of developing the critical faculty, enhancing the individual's personality, and increasing his command over society. While it is not necessary that every student should have even a smattering of all the sciences, it is necessary that he should appreciate scientific thought and be able to communicate with scientists. Similarly, the scientist should understand the widest social and intellectual implications of his discipline so that he can make his maximum contribution to the life and thought of his generation. In other words, scientist and non-scientist alike should feel that they are constituent parts of a common culture, rather than separate cogs in a mass machine. It is a more important task of education in the sciences to contribute to this awareness than to engage in purely technical preparation for specialized careers.

4 The Humanities

If scientists are traditionally optimistic and forward-looking, humanists are very often inclined to pessimism. This may be because they have inherited the Greek tradition of a golden age in the past, after which the times can change only for the worse. Or it may be more simply because they are so well acquainted with the record of human folly through the ages that they cannot imagine any small improvements in technology changing the fundamental situation which governs mankind. Be this as it may, the humanist responsibility for preserving the wisdom of the past and reinterpreting it for the present is a necessary complement to the scientific progress which threatens to destroy the old truths at the same time as it emancipates us from our ancient limitations. But although much of the subject matter of the humanist is derived from the past, it is wrong to think of his disciplines as static. The formulation of a new philosophic proposition, the writing of a new play, the development of a new principle of criticism may not be either as certain or as dramatic as the discovery of a hitherto unknown process of nature, but these humanistic activities are just as important to our understanding of the human condition, and hence to our ability to control it. Despite Aristotle, not all knowledge is necessarily empirical and deductive.

The basic human study is language, which of course includes literature. A command of language is necessary not only for the other human disciplines, but for all studies. We may obtain information from observation, skills from practice, but it is by putting our experience into words that we come to understand it. Similarly, while human experience may be expressed through art or through music, through the dance or through mime, literature remains the most demanding and exact form of expression precisely because its medium, the word, has an objective reference, or meaning, which is common property and does not depend solely on the context which the artist gives to it. Yet, despite the importance of language to human understanding, the deliberate teaching of the mother tongue is a relatively recent educational practice, and the success of this teaching remains highly suspect.

In classical times, the key humanist studies were grammar and rhetoric, which were not so much studies of language as such as studies of rules drawn from the practice of the authorities, the authors accepted at the time. The aim of these studies was not fluency in expression, nor even familiarity with classical authors, although both these results might follow, but rather the acquisition of a formal skill which could be applied to the forensic, dialectic and scholastic pursuits of the age. It was in fact an exhaustive professional training designed for a class of administrators or clerics, and it presupposed rather than inculcated a knowledge of and facility with language. In more recent times, these studies were succeeded by an intensive study of Latin, and sometimes Greek, authors. The principal method employed in these studies was the construing, or translating, of passages from the original, and commenting on the grammatical constructions. The value of this study was held to lie in the acquaintance it gave the student with elevated thought, and even more in its virtue as a discipline of mind and body. Among those who possessed a certain linguistic ability it certainly developed powers of construction and vocabulary, and it promoted the solidarity of the ruling classes by initiating all their members into a common culture which at least provided handy tags to decorate parliamentary orations, but it is doubtful whether many students who were subjected to this stern regime ever left it without feelings of profound relief.

With the development of universal elementary, and later secondary, education, and the steady withering away of the classics, the study of the mother tongue has assumed a new, and twofold, purpose. In the first place, it has the role of making the whole population literate. In the second, it has inherited the role of providing a common culture, not now only for a small elite, but for whole nations. This second role tends to lead to a third, that of cultivating discrimination in relation to such popular arts as films, newspapers and television. In short, the cultivation of literacy turns out to be nothing less than a study of the whole of civilization as it appears in any particular place.

In Australia, we assume that the mother tongue of our students is English, an assumption which can cause difficulties in areas with a large migrant population. We are no doubt correct in this policy, not because of the practical difficulties of providing a different education for different national groups, but because to do so would be to destroy the school's effectiveness as a social integrator. However, we should not forget the price we pay for this. In the first place, children who speak a language other than English are handicapped in all their studies until they master our tongue, and we undoubtedly are wasting some of our educational potential for this reason. Secondly, by giving them a second-rate education in what is, to them, a foreign tongue, we may in fact be delaying that degree of integration into our community which they could achieve if they were educated in their own language and taught English properly as a second language. Finally, by ignoring the contribution they have to make to our common culture, we are reducing our understanding of our own civilization. This is a point to which I shall return later.

The most common criticism of English teachers when they make large claims for the study of literature and the cultivation of discrimination as integral parts of their subject is that, in pursuing these cultural will o' the wisps, they are forgetting their primary function. Just teach them to read and write is the common cry of academics and employers, and let them get on with their job. Shakespeare is all right for the people who like that sort of thing, but the future engineer cannot afford to waste his time on trimmings. All that he needs is to be able to spell accurately, write correct sentences, and get straight to the point of what he reads. The junior executive does not need even this much. He will be right as long as he can write a clear report, dictate a brief letter, and read a simple instruction. As for the typist, she needs only the ability to spell.

All these ideas reflect the conception of English as an instrumental skill, like a knowledge of multiplication tables. The unfortunate fact is that none of the skills mentioned is simple, and that they cannot be acquired by learning formal rules, or even by assiduous practice in linguistic drills. Such techniques can be valuable to correct poor habits of expression or to develop specific skills, but only if the student understands their purpose and underlying principles. This understanding comes only from an understanding of language itself, which may as well be gained outside the classroom as in it, but cannot be acquired by any form of sleight of hand.

The assumption behind the idea of language as an instrument of communication is that all a person has to do is to know what he has to say and then apply the proper rules to say it clearly and correctly. If he is aiming at literary graces, he can then add the adornments which will give literary merit. Similarly, when he reads he should first look for the main point of the passage, then the points which lead up to it, and he will then understand all that has been said. In other words, language is a kind of code by which we communicate with each other. The originator of the thought translates it into the code, and the receiver turns it back again. This analogy is strengthened by the popularity of computers, which can operate in precisely this way. It also provides the logical basis for the type of communications handbooks used in the services and in business, which lay down the forms for every type of message. This distinction between form and content, always inaccurate, has long been discredited in literary criticism, but it still holds sway among those outside pundits who expect the benefits of language without the trouble of understanding it.

Human experience follows a path from chaotic sense impressions to analytic understanding. To the primitive or the child, human experience is a chaotic, incoherent whole which he must explore and organize. His first instruments for this exploration are sound and movement. These sounds are not the bellows with which he attracts attention to his needs, but the babbling, chortling and tuneless singing with which he accompanies his actions. We can imagine how these sounds evolved into a language by observing a baby learning to speak. Quite often, before it pronounces distinguishable words, it will chatter away in a mysterious language of its own. The proud delight with which parents greet the first sound of 'Ma' and 'Da' conceals the fact that its early speech consists not of single words but of complete sentence patterns. Even later, while its vocabulary is still limited, it will continue to accompany its actions with a recitatif of sound, although its sentences of command may be both precise and distinct. What has happened is that its expanding common vocabulary gradually separates itself from the background babble and acquires distinct, analytic meanings. The first step from synthesis to analysis has been taken, and the last will be taken with death, although possibly long before physical extinction. Yet it can take this first step without ever being taught a rule of formal grammar.

Amongst the earliest men speech probably arose in association with ritual, for work or religious purposes. Chanting forms a natural accompaniment to such activities as hunting in packs, hauling such heavy objects as tree trunks, and dancing in religious ceremonies. Gradually the individual parts of these chants would acquire particular meanings. Although the details of this development are necessarily obscure, it seems clear that language is in origin a community possession and a part of an overall system of ritual, myth, and action. But as soon as language begins its separate existence, the individual possesses a tool for analyzing these previously organic experiences into their separate parts and forming new syntheses for himself.

For a long time in the development of human society the modern idea of the individual artist remains unknown. The singers of early societies are a part of their community, and express its common heritage of stories and beliefs in the patterns and even the very phrases which have been handed down to them from time immemorial. The individual bard differed from his fellows in excellence rather than in kind. But even this stage is an advance on the complex but primitive art of the corroboree, where individual and community are one, and the different arts inseparably intermingled. It is only in advanced communities that we find literature becoming an original exploration of personal experience. Yet even the most advanced literature must use the language which has been shaped and passed down through countless generations. In the shaping of the individual languages we can trace something of the same process, as they change in their nature from synthetic, where each word undergoes complicated changes of form to indicate its relationship to others, to analytic, where each word has a simple, unchanging form, and its relationship to others is indicated by its placing in the sentence. Literary patterns share a similar process. The earliest forms are the carefully ordered, traditional patterns of poetry, and only later do the more individual, exact styles develop, where close attention is paid to each element, rather than allowing it to be lost in the whole. Even when modern readers return to older forms they tend to forget this fact, and admire the striking but exceptional excellence of individual phrases rather than observing how each one plays its full role only as one part of a pattern.

In the healthy development of an individual, the growth of language should observe a similar pattern. As he acquires the first elements of a vocabulary which will enable him to express his personal experience, so he should be fed with the wealth of rimes and jingles which both express the traditional wisdom of his race and provide patterns of sound which are interesting in themselves. At various stages of his schoolboy career it is possible that he will learn or invent those strange juvenile languages which are impressive as much as expressive, secret rather than public, and which, by thus limiting the community which shares them, emphasize the primitive communal and even magical elements of language. But as his range of physical, mental and emotional experience develops, so will both his need and his ability to express this experience in language. This growing power of language will not develop in isolation, but will be associated with the rituals of games, with the miming and playacting of elementary drama, and with the delight of drawing and painting. The arts of song, dance and painting were not separate in their origin, and should not be separate in the life of the child. To understand how closely these different forms of expression are linked in the child's mind the adult should listen to a child unfold the story which lies behind his latest painting.

It is within this context that the teacher of English must work. It is his job to lead his students to an appreciation and understanding of the unlimited but often intractable resources of the language to which they are heirs. In the first place this understanding will be developed by encouraging them to explore their experience in words. A lack of such encouragement is one of the greatest handicaps brought with them by children from under-privileged families in sub-verbal cultures, where communication is as much by nod, grunt or shrug as through words. On the other hand, the typical child from a middle-class environment comes with a readiness to speak and listen which has been developed through the verbal barrage with which he has been surrounded from the time he was born. All children can be given something of this advantage in a kindergarten which forces them to put their demands into words. 'Can I have that?' leads to the response from the teacher, 'What do you call it? What do you do with it? What are you going to do with it now?' These questions demand quite complex answers, and force the child to use his latent verbal abilities, but although the technique appears simple it requires time and patience, as well as an awareness of individual needs. These qualities are available usually only in the kindergarten, for the size of the typical class prevents many primary teachers from giving sufficient attention to the individual to overcome the cultural handicaps. Yet kindergartens exist in their greatest numbers in the fashionable suburbs where these problems are least common. On the other hand, the deprived child, whose problem could perhaps be recognized and solved if he were the only one in the class with this difficulty, will probably be in a class where the majority of the children are in the same situation. This means not only that the teacher is unable to give each the attention he needs, but also that the social situation is one where the same non-verbal standard is general, with the consequence that there is no stimulus for any of the children to develop their own fluency. The longer they remain at school, the more intractable the problem will become, the fewer will be the opportunities available to meet it, and the greater will be its effect in other spheres of learning.

Before experience can be explored in words there must of course be a range of challenging and stimulating experiences to explore. In the kindergarten, these are supplied by the range of materials on hand, which practically suggest their own activities. Later, the teacher must show greater ingenuity of contrivance in providing situations and activities which match the developing maturity and interests of the child. The principles of Piaget are as applicable here as they are in the sciences and mathematics. Among younger children the experiences should be immediate and concrete; later they should be encouraged to look beyond the immediate experience to the generalization, and to find the same excitement in the world of ideas that they once found only in the world of physical reality. Their education has been stultified if by the time they leave school they cannot find in the laws of physics or the imagery of Shakespeare the excitement they once found only in a game of hopscotch or a football final. On the other hand, their schooling has been even more disastrous if they have lost the latter enjoyment in the pursuit of the former.

The experiences which the child needs to explore in his English classes are not only, or even primarily, those drawn from his personal knowledge. Possibly their most important source is that range of vicarious experience embodied in imaginative literature. This literature should not be presented as something set apart for admiration, but as an integral part of the talking, story telling, playacting, singing and painting which comprise their normal work in English. The material chosen at each stage should be relevant to the child's interests and valuable for his mental and emotional growth. This can lead to a conflict of purpose in English teaching, for the intellectual aim of the teaching can be seen as subordinate to its therapeutic value in promoting healthy development. Such confusion arises, however, from a failure to distinguish between means and ends. The end of any English teaching is neither mental nor social adjustment, but the mastery of the intellectual discipline of language. Because language is concerned, however, with the exploration of personal experience, its use is inseparable from this experience. Just as we cannot properly distinguish between the form and content of a passage of writing, so we cannot distinguish between experience and expression in the act of writing itself.

The Australian author, Alan Marshall, describes the business of autobiographical writing as being like living one's life over again. That is, the imaginative writer is re-living, or re-creating his life, in words. The new experience may in fact deal with fictitious events or characters, but essentially the same truth applies. When we turn to the more prosaic task of writing a technical report, the position is no different. An engineer had his recommendations rejected several times by a large Victorian enterprise, because the board were unable to understand his scheme. Finally, one of the personnel officers was asked to revise the report. This revision turned out not to be a mere matter of correcting the grammar and straightening out the syntax, but a task of several months' duration which involved collaborating with the author of the project in working through every detail of the scheme from its conception to its developed expression.

The same experience is familiar in everyday life. When someone has a problem, or is upset about something, he likes to talk it over with a friend, not so much to receive advice as to hear himself talk it out. The friend's role is to assist the talking by prompting with the occasional question or comment. But this use does suggest a further aspect of language—what David Holbrook has called its role as 'neutral ground'. It possesses this quality because, although any work of literature is the outcome of personal experience, the product of this experience has an independent and objective character which can be coolly analyzed and dissected. In talking out a problem, we distance it from ourselves and are able to see it so much more clearly. Similarly, in reading or listening, although we become emotionally involved, we also remain detached spectators, able to understand and comment on the very experience we are undergoing.

This fact is of particular relevance in the choice of literature for school use. The nursery rimes and fairy stories of childhood deal, in an objective and mythologized form, with the emotional problems of the child who feels himself the helpless victim of outside powers, dependent for his very existence on the continued goodwill of adults. The fairy stories bring these fears under his control by confronting him with situations where this goodwill is withdrawn, and then solving the resulting crisis. The loving mother is replaced by the wicked step-mother, but eventually love again triumphs through the good fairy. Giants can be challenged with cheeky impunity as long as Jack knows that home still waits as a safe refuge. Above all, the reality of these terrifying situations is limited by the controlling voice of the parent reading about them.

These considerations suggest a proper perspective on comics and such near-comics as Enid Blyton or the Golden Books. These publications have the common characteristic of over-simplifying for the sake of a formula. The Blyton and Golden stables trade on pre-freudian sentimentality about childhood as a garden of innocence, but uneasy moderns do not believe sufficiently in this garden to trust its power to retain its own virtue. Instead of water, they spray the garden with detergent, and instead of digging in the manure they apply only completely deodorized artificial fertilizers. Fortunately, small creatures in neighbouring gardens still hurl sufficient good clean dirt over the fences to ensure vigorous growth and horrify any mother who accidentally oversees her offspring's mind, but this vigour does not entirely compensate for the lack of balance in the basic diet, and leaves the plant susceptible to the drug addiction of the next stage of growth—the comic book era.

These manifestations of commercial art are unbalanced in precisely the opposite direction to the kiddies' books. Whereas commercial books for the younger child are emasculated of any violence, passion or emotion, these products of vicious adolescence contain little else. Their world is one of technical virtuosity in which heroes of amazing physical and mental endowment combat fiendishly malevolent prodigies of evil. Good, of course, always triumphs, and the world is again saved for democratic American manhood. The books are distinguished for shoddy printing, total absence of humour, ingenuity of situation and incredibility of character. They also advertize courses for muscle development and cures for acne.

It is doubtful whether any of these publications do any harm in themselves. Their danger is that their simplicity encourages an addiction which leaves room for no other kind of reading, and so allows the child to grow up with a picture of reality which is distorted more by its inadequacy than by any deliberate falsification. Various critics of comics have fastened on their overtones of racism, their violence and brutality, and these are certainly the features which are most distasteful to the adult mind. The experiment of Dr Maurice Balson, of Monash University[1], in creating prejudice against a mythical race of Javas by subtly slanting all references to them is a reminder of the dangers inherent in this hidden kind of brain-washing. Nor does the behaviour of the Americans in Vietnam, or the willingness of the Australians to send their children to follow them, suggest any reason for confidence in the ability of adults to outgrow their childhood myths. However, the answer does not lie in any attempt to suppress these publications, or their film and television counterparts, although intriguing possibilities are suggested by the thought of applying (under the new New South Wales censorship act) to have Noddy classified as suitable for adults only. Rather, the teacher has an obligation to provide a counterweight to this element of his students' reading, and to develop those powers of discrimination which will enable them to understand their reading matter and reject what is false. This second aim, the task of the later secondary years, can, however, be accomplished only if the students have made the acquaintanceship of a wide range of worthwhile literature throughout their school years. The simplest test of whether a book is suitable for a child is probably to decide whether it is of interest to a mature adult. If it is not, there is no reason to ban it, for only the rashest of mortals would assume that his taste is sufficiently trustworthy to enforce on another, but there is every reason to refrain from offering it to the child for his use. To do otherwise is both patronizing and degrading.

The technicalities of English are subordinate to the basic activities of reading, speaking, writing and drama. The desire to read or write should precede the practice if the latter is to be effective. In the field of reading, in particular, modern techniques and practices have removed a great deal of the drudgery. The principle behind these techniques is that of removing unnecessary and distracting difficulties while drilling essentials. The Initial Teaching Alphabet accomplishes this by providing a single symbol for each sound, so that the child can master the principle of translating symbols into sounds before he has to deal with the complications

[1] See bibliography.

of English orthography. The system of words in colour achieves the same effect by using a single colour for each sound. Present research does not suggest that either of these methods is superior to the other. However, investigators are still interested in the problem of precisely what causes the jump from incomprehension to understanding, and how these early experiences of reading affect the child's later performance.

The practice of carefully controlling the vocabulary in the reading material also promotes confidence and reading speed by ensuring that the child is not caused unnecessary difficulty by meeting a word which is right outside his experience and which he is not likely to come across again for some years. Time spent in mastering this word may well be wasted, and too frequent repetition of the experience can jeopardize his chances of achieving any real fluency and cause permanent retardation. So the readers used in early years are carefully limited to those contained in lists compiled from the vocabulary of children at each age. When new words are introduced, they are repeated shortly afterwards so that they quickly become a part of the child's working vocabulary. Mathematical techniques are now being developed whereby any passage of reading can be graded for its level of difficulty according to the range of its vocabulary.

A similar technique is used in the reading laboratories which have become so fashionable lately. The reading cards in these sets are graded according to the difficulty of the vocabulary, sentence structure and ideas. An initial test shows the child's starting level, and intensive practice on a variety of material within this range builds up his ability and confidence. When he reaches a certain standard of performance, he moves to the next level. In this way, each child is able to work at his own speed, and does not have to waste time on work intended to deal with troubles being encountered by other students. However, the material used in these laboratories is limited in its range and tends to be snippety in its content, the practice of giving each child his own material deprives the class of a common body of experience as a basis for other work, and the use of the laboratory for reading creates a divorce between this and the other parts of the English course.

Finally, too few teachers realize that the laboratory is only effective if every child is given close individual guidance, and only then for limited periods of time. Too often the use of a laboratory becomes merely an easy gimmick which avoids both teaching and learning.

The principle of limiting difficulties in order to bring about effective learning is itself open to criticism. One of the marks of the effective reader is that he is able to deal with the unfamiliar as it is encountered, either by guessing from context or from his knowledge of cognates. Once basic fluency has been achieved, any deliberate restriction of the reading material smacks of the practice of some New York kindergartens which employed teachers to unteach children who could already read so that they would be ready for the scientific methods of the primary school. However, the methods are of undoubted value in promoting this basic fluency in the first two or three years of primary school, and for students in later years who for some reason have failed to take this initial step.

Attempts have also been made to produce programs to develop writing skills. It is doubtful whether these can work, because writing is, or should be, an essentially personal matter, and a program can only develop a facility to spin words according to external criteria. However, useful drill programs have been designed to correct specific weaknesses, such as spelling, or to provide crash courses of vocabulary extension. These aids are valuable as long as they remain supplementary.

The pattern of any work in English should be from the basic experience, whether it is a classroom activity such as reading, story-telling or drama, or some experience from outside the English classroom, to talking, to writing, to criticism. It is at the third of these stages that the technicalities can be emphasized. An English sentence which says nothing is as useless as a mathematical equation which does not balance. But the child can be brought to understand this not by learning rules of grammar but by realizing that a sentence is incorrect when it does not accurately describe the experience with which he is concerned. The rules of grammar are a description of what actually happens in

English, not a prescription for writing it correctly. Their study is useful as a means of understanding the workings of the language, but is an advanced rather than an elementary study. Moreover, linguists are coming to realize that the traditional rules of grammar are an attempt to apply a Latin formula to the essentially germanic English, and as such are both inaccurate and misleading. Their disappearance from the syllabus will not be followed by any deterioration in the standard of written English.

The practice of English, then, starts with acquiring a fluency in the use of words. Rigour is developed by practice in accurately describing experience, whether this experience be immediate or vicarious, a matter of feeling or observation, activity or knowledge. At the same time, the child's own experience is enlarged through reading, which means entering into the mind and experience of others. At first, such a conscious distinction is meaningless to the child, and he enters into a story with the same zest as he would embark on an actual adventure. Later, he develops the ability to criticize, at first by discussing the behaviour of the story-book people, much later by questioning their reality. As the end product of self-expression is the ability to write fluently and correctly, so the end of reading is literary criticism. But this distinction is false unless it is remembered that it marks a difference of emphasis, not of nature. The effective writer must practise self-criticism; the effective critic is practising the exploration in words of his experience of reading.

Criticism is the logical consequence of the experiences in reading, writing and speaking which have been the child's life from the time he first enters school. It marks the ultimate stage in his awareness of language, for now he is not only able to enter into the experience of another through the words which describe that experience, but as a result of his own practice with words he is able to evaluate their relationship to that experience. For although language is primarily a tool for the exploration of experience, we have seen that it also has a life of its own. This enables the manipulator to simulate experience by a clever net of words. It also enables words to be used, not as instruments for revealing the truth, but as weapons against others and as tools for using others for our own purposes. The person who is aware of language will be less likely to fall a victim to either of these practices.

It is within this context that we can see the place for a study of films and television in the school curriculum. The usual argument offered in favour of including these arts among school studies is that children today spend so much time watching them. The same chain of reasoning would suggest that the major study on the curriculum should be sleep, because we spend so much of our life at it. The reason for including any study in the school course is not its importance in later life, but the importance of the skills which this study cultivates. In the school situation, drama offers far more possibilities than do films and television, even if the students never attend a theatre after they leave the schoolroom, although such an outcome indicates a very poor standard of drama teaching. The method of drama teaching now being developed in schools cultivates the natural acting and improvization abilities exercised by children in the normal course of their play. During primary and early secondary years no scripts are used except those the children devise for themselves, and then only on special occasions. The normal drama activities consist of miming, acting and improvization to music, or around given themes. This develops the children's natural speech and acting abilities, provides an activity on which to base other parts of the English work, and lays the basis for a formal study of drama in later years.

The study of films and television can be developed from this study of formal drama, both because they are an interesting branch of the medium in themselves, and because they all depend on words for their total effect. They also offer an illuminating contrast to the theatre, for the word is no longer the dominant factor in the exploration of experience, but co-exists on equal, or even inferior, footing with the visual image and with sound. Nevertheless, the technique of criticism developed in a purely literary context is an equally effective instrument in this field. Even in earlier years, before it is appropriate to encourage formal criticism, the children's experience of film and television can be used as a basis for their own writing. Finally, a number of teachers are now exploring film as an art medium by working with their classes to produce their own films. This is an activity which brings together the skills and techniques of the practical arts and crafts as well as of literature, and its extension could have most significant effects on Australia's culture. However, it cannot fill the place of the more traditional activities of the English classroom.

A major obstacle to the development of English teaching is the uncertainty of purpose which afflicts teachers of English in much the same way as it affects those in the sciences. This is an uncertainty whether the subject is being taught for those who are to pursue it as their profession or for the average student. This difficulty is compounded in the case of English by the refusal of many academics to admit that there is any critical specialization. The accomplished critic, according to their argument, is just a skilful reader. This is in essence true, but they forget that the professional critic, or the student taking English as a major study, has far more time in which to develop the skill of reading than does the general reader. The specialist has the opportunity to acquire a far broader background of general reading, to acquaint himself with a far wider selection of critical reading, and to devote far more thought to the individual works he is studying. But if the critics are right in believing that their concerns are the same concerns which should interest every reader, they should be prepared to recognize a lower level of technical accomplishment as a worthwhile school attainment at least among those students who do not intend to take their English studies further.

The failure of the school English course to meet this need for different standards has led to different results in the separate states. One response is typified by the Victorian matriculation course, which offers English Expression as a compulsory subject and English Literature as an optional. The former is examined for pass only, and tends to be an arid technical course which, while offering the interested teacher the opportunity for covering a lot of valuable work which is only marginally relevant to the examination, does not prevent the hack from effectively coaching his quota of students through each year without ever inspiring them to an original thought or a pleasurable reading. Recently, however, a section of wider reading has been introduced which will at least force students to consider what writers have to say about the world they live in. The Literature syllabus, on the other hand, is usually taken only by students specializing in the humanities, and demands a degree of competence in the techniques of formal literary criticism which is perhaps beyond the scope of the normal matriculation student, although expert coaching can develop an effective simulation of these techniques.

The New South Wales syllabus has until this year been a single course covering both literature and expression, but, to judge by the number of cribs on the market, lending itself to the worst techniques of the crammer. It demands formal knowledge rather than understanding, and it is not surprising that the survey at the National University showed that many of the students who passed in it were not capable of handling the language of university studies. From 1967, however, a sixth year English examination will be offered at three levels, and this could possibly meet the needs of the specialist without sacrificing the potential scientist and engineer. However, it would seem that the students who elect to take the middle level of the examination will still be required to undertake a course which has sufficient breadth to require cramming without enough leisure to obtain depth. More seriously, those who take the higher levels are offered a rigidly academic study of standard classics which must reinforce traditional ideas of the dullness of literature.

The problem of teaching literature to non-specialists, which includes all junior students and a good proportion of seniors, is to decide what standards can be observed by the students as the basis of judgement. This question did not arise in the earlier years of literary studies, where it was assumed that a work was profitable in proportion to the elevation of its sentiment, and the task of the teacher or examiner was to ensure that the students had a scholarly acquaintanceship with the prescribed books. By this was understood an ability to quote lengthy passages, to paraphrase complex arguments, and to explain abstruse references. But modern literary criticism is concerned with the moral values of literature as experience, not as inspiration. By abolishing the classical distinction between form and matter it has made reading a more demanding and a more rewarding art. But it has also introduced questions of the moral health of the reading material, which tends to be assessed according to the individual critic's judgement of what is life-promoting and what is life-inhibiting. Lawrence is in because he demonstrates in concrete terms the complex vitality at the centre of healthy human beings. Milton is out because he writes in a style of lofty sublimity which serves only to conceal the muddled thought and perverse philosophy at its centre. Only by understanding such matters, it is proclaimed by the more extreme, can the individual achieve moral balance in himself.

Unfortunately, the degree of literary judgement needed to assess such verdicts as these is one which can only be developed after many years of practice. It requires not only the ability to respond to literature, and to make fine discriminations between different pieces of literature, but also the ability to analyze these responses and discriminations. It is this last ability which is beyond the majority of school students, and the practice of examiners in demanding an ability for close analysis does not produce literary critics, but rather students trained in the simulation of literary criticism.

What can and should be developed in the schools is the ability to distinguish between false and true uses of language. We have seen how language has a reality and existence of its own, independent of the experience it may be describing. We all take advantage of this quality when we compose nonsense rimes or exploit a gift for punning. On the other hand, a part of a poet's technique is to harmonize the independent behaviour of his language with the shape of his thoughts. The school student can learn from both his own practice and from wide reading to recognize where the writing departs from experience, either by acquiring its own impetus, or by a falsity of tone or emphasis. He can then learn to apply this same critical discrimination to character studies, from film and television as well as from books, to emotional situations and developments, to human action and to argument. The English teacher can assist students to develop these powers of logical analysis, but they should not be expected to demonstrate them prematurely.

We still may encounter the critic who would agree that the initial understanding of language is gained from a wide experience of its use for every purpose, but who would argue that once a student's interests have matured in the later years of his school career he should be allowed to concentrate on its technical and practical uses to the exclusion of literary fancies. Surely there is enough work for him to do in reading the literature of his own subject, and learning to express his specific understanding of his specialized interests.

One answer to this claim is that the cultivation of the imagination is at least as important as the development of the faculty of reason. If reason alone governed man's decisions, there would be unanimity of opinion among students of any single area of human conduct, and we could safely entrust major decisions to these experts. However, the human reason is normally the servant of emotion, and we in fact develop our arguments only after we have adopted our basic position. The most that can be expected of our reason is that we may be open to conviction of error if we can be shown to be wrong, but history offers little reason to suppose that this will ever be a common occurrence. A more reasonable aspiration is that man's imaginative growth will lead to increased sensitivity to others, and an increased ability to understand the situation of others, which will give a greater chance of the initial position being soundly taken.

But an equally serious objection to narrowly technical studies of language is that this practice elevates the analytic above the synthetic quality of language, and leads to an erroneous understanding, not only of language, but also of the experiences it is used to describe. We have seen how the development of language is largely a development of its analytic capacity. But this capacity is valuable because it creates a greater potential for making new syntheses. The closely analytic language of the scientist, which restricts every term to one precise meaning, is useful only within its proper context. Once these terms seem to show the whole of reality, they become dangerous, for they both restrict their user's understanding of his subject and blind him to the understanding of others. This tended to happen to physicists in the nineteenth century, who saw all reality in terms of their own discipline. It is happening to psychologists today, who not only fail to see the limitations of their discipline in relation to others, but also fail to understand that their jargon embraces only a single aspect of the truth it connotes. There is probably no field where this distortion is as dangerous as that of education

The role of the literary artist is to remind us constantly of the wholeness of things. He is concerned, not with the single meaning of a word, but with everything it can say to us. He is as concerned with the physical reality and geological implications of a grain of sand as is any scientist, but he can also see the world implicit in it. This synthesizing view is necessary to the scientist not only as a corrective to his analyzing approach, but also so that he can understand the full context of what he is doing in his own narrow field. It is in this sense that literature belongs to all, and so cannot be left as the exclusive field of the professional experts.

A major reason that a study of English rarely achieves its potential is that its teaching has not normally been considered a job for experts. In the primary school, and at the lower levels of the secondary school, it is believed that anyone can teach English, and anyone does. This is not perhaps as serious in primary schools, where at least all the teachers have had primary training and the miniscule English studies which are a part of it, but it can be disastrous in secondary schools where the course becomes more demanding at the very time its teachers become less qualified. Even if the training of primary teachers could be improved so that they would all be required to undertake rigorous studies in English before being allowed to teach it, their efforts would be largely wasted unless there were fully-educated secondary teachers to build on their foundations. The teaching of English at any level is an exercise requiring critical skill if the teacher is to understand the possibilities the subject matter holds for his students. It is one subject which should not be taught by anyone who has not himself studied it fully.

But if the state of teaching the mother tongue is alarming, the state of teaching foreign languages is catastrophic. Australia is perhaps the most isolated country in the world, and it has taken advantage of this isolation to develop a culture which complacently assumes that all good things come in English. Now it finds itself becoming involved in the affairs of Asia, it is unable to staff its diplomatic posts with men able to speak the local language. Although it has been the beneficiary of a vast post-war migration from Europe, the onus is placed wholly on the newcomers to learn our language. Although this same post-war period has seen globe-trotting become a way of life among young people, the vast majority of them are quite happy to tour the world speaking nothing but English.

These circumstances would scarcely suggest that language teaching has always occupied a place of honour in our secondary schools, yet such is the case. In New South Wales, until recently, all children have been graded into two, one and no-language streams. In Victoria, the majority of children have been forced to labor over at least one foreign language. In the other states, a language has been a recognized part of any secondary academic education. The most common of these languages is French, but a certain amount of German is also taught. Latin has maintained its place in Catholic and, to a lesser extent, in other church schools, but has been declining in importance in state schools. Italian has a small, but growing, place, and there is now an increasing interest in learning Asian languages. With all this activity, then, what has gone wrong?

In the first place, the language teacher probably has to face greater hostility from his students than does any other. The majority of secondary students do not intend going on to higher education, and even those who do are more likely to be interested in the histories or technology. Their attitude affects the minority who might otherwise be interested, and the teacher is forced to spend a great deal of his time on publicity and propaganda rather than on teaching.

In the second place, few schools allocate sufficient time for an adequate program of language teaching, and very few students have the chance of commencing their language studies before secondary school. This means that it takes a very long time before the student feels that he is getting anywhere. It is probably not until the fifth year of secondary school that he has learned enough of any language to read in it anything of great interest, and not until even later that he is able to speak or read it at all frequently. In addition to this, the few able and interested students are forced to proceed at the pace of the slowest. The result is that for a number of years language can be nothing better than a dull grind of vocabulary and irregular verbs.

Finally, there is a great shortage of qualified language teachers. This is one of the reasons for the continued dominance of French, for there are so few people capable of teaching any other language. Even if a headmaster is fortunate enough to have on his staff someone capable of taking French or Latin, he is reluctant to introduce a new subject in case this specialist is transferred and the students who have commenced the subject are left stranded. As most Arts faculties still require a language other than English as a desirable entrance qualification, this could restrict the future prospects of these children. Thus the very stipulation of the university which has kept a place in the schools open for a language operates to restrict the language actually offered.

The great shortage of language teachers is, however, entirely due to a total lack of imagination on the part of administrators, together with the rigidity of rules of employment in state schools. The immigration boom has offered Australia its greatest chance ever to make a final break with the insularity which has hitherto characterized its history. Among the first wave of displaced persons were very many with teaching and other professional qualifications. These men could have been offered special courses of training and sent to the schools to act as special language teachers. They could have both preserved the languages of migrant students and helped Australian students to acquire a similar bi-lingual facility. Similarly, there is no reason to delay the introduction of Asian languages until we can give enough of our own teachers a smattering of Indonesian or Chinese. The Colombo plan offers a framework which a visionary government could easily use to place an Asian language teacher in every Australian secondary school. The results would be even more dramatic if we in our turn exchanged Australian teachers to teach in Asian countries.

These foreign teachers of language should not be regarded as a mere way of meeting a shortage of Australian teachers. Rather, they should be regarded as supernumerary experts to give small groups of students intensive work in a foreign language. Meanwhile, the present language teachers could work with larger classes on courses of general language studies, which would include grammar, history of language, development of vocabulary and phonetics. These courses would have to be carefully designed so that they contributed to understanding and did not merely convey a body of facts, but properly taught they would provide a basis for the practical study of any language.

Finally, it should be understood that facility in several languages does not require any exceptional talent. Our own experience with migrants should be enough to convince us that, given the need and the opportunity, most people are able to acquire at least a working knowledge of a second tongue. I would suggest that any secondary school should offer its students the chance of learning up to three languages chosen from Latin, French, Italian, Spanish, German, and Malay or Indonesian. In addition, we should aim to give each school the facilities to teach one of Greek, Chinese, Japanese and Russian. Any student following a normal secondary course should obtain a reading and conversational knowledge of at least one foreign tongue, and at least the better students should have the chance to begin their foreign language studies in primary school.

Present experience would suggest that these ideas are utopian in the worst sense of the word. The most skilled language teacher would probably not claim to give a working knowledge of his tongue in even four or five years of study. There is not enough interest in the community to support such a program. Moreover, there are more pressing needs in other subject areas, and a need for new subjects, and these needs will not allow any extension of the time given to language teaching.

The question of community interest and need is one that will possibly resolve itself with time. I believe that British manufacturers are finding, in their dealings with the common market, that their clients are remarkably adept at English when they are selling to England, but that they suddenly lose this facility when the Englishman tries to persuade them to buy. As Australia's traditional markets dwindle, Australian businessmen trying to pioneer new countries are likely to encounter the same phenomenon. Furthermore, the increasing internationalization of business means that Australians of executive rank will be liable to be given overseas postings. The greater their knowledge of languages the wider their scope for seeking such promotion. At least one big oil company has already been forced to introduce language training schemes for its senior employees.

But the greatest reason for the teaching of foreign languages is the potential contribution to human understanding. We need to know at least one other European language to understand our own European culture. As we are brought closer to Asia in business, politics and personal dealings we need to know a major Asian language to understand something of the culture of this continent. Moreover, if our dealings with our neighbours are to be based on an adequate knowledge, we need great numbers of Asian language speakers in the government and public service, in universities and newspapers, and in our community at large. Finally, if our scholars and research workers in all fields are to keep abreast of world developments in their different studies they need the assistance of large staffs of translators.

An effective project of language teaching need not be very expensive in terms of time. The greater part of the effort put into language studies at present is wasted because of the interval between classes, the size of the classes and the range of abilities and interests within each class. The introduction to a new language is most effective if it is intensive and continuous. This can be most easily achieved with full-time courses. This would mean that, instead of taking three or four periods a week throughout the year, students would be given an intensive course, possibly conducted by itinerant teachers, of two or three weeks. Their further progress could be ensured through general language classes and small specialist teaching groups, and through the use of language teaching machines.

These teaching machines, or language laboratories, give each student the opportunity to work through a teaching program at his own speed. If he encounters a particular difficulty, he is given sufficient drill to master it. The machine feeds him with patterns of sentence structure which he memorizes as models for further use. This approach has been criticized by some linguists on the grounds that it over-simplifies the structure of language, but such criticism would seem to be confusing the way in which we analyze a language scientifically and the way in which we learn it in practice. The empirical evidence does suggest that these machines achieve better results than existing methods of teaching, although this may be due as much to the intense practice they give as to the principles behind their programs. However, it seems certain that their widespread use is the most likely method we have to achieve the breakthrough in language teaching which we must have if we are to overcome the disadvantages of our insularity.

Finally among the humanities we have the histories. Here we face the irony that, while history is the most popular study in the Arts faculties, and hence among potential teachers, the subject history is given a smaller allotment on the school timetable than either of the other major human disciplines. Such a statement is, however, misleading unless we remember that, while some senior students may be studying two, or even three, histories, many other students, including all those in the lowest streams, will drop languages altogether. This situation, which is probably due to the thriving state of historical studies in Australia, is, however, possibly a reason why history teachers are in better supply than those in most other academic disciplines.

Despite its popularity, it is doubtful whether we can justify even the amount of time which is given to history in junior forms. Certainly, where there is no qualified teacher to take it, it is probably better not taught. History teaching which consists merely of the dictation of notes from last year's notebook is at its best useless and at its worst dangerous, for it succeeds in perpetuating myths without encouraging historical understanding. Even the qualified history teacher is not of much use unless he has the time and opportunity to steep himself in the local community and its past so that he can show the relevance of history to the daily lives of his students. Alternatively, by skilful use of story-telling from the past, he can convey some idea of the grandeur of man's history and the relative importance of our own time. The most important function of junior history teaching is probably just such story-telling, combined with personal investigation of the immediate locality, for by filling his students' minds with such ideas the teacher can prepare him for the time when he will be able to develop a historical understanding of his own. Any attempt to do more in early years can only lead to over-simplication and myth-making. If the teacher is interested in myths, it is better that he use the stories of Greece and the north than that he construct his own about aborigines, rum, and Governor Bligh.

It is from third form onwards that history teaching can really come into its own in the hands of a capable teacher. However, even at this stage it is doubtful whether there is much point in teaching it to students who have not already developed a command of English, for without the ability to handle ideas they cannot be expected to profit from a subject which demands a higher level of abstraction than any other humanity apart from philosophy. For a mere knowledge of facts is only, at the best, chronology, not history. An understanding of history depends on the ability to interpret the concrete facts in order to discover the underlying patterns. If it is taught prematurely, the temptation is for the teacher to give both the facts and the theoretical pattern, so that the students learn not so much history as archetypal models. It is not an advance on teaching a series of facts to inform the class that a particular event, such as the outbreak of the first world war, occurred, and that the reasons for it were one, two and three. True history teaching must include the same element of uncertainty which characterizes historical studies. The danger of doing otherwise is not only to perpetuate misconceptions about the past but also to give a completely false idea of how events are shaped in the present. The English invasion of Suez, or the domino theory of communist aggression, are just two examples of how stereotypes from history prevent people from observing the facts, and the essential differences, in contemporary situations.

Perhaps the greatest value of skilful history teaching is to inculcate an idea of the complexity of human behaviour, as well as its unchanging foolishness, and to provide a perspective from which today's worries can be seen in their proper perspective. One of the new aids for this kind of teaching is the Jackdaw series of wallets containing reproductions of documents relating to historical events. These documents encourage the students to make their own reconstructions of the past rather than being given someone else's construction as a form of holy writ. Equally importantly, they enable the student to put himself back into the state of mind of a past time, and so to return with a refreshed insight into his own time. The wallet on the Gunpowder Plot, for example, enables him to understand how society was once as bitterly divided between Catholics and Protestants as it is today between anti-communists and others. The reproduction of a bloodthirsty contemporary print of the execution also offers a salutary lesson on man's self-righteous inhumanity.

Apart from bringing about an understanding of the present by developing an understanding of the past, historians claim to bring the more direct benefit of showing how contemporary institutions have developed their present form. So the history of the eighteenth century gives the student an understanding of the origins, and hence the present functions, of parliamentary government. The history of the Pacific provides the basis for understanding the present roles of America, Japan or China. The study of Australian history enables us to understand ourselves today. These claims are justified when the subject is handled by capable teachers, but again they are misleading when the subject is taught by the less than competent. In such circumstances, even an accurate account of the development of an institution can merely serve to obstruct an understanding of the performance of that institution today. Australia and Commonwealth Day ceremonies offer the ideal example of the way in which historical charades can be so mounted as to completely obscure current reality.

It is around the third and fourth years of secondary schooling that the most important attempt is made to give students some knowledge of our northern neighbours. Whereas a generation ago the emphasis of detailed history teaching was on the development of the great and glorious British Empire, today this has largely disappeared from the secondary schools, which usually lag only about twenty years behind the world, and is on its way out in the primary schools. The place of British history, taught for its own sake and as a background to Australian history, has not diminished, but Empire history is being replaced by Asian history. Unfortunately, this lacks the clear-cut whig theme which marked the older books that were able to trace man's growing enlightenment from the stone age to the Pax Britannica. The need of a theme is too often supplied by an emphasis on the quaintness of our coloured friends, whose political aberrations need to be tolerated until they reach our stage of advanced decency. It is difficult to see how this attitude can be combated within the strict limits of history teaching, for the subject of Asian history is so vast and diffuse that it is difficult within the inherent limitations of the school to do more than give a smattering of facts which inevitably emphasize the exotic rather than the human.

One way of reducing the topic to manageable proportions is to concentrate on one or two countries of central importance. This enables more attention to be paid to the developing strands of nationality and reduces the danger of obscuring the human reality underneath a vast mish-mash of superficial factual detail. Even so, the pressure of contemporary events makes it desirable to concentrate on later modern, or colonial and post-colonial, history, and it is difficult to convey any idea of the long and complex histories which preceded the Da Gama era. Furthermore, the conscientious teacher who attempts to bring his class to understand that the material and social conditions of these countries are so different from our own that it is unrealistic to impose our own standards of judgement is liable to convey the opposite impression to what he intends. It is so natural for children to regard their own environment as normal that to suggest that someone else has different circumstances is almost to suggest that he is sub-human. To suggest that another people might have different aspirations to our own is to suggest that they belong to another planet. In these circumstances, it is very difficult to go from the stage of recognizing a difference of environment and tradition to the further essential stage of understanding the common humanity behind both traditions.

It may well be that the schools should in this respect learn from the university courses in 'area studies', which attempt to combine a study of the language, literature and society of a foreign country with something of its history. At present teachers do often make a gesture towards the 'cultural heritage' of other countries by giving out lists of their great artists and writers, and there would not be any textbook published today without a couple of photographs of mysterious eastern temples, but such extrinsic attention is probably of no more value than a television revival of Fu Man Chu. What we do not attempt is any use of the work of Asian writers to convey an understanding of their own countries, yet it is precisely here that the work of the history and literature teachers could be integrated meaningfully. Selected fiction and poetry of a neighbouring country could be studied, in translation, in the English classroom in exactly the same way as any other work is considered. This would remain a part of the English course, but would also provide some of the necessary background of understanding when the same students came to the equivalent section of their history course.

Another line of development in humanities is suggested by the new course in general humanities which is being introduced at Latrobe University for all its students. This is a course of reading and discussion of the best of human thought from Genesis to Armageddon. It includes works of literature, philosophy, history and science. It enables students to develop their own specialties and to gain some insights into the fields of others. Above all, it enables them to bring their specialist skills into a common field of endeavour. If it achieves the success hoped for by its sponsors it could well indicate a way ahead for humanities in the secondary schools. But such a prospect should be treated with caution, and should certainly not be regarded as a substitute for developing the standard of teaching the present subjects, for to pin our hopes on some new synthesis is to risk destroying the potential of the present system for the sake of some course of amateur dabbling which is too broad for understanding and too shallow to satisfy any serious student.

One of the distinguishing characteristics about the humanities in our schools is that the administrators consider that they can be taught without any special equipment. Consequently, although the domestic science wing may have twenty thousand dollars' worth of apparatus in use by twenty girls at a time, and the Commonwealth government itself is prepared to pay to build and equip new laboratories for science, the humanities teacher in even the most modern schools quite frequently has to start from scratch, with nothing more provided than the classroom, chalkboard and desks. It is not surprising, in these circumstances, that so many opt out of the responsibilities of teaching in favour of a dull routine of dictated notes for rote learning.

It is certainly true that a great deal of the humanities are concerned with abstract ideas, and that elaborate mechanical aids like overhead projectors and tape recorders in every classroom may merely be handy toys for the teacher to play with instead of facing the challenges of his subject. However, such aids are necessary so that the most effective method of visual or aural presentation can be used for any aspect of the work. It is only when these aids are unusual that their novelty is likely to exaggerate their value, and when they are not readily accessible that the teacher has to devote time and energy to arranging ahead for their provision when he should be doing more serious preparation of his subject matter.

But the most effective and necessary aid for the humanities is a library. This does not mean that the school library should be regarded as the property of the humanities departments, for its role in providing information and ideas is equally important to all parts of the school. However, for the humanist it is also the primary locale of research, and fulfils a similar function in his work to the laboratory in a scientific discipline. The effective teaching of any of the humanities requires both a ready supply of books, newspapers, periodicals and charts in the classroom, and constant access to a central library where the student can pursue any particular topic at his leisure. Without these facilities the teaching can never get far from talk and chalk, textbook and notebook, cram and exam.

This brings us back to the central problem of all the humanities, which is to encourage the student to recognize that there is rarely if ever any right answer to a human problem, but that this very fact imposes on each individual the obligation to explore all the relevant evidence thoroughly and to make up his own mind on this basis. This exploration may be handicapped by purely technical deficiencies in the mother tongue or another, and so it is a part of the responsibility of the school to supply the need for such basic fluency. But too few teachers realize that such merely technical facility in a field is only the beginning, not the end of the task. Too many individual explorations result in a distorted map because the explorer lacks the wider perspective which would relate his own discoveries to their wider environment. In an intellectual discipline, this wider perspective can be given by authoritarian dictation, and a teacher could grave the lines of his particular intellectual universe indelibly on the tablets of his students' memory. This is done when a subject is taught as a series of notes to be learnt, facts to be memorized, and rules to be mastered. But such teaching must either render its subject matter irrelevant to the ever-changing reality of the students' lives, or so affect their vision that they will fit their perception of life to fit predetermined stereotypes.

The only way we can escape from this dilemma of prescription or chaos is to change our notion of education from the traditional idea of the teacher standing in front of the room and instructing his class to a model of the teacher and the class co-operating in the study of common problems. This does not mean that the teachers' authority is destroyed, or that the children usurp the right of steering the ship before they have learnt to read the existing maps, let alone make new ones. It is the teacher's responsibility to choose the problems and to organize them so that in the course of their solution the students will cover the area of learning which is his charge. But during their studies the students should be making some genuine discoveries of their own, and at their conclusion they should not only have developed their personal intellectual maps but should also feel the urge to set sail on further similar voyages. They will share with their classmates a common body of newly-visualized fact, but each will see these facts from his own particular perspective, and thus discussion and controversy will arise naturally and the students will be introduced imperceptibly to the realities of intellectual and public debate. It is to these ends that humanities departments should be supplied, not so much with elaborate gimmicks, but with vast supplies of reference material of every kind. It is for these reasons that humanities teachers should be well qualified explorers in their own right. It is only in these terms that the teaching of humanities can be justified.

5 Arts and Crafts

The practical subjects occupy an ambiguous place in Australian schools. On the one hand, they are regarded as luxurious trimmings which have nothing to do with the serious business of education. On the other, they are considered as the ideal subjects for less able students who are destined for the manual trades. The common assumption behind both of these theories is that proficiency in practical skills requires no mental effort, a thesis which scarcely does justice to the close relationship between hand and head which has distinguished man from other beasts of nature.

There is a good case for reversing the normal school priorities in regard to the arts. If they are not fundamental there can be no reason for allowing students who are not already proficient in the central disciplines to waste their time on mere extravagances. On the other hand, if they have any importance to a balanced education the most able students should not be denied the opportunity to develop their talents in this particular direction. But such an extreme view overlooks the fact that the student who does least well at school is usually the one with the least verbal skill. The practice of manual crafts can give him the opportunity to develop his self-confidence, can further the development of the co-ordination between eye and hand which is necessary for the performance of the simplest tasks of everyday living, and can give him the chance to express himself, and so to grow in his understanding of himself, through non-verbal media. The task of the art teacher can therefore be seen as twofold. On the one hand, he gives the better students the chance to develop an important element of their personality which might otherwise be neglected. On the other, he gives to the less able students an alternative road to the central concerns of education. This alternative medium, although it can never share the precision of verbal expression, has other qualities which make it no less rigorous in the demands it makes of its students.

The term art is itself one of the most difficult in the English language. It can mean all those activities which were presided over by the Greek muses, or those which are now found in a university arts faculty. Alternatively, it can mean only those activities which are not found in an arts faculty—the practice of drama, music, painting and sculpture, and such related activities as printing or film-making. Finally, it can mean the practice of any skill, the sole meaning until the romantic revival, and one which is retained in the word artisan. But even this idea has changed as it has been extended from the purely manual skills to such usages as the art of addressing a jury or the art of teaching. In school terms, the subject known as Art includes practical work in drawing, painting and modelling, the history of art, and the theory of aesthetics and design. In this chapter, I shall use the word Art to refer to the subject, and arts to refer to all the practical arts taught in a school.

Drawing and painting is one of the earliest means a child uses to express and understand its reactions to the world about it. A lot of nonsense has been written about the natural aesthetic value of child art, and any understanding of the finger paintings children bring home from kindergarten depends on the realization that they are both attempting to portray their environment as they see it, learning to co-ordinate their muscular movements to obtain desired results, and watching with delighted absorption the pretty pictures which the paint spontaneously produces on the paper. The strange pattern of vertical lines may in fact represent the legs of a crowd from the perspective of a three-year-old, but they are far more likely to represent nothing except themselves. This is one of the qualities which has so appealed to certain schools of modern artists.

Through these early activities the child simultaneously develops its own expressive powers and its understanding of the medium. But after kindergarten, or if he is exceptionally fortunate, after the first year of primary school, the child runs into the laws of life which govern school conduct. The first and most important of these commandments is that he shall not cause a fuss or make a mess, and painting is liable to do both of these. The second is that he must have a neat and colourful book to produce for the annual visit of the inspector. The interaction of these two rules brings the result that gay paints and large pieces of paper are forgotten, and the child instead is encouraged to draw, or trace, careful outlines and colour them in with coloured pencils. Despite imaginative Art syllabuses for primary use, the occasional Art lesson produces little more than tiny sheets of coloured paper scribbled over with pastel or Craypas, or pasted up with even tinier pieces of other coloured paper. In this one field, the primary school is not inferior to the secondary school in its ability to suppress the imaginative freedom which is the child's natural endowment. Ironically, it is also the field where secondary teachers are most anxious to cultivate this native endowment.

Art in secondary schools has undergone a complete transformation from the days when students were required to spend endless time making model drawings of pots and leaves, composing overall patterns, and painting the occasional free design. They are now encouraged to try their hands on all types of material, including paint, wire, paper, clay and wood. The lesson starts when the teacher gives the class its subject and its materials, and the students then make the most of it that they can. Even the subject is not so much prescriptive as inspirational. They are not told to paint a picture of a gum tree, but are asked to imagine fire, or a rainy day, or fear. When they do field-sketching, their attention is not drawn to specific features of the landscape to reproduce on their paper, but they are taken to an interesting spot and encouraged to explore its possibilities. The aim of the work is not the exhibition of technical proficiency but the development of an understanding of the potential of various materials. It is through this interaction between materials and subject matter that the work of art is created through the child's discovery of a pattern which brings the two into a new relationship. The quality of the work depends on this inner unity, and not on any merely representational value it might possess.

The child's exploration of being through the various plastic media available to him extends his imaginative powers and develops the basic understanding which serves as a starting point for a similar exploration of the work of mature artists through the ages. The first task of the teacher is to rid his students of those preconceptions which will stand between them and the works of art they come across. They need first to be able to approach each new work of art with the open capacity to perceive for themselves what the individual artist has discovered in his particular environment. When a sufficient wealth of such experience has been accumulated they will naturally grow to some understanding of the way mankind's perception of his environment has grown and changed through the ages, and of what understanding of this age contemporary artists have to offer us.

From this interest in the visual qualities of the environment develops that awareness of architecture and design which can grow to a concern for the whole question of industrial and urban aesthetics, town planning, the preservation of our natural and human heritage, and the quality of life in contemporary society. This awareness is fostered, again only in the later years, by the formal study of design and the history of architecture. Introduced too early, such study can consist only of dreary exercises in copying the designs of Attic cornices and memorizing summaries of the three stages of Gothic. Once the elegance of the Parthenon has been transposed into the crudity of the schoolroom sketch we can be sure that the spirit of architecture has been so well embalmed as never to disturb the complacency of suburban cut-glass parlours, and that the next generation of municipal councillors will be as deaf to the demands of visual decency as the present.

It should not, however, be thought that all, or even most, secondary teachers achieve the aim of developing the children's understanding in the fashion envisaged by the new Art courses. Most are restricted by their own meagre understanding, by the exigencies of the timetable, by the apathy of the students or the need to curb unruly classes, or by the pursuit of irrelevant distractions. It is far easier to produce a colourful display for parents' night or the board of inspectors than it is to ensure that the students who produce this work have understood what they are doing. The absence of firm standards can be an excuse for the laziness which allows students to do whatever they like rather than keep them working at a demanding task. Even apparently heterodox results can be produced by rules as rigid as any used in the old technical discipline. As in other subjects, the very freedom of the new approach makes demands for self-discipline and intellectual rigour on the part of the teacher which he is too seldom prepared to meet, and the novelty of the methods shields him from the criticism which once would have instantly attended any slovenly attitude to his craft.

Yet even in the hands of capable and dedicated teachers the new approach carries the inherent danger that the abandonment of external standards will lead, not to the substitution of internal standards, but to a heady dedication to the cult of self-expression, which can only produce a chaos as unhealthy as was the inflexible order of the previous generation. The demise of the rule-book does not mean that we must substitute nonsense for sense. While students should by all means be encouraged to work things out for themselves, it should be made clear to them that the characteristic of a work of art in any field is that it says something. The kindergarten pupil has no doubt that his picture has a meaning; there is no reason why this common-sense should be lost with maturity. If the secondary student wishes to slosh oil and water all over his paper and watch the pretty effects, he should be encouraged to go ahead, but he should not then be allowed to exhibit the result as anything other than an experiment in accident.

The cult of chaos has already led to criticism from some sources in gallery schools of painting and university and technical schools of architecture that the students who come to them from secondary school Art courses are the least well equipped to follow higher studies in their field. Although they are adept in the use of elaborate swirls of colour, they know little or nothing of the fundamental techniques of drawing and design. This criticism need not imply a return to the older methods of starting with the discipline and allowing the self-expression to come later. It does, however, suggest that Art teachers are failing to develop the interest they arouse in their students. No painter can be successful unless he has the skill to execute on canvas the conception he holds in his mind. Similarly, school students should realize that if they are to pursue their understanding of the medium they must master some of its technique. The fact that this technique should follow rather than precede an interest in the subject does not mean that it can be totally disregarded.

The tendency of apprentice architecture students to obscure their designs with prettily artistic elaborations suggests an even greater weakness in the discipline of secondary Art studies. Architecture is essentially a matter of solving functional problems by creating spatial structures, and to confuse this with the neighbouring, but distinct, field of painting is to betray a lack of respect for either subject. Although the architect's personality is a necessary and invaluable element in any of his designs, he is neither artist nor architect who regards building as an appropriate medium of self-expression.

Such a fault in budding architects need not, perhaps, be of great concern in itself, for the architects receive a rigorous professional training which corrects such excesses before they are let free to inflict their ideas on the community at large, and at any rate they constitute only a tiny proportion of the students who study Art at school. Few of these will ever use the services of an architect, let alone join the profession themselves. The majority of them will therefore carry the misconceptions of their school Art classes with them through adult life to the grave, whither they will be accompanied by sheaves of plastic flowers and where they will rest their bones under six feet of clay topped by a gilt-encrusted tombstone. No part of their lives will suit them so well as their parting, which will epitomize all that tawdry glamour which separates them from reality from the day of their birth. The very coffin in which their corpse is carried to the grave becomes a silver-knobbed casket in which the relatives carry with varying degrees of emotion and indifference the last earthly remains of him whom death has suddenly made universally beloved.

At first glance it seems that the values of the Art room are far removed from these shoddy manifestations of the neon and plastic age, which would seem to have more in common with its Victorian ancestors than with the artists who have for fifty years rebelled against every form of stuffy hypocrisy and conformity. The difference, however, is that whereas artists have thrown aside the external trappings in their pursuit of the inner reality of existence, their host of followers, among whom we must number the teachers, have merely exchanged one suit of clothes for another. The teacher who enthuses over a student's mindless chaos of fashionable colour is no less confined to the superficial than the philistine who believes that every work of art must look like the kodachrome he took on his last boat trip. Moreover, while the philistine harms only himself, the teacher contributes to the contemporary obsession with meretricious novelty, and so becomes an accomplice in the debasement of public taste and the destruction of any sense of values.

Nor is this merely a question of the quality of life. A visit to the Design Centre conducted by the Council for Industrial Design will show what a pitifully small number of Australian products conform to the principles of utility, let alone beauty. If we walk from this exhibition to any hardware or electrical goods store we will see what the Australian manufacturer regards as good design—streamlined chrome and plastic exteriors concealing with their glitter the fact that the object has been thrown together with no conception of its purpose or likely use. So we find motor-mowers whose blades rotate only inches from the users' feet, with no safety-guard between, electric jugs whose handles cannot be tightened without either a specially-designed tool or a remarkable degree of manual dexterity, drink-vending machines which cannot be cleaned inside because the surface which catches the overspill is surrounded and studded with raised flanges. Anyone who has furnished a house could extend the list indefinitely. The existence of this attitude to industrial design may be an indictment of public taste, but its cost is an economic burden we should not have to carry. A product which is so designed that its life-span is only that of its weakest parts may add to the manufacturers' immediate profits, but by diverting resources into unnecessary production it wastes the community's assets. A household utensil which does not operate with maximum efficiency wastes its user's time, and to the extent that this waste of time is reflected in speed or impatience on the road or irritation in the office its cost is borne by all of us. Finally, and perhaps most obviously, the neglect of industrial design at home costs us money for overseas licences on the one hand and loses us export markets on the other.

Yet this manifest failure of Art teaching to influence the community at large must largely be attributed to Art teachers themselves, for Art is the one subject where there is a comparatively adequate number of teachers. This is partly because the Art training course has lower entrance qualifications than most other secondary teaching courses and partly because those who complete the course are not qualified for any career other than teaching. The course is also shorter than most courses of secondary training, a fact which in some states has the gravest effects on the promotion of Art teachers. The departments concerned meet any criticism of this handicap by pointing out that there are alternative courses through which these teachers can qualify for higher positions, but they do not feel obliged to explain the relevance of these courses to the responsibilities which those who pass them will be required to undertake. Nor do they bother to explain that the burden of such a course is often more than a married man with family responsibilities can undertake, particularly if he is teaching in a country school without local facilities for higher study. The consequence of this is that Art teachers tend to be both the most numerous and the least contented members of a school staff, and are frequently called on to undertake a wide range of duties which technically they are not qualified to perform. Proficiency in the execution of these duties has no necessary bearing on their prospects of promotion.

The more serious obstacle to the achievement of a high standard of Art teaching is the nature of the facilities available. In more recently built schools there is usually a specially equipped art room with sinks, benches and display boards, and probably a storeroom. This is the minimum equipment necessary, but it is not unknown in older buildings for Art to be taught in ordinary classrooms with no storage space and not even running water. Before a lesson can begin, buckets of water have to be carried in by the students, and long before the period ends cleaning-up must commence so that all the material can be removed to remote storerooms and cupboards. But even in the newest buildings, the Art teacher is handicapped by the notion that Art as a subject must be taken like any other, period by period, with forty children crammed into each room and told to go ahead and create.

The ideal Art room would be a large workshop area with a number of small work carrels devoted to different activities. As well as benches for painting, drawing and modelling, there should be a kiln for baking pottery and clay models, a potter's wheel, looms, a printing area, facilities for soldering and welding, and woodwork benches. These would be around the periphery, while in the centre would be space for class lessons and demonstrations. Finally, there should be display facilities for experimental work and specimen exhibits, and storage room for unfinished work. Normally, the best students' work, together with a wide range of prints of standard artists and some originals, should be displayed throughout the school area.

Such an Art centre should not be used only, or even mainly, for scheduled classes. Art is not an activity which fits easily into the standard timetable, and will achieve its best results when students are free to pursue it in whatever time they have available outside their classes in the basic disciplines. The Art centre would be staffed continuously, and students guided individually or in small groups along the paths best suited to them. Classes in History and Appreciation of Art would be held at scheduled times, but need not be part of an overall school timetable or restricted to any particular class. Any such arrangement would, of course, presuppose that the school timetable left students free outside the time devoted to the basic disciplines to spend their time in the library, on practical work, or at sport, as they felt inclined. The responsibility for guiding them to achieve a balanced use of their time would then depend on student counsellors rather than on an arbitrary timetable.

If Art has abandoned the old rigidity without yet developing the potentialities of the new approach, woodwork demonstrates what good craft teaching can mean. Because it is an applied craft, any weaknesses of design or construction are quickly made evident by use. The material and the purpose of the task provide their own inescapable discipline. Moreover, the nature of the work is such that each student is able to proceed at his own pace. Whereas this once meant that the slower students spent years trying to plane down a face edge for a garden stake, an exercise of value only to develop a particular skill, they can now start straight away on simple objects of use. If their crudity of execution never improves, they will continue to construct such simple objects as long as they are at school, but this exercise need be neither boring nor futile. Nor are they prevented from using such new aids to carpentry as vinyl coverings and factory-turned legs which enable them to achieve a reasonable standard of finish and efficiency despite their own lack of skill. Yet such results are not confused with ability, and the more adept students who are able to proceed to such elaborate projects as boat-making or furniture construction achieve their due reward in marks as well as in satisfaction.

The teaching of needlework has probably not changed so obviously, except that samplers and endless miles of hemming are out and practical garments are in. The atmosphere of the sewing circle, moreover, gives the teacher the opportunity to discuss many matters only indirectly related to the task in hand, and so develop the awareness of dress and knowledge of fashion which will enable the girls to attract a husband, as well as the understanding of economy which will enable them to keep him. Furthermore, like woodwork, it offers to the otherwise indifferent student a field in which he may be able to shine, and to those who are exhausted by more academic studies a time to relax at an entirely different kind of activity.

Both needlework and woodwork are now taught as hobby rather than vocational subjects, and aim at giving their students a degree of practical ability and an interest for their leisure hours rather than a means of earning a living. Their place in the school curriculum is, however, limited by the lack of time for students in the academic disciplines to continue them beyond the lower forms of the secondary school. This is one of the problems to which the Wyndham committee addressed itself, and as a result New South Wales now offers these subjects, like all others, at three levels, the lowest of which is intended to cater for those who wish to pursue it as a general interest rather than as vocational preparation or as a way of finding an extra subject to make up the requirements of a school certificate. But whether this intention of the sponsors will be fulfilled in the face of pressure on the academic subjects from the universities remains to be seen.

The other limitation on the effectiveness of these crafts in the schools is their separation from the subject of Art. Although most Art teachers are also craft teachers, and vice versa, many of them come to specialize in one branch or the other. Furthermore, in the larger schools even the teachers who take both parts of their discipline may not take the same class for each. This leads to a lack of correlation between what should be virtually two parts of the same subject, with the result that even those students who can claim a sound understanding of design in the Art period will turn around in their needlework or woodwork class and produce works in which a fundamentally sound design is completely obscured by irrelevant decoration.

As well as the plastic arts, the schools concern themselves with drama, music and dancing. These three activities, which should form a common body of experience, are split up into separate subjects even at the primary school stage. Drama is regarded as an extension of English teaching, a placing which rightly emphasizes the priority of the word in mature dramatic works but can lead to a neglect of the skills of movement and choral chanting, which are equally a part of the primitive dramatic experience which should precede any attempt to study plays at a more sophisticated level.

Music teaching is usually confined to a tiny part of the school timetable, and even then is limited to singing, unless the school happens to possess a recorder or drum and fife enthusiast who takes the band at lunch hours. A few schools have formed orchestras, but although the instruments are available the opportunities for individual instruction are usually limited. Such methods as those of Carl Orf, through which primary children are introduced to both singing and instrumental playing through a limited scale, are starting to find acceptance among a small band of enthusiasts, but the overall picture remains gloomy. School choirs are more often than not all female, and appear only for such grand occasions as the speech night. The repertoire of both classes and teachers seems limited to the more effete productions of nineteenth century gentile, or to rollicking imitations of the ballads, and their musical vacuity is matched only by their poetic triviality. The one quality which you cannot expect to find in a school music class is joy.

The only remedy for this situation seems to be a vast increase in the itinerant music staff in primary schools and an extension of the voluntary principle in secondary. The first of these measures would ensure that even those students with tone-deaf class teachers would be introduced to at least the elements of music, while the second would allow those children who showed this particular interest and ability to develop it at leisure. Instead of everyone being required to take in all their music in one single period a week, the few who were interested could spend a number of periods in the music room as an alternative to sport or to one of the other arts. There would be no need for such a choice to be permanent, for students could be given the opportunity to swap around these voluntary activities at regular intervals. Meanwhile, teachers of such subjects as Art, English and physical education could be encouraged to use music as a normal part of their activities, and lunch-hour recitals by school choral and instrumental groups could use the talents of the specialists to entertain and enlighten the rest.

There is little to be said about dancing in the school curriculum. When it appears in the classroom it usually takes the form of an emasculated folk-dance being prepared as an elaborate but meaningless ceremony to precede the entry of the choir on speech night. Otherwise, it is left to ambitious parents to enrol their agile little girls and precocious little boys in privately conducted ballet schools. A few of these may graduate to professional dancing on television, the rest will join the majority of their countrymen in regarding all forms of dancing as something fit for small children, society women, and effeminate Europeans.

The generally unsatisfactory condition of the arts in schools reflects the inability of Australians to recognize them as anything other than pleasant hobbies. The result is that students are given a smattering of too many in their early years, and are able to study too few in their later. At the same time, art teachers are frequently regarded as lesser members of staff, and are uncertain about their own aims. Such hope as exists for the future lies not so much in the schools themselves as in those arts which have managed to flourish in Australia despite the hostility of the community and the indifference of the schools. When their lessons have been absorbed by the schools, the lessons in the classroom may become satisfactory.

Perhaps one of the most effective ways of improving the status of the arts in schools would be for education departments and private schools to offer facilities for practising artists to work in the schools, not as teachers, but as artists. A studio would be provided, and the job offered to someone who had already shown talent but who could benefit from an opportunity to practice without financial worries. He would be employed as a full member of the school staff, but would have no specific duties. If he chose, he could take particular classes by arrangement with the teachers responsible, but his chief value to the school would come merely from his presence and from a limited accessibility to staff and students to talk about their work and his. In this way, while his talents as an artist would be available to the school, his school duties would not be so onerous as to inhibit his art.

The problem of the arts in school goes right back to our fundamental concept of what should be the purpose of the school itself. As long as we envisage it primarily as a vocational training and selection institution the arts will remain on the periphery. Once, however, we pay more than lip-service to the concept of educating the whole man the arts will move to the centre of the school program, for it is through the arts that man comes to understand himself and his environment, and it is chiefly through the arts, in a pluralist society, that he can establish any sense of community. The school which takes its responsibilities seriously will be a flourishing centre of both creative and performing arts, and the interest and curiosity which it awakens in its students through these media will be satisfied by the teachers in the more academic disciplines, including the history and principles of the arts themselves. Nor should this artistic activity be limited to the school, for this is one way in which the school can function as an integral part of the wider community, both taking its performances to it and bringing community performers into its own environs.

The place of the arts in schools is particularly important in view of the revolution in mass entertainment which has occurred during this century. On the one hand, this revolution threatens the very notion of individual personality and social community, and substitutes an undifferentiated and international mass of consumers reacting in a stereotyped and utterly predicable fashion to a constantly changing pattern of external stimuli. Already television advertising men test their products in front of carefully selected typical audiences around the world, and if any one of these audiences shows an individual reaction it is dismissed from calculation as unrepresentative, the twentieth-century equivalent for heretical. Theoretically, we only need this information to be programmed into a bank of computers housed in some international communications centre and we will have solved the problems of human nature forever.

So far, however, human nature has remained unpredictably resistant to the attempts to mould it into a single pattern of stimulus and response, and the last ten years in particular have offered a singular demonstration of the subjection of the mass media themselves to the human factor. Although the television age would seem to have absolute resources to control human behaviour, it is the generation which has grown up in front of the electronic screen which has used electronic technology to challenge its adult masters more radically and more successfully than any other this century. The twanging sounds of the electronic guitar have cut through the norms of belief and behaviour to establish an entirely new pattern of living in which older responses are not so much uncomprehending as irrelevant. The older gods are dead, Prometheus has returned, and McLuhan is his prophet. The new generation has abandoned the habit of logical analysis with which western man has lived for three thousand years, and lives instead by a total response to a total environment. They know more of the world than their fathers, for they use and trust all their senses and all their feelings, but they understand less, for they distrust reason.

This is where the schools are important. At present the new arts are the poor relations of education, allowed to visit the schools for fetes and festivals, but pushed out of sight for the rest of the year. We acknowledge their existence, but find it a rather worrying fact and prefer to forget about it as much as possible. When we mention television, it is in terms of high praise for the more highbrow and literary programs that we hope our students will watch and through which we expect them to be unwittingly led on to higher interests. We may take a class to the local cinema to see the film of a play which has been set for examination study, and we may even teach them the elements of montage and so on in the vague hope that we are giving them a prophylactic against the vulgarity of most Australian television, and in the confidence that by reducing the whole matter to verbal, and therefore literary, terms we have understood it ourselves. This, however, is as far as we go.

Admittedly, there are great difficulties in doing any more than this in school. Although parents are tolerant of the behaviour of their offspring, and oblivious to the implications of the blander forms of entertainment, they still react with all the horror of a backwoods politician to any suggestion that the school is endorsing smut. A misguided request to a class to watch Maigret on an evening when the plot happens to revolve around a brothel can have disastrous consequences for a carefully planned unit of television study. But so it should, for the teacher who proceeds in this directive manner is in fact attempting to impose his own taste on the class. If the schools are to encompass the new arts, they must start from the present knowledge and interests of the children, who are more expert in this field than their mentors.

This does not mean that the school should condone the values expressed in the popular media, but the understanding which leads to criticism cannot come before the understanding which comes from practice. At present, the popular arts enter our schools only on fete days and at school socials, where they appear in their most extreme forms to the obvious bewilderment of the teachers. One day their charges are sitting in neat rows in their departmental desks, all clad alike in regulation uniform and wearing standard smiles for easy identification. The same evening they appear in the school gymnasium clad in clothes which reveal as much of the body as they conceal of the personality, there to sway and swing in rapt ecstacy to the pounding of the electronic band. The staff suffer this in the name of relaxation, and the next morning the streamers are packed away, the uniforms resumed, and the two worlds safely separated for another term.

If schools are to communicate meaningfully with their charges this barrier between worlds must be destroyed. The first initiative for this will need to come from the teachers themselves, who will have to learn something of the new idiom. When the electronic bands are allowed to thump in the classrooms education can begin. Only when the teacher understands the attraction of the vigorous selfishness of such phenomena as boots made for walking all over you can he presume to talk with, not to, his classes about the cruelty which is equally evident in these lyrics. If he can encourage his classes to extend their interest, and creative abilities, from pop music to art and drama, still using the same idiom, he can then start to lead them to discussion of what they themselves create, and what is created for them by radio and television, at a higher level than the usual patter of disc jockeys and teenage 'experts'. In this way the schools could free the creative vigour of the new generation to find its own true flowering, instead of being harnessed to a vast commercial machine which feeds it with the illusion of revolt without the satisfaction of achievement, and which, by permanently impoverishing the vocabulary and sensibility of its addicts, incapacitates them for adult life. These potentialities will not, however, be realized as long as teachers regard the whole teenage thing as a threat to their own established values, and fail to see the real moral energy implicit in it and struggling to escape from its commercial cage. Nor will it be achieved by those happy souls who go overboard with excitement at every new fashion, remaining with-it teenagers into late middle age, and by their self-adulation blinding themselves to the fact, evident to everyone else, that they are as much an object of ridicule to the younger generation as they are to their own. The difficult task of the teacher is to encourage the young in their enthusiasm without losing his own grasp on the values he has himself inherited from the past.

This is where the scholarly and critical function is relevant. To argue that art is what artists do is temptingly easy, for it enables us to avoid the most difficult problems of discrimination among the products of creation at a less self-conscious level than that of the artist. But such discrimination is a primary function of the teacher, who must be able to recognize the honest and original in his pupils' work and encourage them to develop this at the expense of the popular clichés and the derivative forms beneath which it will be obscured.

It is important to have practising artists in the schools, as it is important to give trainee art teachers the opportunity to develop their own creative skills and talents, but it is of equal importance that the teachers of any art have a thorough grounding, during their training, in its history and critical principles. This means that the training of art teachers, as of music, literature or drama teachers, should be accepted as a university function, rather than being relegated to the old technical school type of instruction in craft skills which is becoming obsolete even in the traditional technologies.

The current state of the arts in the schools is, therefore, encouraging, if only because they have shed more of their conservatism than have subjects in most parts of the curriculum. However, they still suffer from the suspicion that they are just a luxurious piece of ornament on the true structure of education, and from a lack of critical principle in their own practice. There is still a dichotomy between arts and crafts; music, drama and dancing have scarcely a toehold; and the newer arts of cinema and television, as well as the popular arts of all varieties, are normally regarded with hostility. But there is possibly a higher level of creative achievement among art teachers than among teachers in any other discipline, and there is also a lesser shortage of numbers already trained and coming forward for training, so, provided that the administrators will provide the opportunities, there is every prospect of further strides being taken in this particular field of education.

6 Practical Subjects

As we have seen, state education was in its origin vocational. It was primarily intended to produce industrious recruits for the manual trades, and only later was it extended to give the more able menials sufficient further training to enable them to qualify for initiation as teachers. Although since then the notion of education has widened and the concept of secondary education for all has been generally accepted in the community, the vocational tradition remains strong, even if in some respects our ideas of vocational preparation have changed. We no longer envisage the fresh-faced infant laboring over his writing so that he may indite a neat copperplate application for an apprenticeship with one of the local worthies; instead we think of the scholarly ascetic burning the midnight electricity and slaving to the sound of an electronic band so that he may raise his knowledge to the level of a university quota and thus embark on the royal road to fame, skill and the certificate which will enable him to fleece his fellow taxpayers without scruple or challenge. This aim is no less vocational, but it does allow the teachers an excuse to pump in a little learning for its own sake, however disguised beneath a veneer of utility it may be.

Nor is there any less vocational ambition in those students who pursue pure humanities courses for five years and then seek a job behind a desk or a counter. The subjects are perceived as having value not in themselves but in what they lead to. This is the cause of many complaints by employers about the standards of the students who come to them, for while they demand increasingly higher qualifications they often have little idea of what they are seeking. In theory, the student who has obtained his fifth-year certificate should be more adept at learning a new job or coping with the various demands of an office than one who has had only four years of secondary education, but it may well be that his standards of spelling and punctuation, the great visibles which delight the middle-aged, are even lower. If, as is possible, he starts with a routine series of tasks which make no demands on the abilities developed by his school, it is very likely that he will prove incompetent and give his employer cause to wonder what is the meaning of all the fuss about education. On the other hand, if he has in fact pursued his studies with no other aim than the certificate at their end it is very likely that the only skill he will have developed is that of passing examinations, and his employer will find no evidence of any of the qualities which higher education is alleged to produce. These experiences help to maintain that scepticism among practical men of affairs which leads to demands that the schools give up their frills of art and culture and concentrate on the down-to-earth task of teaching the skills which are necessary to earn a living.

The most obvious response of state schools to this demand has been through the provision of technical courses. In two states, Victoria and South Australia, these are still offered in separate schools, but in the other states technical training is either already a part of the ordinary high school curriculum or is in the process of becoming such. Apprenticeship training, together with tertiary courses for technical certificates and diplomas, is given special facilities in every state, but these matters lie outside the scope of this book. Several states also provide agricultural and farming courses in country high or technical schools, and there are of course the residential agricultural colleges for specialized tertiary training.

The great advantage of junior technical courses is that they are obviously related to the students' future lives and so appear meaningful in a way which is often foreign to subjects in academic courses. This characteristic extends even to the general subjects in a technical course, for the teacher is faced with the challenge that his students are not normally going to continue to an academic qualification, and so are not going to be concerned very much with what he has to offer them unless he can make it immediately relevant. He is also forced to justify his subject to himself in terms of the needs of all his students, and not just of the few who may continue their education, and this consideration in turn affects both the content and the manner of his teaching. It is not coincidental that the schools which make the most determined efforts to shape their courses to the needs of the average and below-average students are the Victorian Junior Technical Schools.

Yet these advantages carry with them corresponding disadvantages which in the long run prove insurmountable. In the first place, the fact of difference leads to imputations of inferiority, and the technical schools, and technical streams within high schools, tend to be regarded merely as dumping grounds for the incapable. This reputation in turn makes a social division of what should be an educational alternative, and this division in its turn limits the career opportunities of both technical and high school students. It is bad enough that students with managerial and administrative potential are limited to manual trades because they hold only a technical qualification, but it is worse that manually proficient workers are wasting their time as clerks and counter-jumpers because they feel that only a white-collar occupation befits the dignity of a person who has attended a high school.

These restrictions are self-imposed, for there is nothing in either the technical or the general school course which need determine the eventual colour of the student's collar. Junior technical courses can lead on to technical diploma or university studies, providing the student has sufficiently developed ability and does not take only the soft options. Similarly, mathematics is an important prelude to most apprentice training, and the high school graduate need be at no disadvantage to his technical brother in seeking an apprenticeship. For it needs to be understood that no junior secondary school can give professionally adequate training in purely vocational skills. It can teach woodwork or metal-work, but as subjects which may fit the student's interests, not as technical disciplines which will fit him for professional practice. Even if it were practicable and desirable to do so in the school, the great variety of technical fields and the multiplicity of students' interests would make it impossible to do so for more than one or two trades, and the age at which the student would have to decide on one of these as his career would be too young for the decision to be meaningful. The place for specific vocational training is on the job and in the specialist apprentice and senior technical schools, not in the junior secondary schools.

The value of technical schools and courses then is not in any specific preparation which they might give for particular occupations but in the way in which they harness the student's vocational interests to his general education, as well as in the way in which they suit their teaching to the particular talents of their students. But it must be emphasized that this adaptation should be to present needs and not to future possibilities. The student perceives his needs as being related to the future, but the fact for the teacher is this present perception, not the eventual objective.

A further objection to basing a school course on too narrow a range of specific vocational objectives is that he who knows only his own job knows nothing. It is true that a person can learn to go through the motions of a particular craft quite satisfactorily without in the least understanding what he is doing, or caring. Many teachers are a standing example of the success of such a technique. But such unreflective skill is essentially imitative, and requires not schooling but merely practice to achieve its greatest development. Nor will such a person have any power to adapt to changing circumstances. If he does not understand what he is doing, he will not be able to evaluate possible new alternatives, and a great deal of his time will eventually be wasted in the performance of superstitious routines which only he believes have any necessary connection with the aim he has in mind. These qualities can be admirable in an unchanging peasant society, but they are quite inadequate to meet the demands of a society whose very being is being altered by an advancing technology. It is impossible to say today whether any particular one of the familiar occupations around us will still exist in twenty years' time, but we can be quite sure that most of the students we train to follow that occupation will remain alive until then, unless mankind loses all control of itself. We do know that today's students will have to learn new skills, and many of them entirely new jobs, within their working lives, and that their capacity to make these changes will be closely related to the quality of their education, which may not, of course, be identical with their schooling. But unless we are going to rely on the chances of life to develop this adaptability, and the figures show that it will not do so for many, our schools must (before we expect students to commence their practical vocational training) provide the understanding of the disciplines of human learning which underlie all our technologies.

The conflict between vocational and general education arises from a deeper conflict of adolescence. This conflict is between the desire to extend the horizons of our understanding until we embrace the whole world, and the need to find a clear goal in life and to concentrate our endeavours on achieving this goal. For the academically inclined, the conflict is not serious, for the goal at which he aims contains also the wider promise, but the less successful student is under constant pressure to settle for the lesser ambition. His very lack of school success has taught him not to expect too much, and his reduced expectations are fulfilled when he discovers, not to his surprise, that the general subjects of the school become less meaningful the further he pursues them. So he decides to seek a job and the practical subjects which will lead to it, and his teachers encourage him with comforting noises about him having reached the limits of his abilities, and a job making a man out of him, and so on. His discovery of an attainable goal in turn gives to his school life a meaning which has previously been lacking, he settles down more contentedly in his classes, and everyone is happily confirmed in his opinion that the poor student needs practical subjects.

The extreme example of this line of thinking was the Area School in Tasmania, which was geographical as well as vocational in its foundations. Victoria made a brief attempt at emulation with its Consolidated Schools, which similarly were placed in rural areas. The courses students followed were based on local interests and designed for local occupations. These schools could be spectacularly successful, for their students worked with materials and concepts which were familiar and meaningful to them, and the work they did extended their understanding of their lives and environment, and prepared them to follow eminently successful careers as farmers and shopkeepers. The courses looked outwards from the immediate situation, and thus extended understanding rather than limited it, but nevertheless their centres remained local and parochial. The great matters of living were approached, but only in so far as they impinged on the local life. For those who remained at home, this may not have mattered so much, although it probably helped to keep them rather slow to understand, and suspicious of change. However, many did not remain at home, but went away to chase life and money in the big cities. In an increasingly mobile society, the numbers of these are increasing, and a narrowly conceived local or vocational education, satisfying as it may appear at the time, is an inadequate foundation. Yet schools based on the principles of the Area School do have a valuable place to fill, provided that they use the immediate area and interests as a starting point and not as a boundary.

The most consistently vocational courses in secondary schools are the various forms of commercial training offered. Shorthand and typing are subjects which would appear to have no possible educational value, yet highly trained and reasonably paid teachers stand for hours in front of benches of frantically typing girls, holding watches, playing records with the fastest beat, commenting on personal carriage and chiding the insufficiently diligent. This vast effort is undertaken to save office managers from the responsibility undertaken by employers in other fields to pay their share of the costs of the technical training needed in their own industry.

In business colleges which provide this kind of instruction professionally, most of the instructors are women who are themselves experienced typists and stenographers. But in Victoria, at least, most of the typing teachers are men who have done the course for Bachelor of Commerce, and who are therefore considered to be proficient in all aspects of commercial teaching. No matter that one man may do the greater part of his Bachelor of Commerce course in Economic History and Politics, he will have to cede the history teaching to the Bachelor of Arts, who may have squeezed in only one year of Ancient History, and devote his efforts to the relaxing, if tedious, business of watching fingers on machines. In compensation for this, he will be given preemptive rights in Economics, even although an Arts graduate may have superior qualifications in this particular field. It is the label of the qualification, not the content, which counts with administrators. The final irony is that this subject, which in junior forms is taken mainly by girls, is taught mainly by men, probably because the university commerce courses are followed in many cases by men who dropped a language in their early years in order to follow a science course, failed in this, found themselves excluded from the humanities, and took what was left. The girls who matriculate, on the other hand, being both more studious and less practical, are likely to have preferred a language to mathematics, and thus finish up teaching the English and History. Meanwhile, the males who enter the commerce faculty at government expense are required to study sufficient shorthand and typing to qualify to teach the skills, although not to practise them. Their university studies are valued more as a means to future promotion than as an aid to teaching, although they also have significance as a marketable asset.

The commercial subjects are of wider than purely vocational interest, although, since they are usually yoked to office shorthand and typing, they are, as we have noted, followed in the junior forms mainly by girls. In these forms the content ranges from instructions about how to post a letter to elementary bookkeeping. To the extent that they are purely vocational, they tend to consist more of facts for aspiring office girls than of any coherent discipline. However, by the later years of the course many of the girls have dropped out to fulfil their destiny in the local offices, and have been replaced by boys who have failed in their mathematics or languages. This trend is reinforced by the prevailing practice of timetabling commercial subjects as alternatives to what are regarded as the more demanding disciplines. In fact, senior commercial subjects require a quantity of technical knowledge and a quality of abstract understanding which is at least as great as that demanded by any other discipline, but the commercial teacher must inculcate this mastery in students who have either come fresh to his field in their public examination years or who have in past years been following a course which has made less rigorous demands on their capacities and has thus less well fitted them for higher learning.

The commercial teacher thus often finds himself in the invidious position of teaching the least esteemed but most difficult subjects at senior levels and going through an undemanding routine of vocational coaching and general knowledge at lower levels. As the calibre of commercial teachers has risen with the increasing rigor and sophistication of university training given to them, so have there been increasing attempts to raise the status and value of the courses they conduct in schools. Consequently, modern commercial courses are changing their emphasis from a mere knowledge of the facts of business practice to an understanding, gained through practice, of the principles underlying not just office routine but commercial activity itself. So the students may now learn to gamble on the stock exchange, buy on the lowest market and sell on the highest, manage an office, prepare a balance sheet, produce a profit, as well as the older skills of keeping the books which record these activities. These techniques are learnt not as separate skills but as integral parts of a single process.

But the scope of commercial subjects is changing as well as their emphasis. They are coming to be seen not merely as vocational, but as an important part of general education. Both consumer education and language skills are now seen as a proper part of a subject whose aim is both to prepare people for careers in the commercial world and to increase the student's understanding of commercial processes. The function of consumer education is to prepare the student to ward off the dangers of the jungle of commercial salesmanship and to steer his way effectively towards the goal of better value. It will develop not only a knowledge of the law of contract and the ability to resist the blandishments of the doorstep salesman, but also an understanding of the principles of design and of family budgeting. As it excludes no field of contemporary life, the teacher may find himself covering everything from the morality of packaging to contemporary teenage fashions.

An alternative development has been to offer some commercial studies to all junior students as a normal part of their course. Again, the exigencies of timetabling and the demands of the academic courses often mean that this ideal is not achieved, and that the subject is offered only to the weaker classes, but nevertheless it does break out of the vocational mould which has restricted older conceptions of commerce. Such a subject may have its own form of vocational relevance by including such aspects as farm bookkeeping in a rural area, but it will also cover topics of value to any student, such as family budgeting and accounting, and personal typewriting. It can be a purely practical subject, it can be linked to the wider concerns of consumer education, or it can be used as an introductory subject for those who wish to specialize in the commercial area as well as a general subject for those going on to other fields.

If the development of courses in consumer education and general commercial studies is intended to widen the scope of commercial teaching to meet the needs of the ordinary student, the extension of senior courses in typing and shorthand to the whole field of business communications is intended to provide a specialist course which will give the widest possible education to its students without losing sight of its practical objectives. As it is intended for senior girls determined on a business career, its vocational content is not only justified, but provides an opportunity to develop a model which will bridge the gap between general and vocational courses by providing an education which both develops the all-round ability and interests of the student and evidently fits her to fill an economic niche in the community. The people responsible for the design of this course see the typist not just as an employee with a narrow technical facility, but as a professional colleague who is able to assist her employer in every aspect of his correspondence and recording, from composing reports and letters to preparing displays of statistics and factual information for prospective clients or suspicious shareholders. In addition, her professional competence should make her a socially useful citizen who can play an expert part as secretary or treasurer in local clubs and societies.

The most obvious danger in this extension of commercial teaching is that it is encroaching on other disciplines which may not be fully mastered by the commercial teacher. As a consequence, he will tend to emphasize isolated rules and techniques of correctness which may not promote any real understanding. It is notable that the language parts of the typewriting course contain the kind of admonition which has been painfully discarded by English teachers. On the other hand, the attempt to connect the formal skills of one subject with the principles of another could lead to a better command of both as students are forced to apply one set of skills in a new context, rather than pursuing their normal pattern of carefully shutting the content of each instructional period into a separate and watertight compartment to remain untouched and unharmed until the next lesson in that subject. Moreover, if teachers respond to the challenge of new courses by abandoning their professional aloofness and co-operating to pool their different resources of expertise through various forms of team teaching, this provision of courses calling on the different disciplines could lead to a deeper understanding of the teacher's own role in education.

On the other hand, any attempt to provide courses which overlap the traditional subject boundaries is likely to lead to the smorgasbord style of curriculum, where each student picks out from a common offering only those morsels which tempt his fancy or suit an already jaded palate by promising ease of digestion. If this risk is avoided by keeping the vocational aim firmly in the centre, we are faced by the alternative prospect that the whole course will be impoverished by arbitrary attempts to relate it all to a single end, an end which is itself too narrow to embrace all the interests of a healthy individual.

The truth which is so often overlooked by advocates of the latter view is that few, if any, of the aspirants in the commercial class are primarily interested in the office as a vocation. At the best, it is a place where they can spend a few years before they marry, a place made more interesting by the prospect of sharing it with eligible bachelors. At worst, it is a place which will provide an easy occupation and a sufficient income for them to pursue their main interests. So an education which fits them only for the business world will be only slightly better than the education which fits them for nothing, which is how they will see the other courses the school offers. The development of specialist vocational courses is, then, not an answer to the problem of these girls, but only an opportunity to find an answer. It is nothing other than educational irresponsibility when, as so often happens, the girl who chooses such a course is, as early as form three, debarred by the school organization from also taking part in the classes in art or needlework which are equally relevant to her eventual needs as a human being.

The greatest danger in the development of new and wider courses is not, however, merely shallow or narrow teaching. The world of commercial studies revolves uneasily between the two poles of occupational competence and personal development. On the one hand, the commercial teacher is attempting to shape his rough human material into pegs which will slide smoothly into the holes waiting for them in the business world. On the other, he attempts, by teaching them the nature of commerce, to enable them to preserve their individuality, personal and financial, against its encroachments. In his role of instilling business principles he finds himself committed to the business morality that everything has a price and nothing a value, yet he also hopes that, by teaching the students to manage their own affairs, he kill enable them to obtain value rather than appearance. But he lacks the resources to solve the problem of value, for his professional commitment to the world of today and the job of the future excludes the notion of any roots in the past and becomes essentially empirical and pragmatic. He is concerned not with what is true but with what works. By his very concern with the things of today he denigrates them, for if something new happens tomorrow then the affairs and values of today will no longer be important. To the extent that the course transmits its own inner logic it must produce either sentimental optimists who accept everything or hard-faced cynics who believe nothing.

These dangers will be less serious if the senior commercial courses as a whole are carefully designed for people who intend to enter the commercial world, and not just as a vocational preparation for entering this world. As well as the skills which they will exercise in their jobs, the students need to develop the powers of analysis which will enable them to understand their job in relation to other fields of human activity and not as either a mere means of making a living or as the one absorbing task in life. A course which seeks these ends in the senior school will need in its turn to be based on a broad course of commercial studies for all students in the junior school, which should go beyond providing a little prophylactic skill for the consumer and a modicum of business routine for the employee to a consideration of the fundamental roles of man as producer and consumer, as worker and as a creature of leisure. This course, too, has within it the seeds of degeneration into something resembling the American courses in democratic citizenship, but it need not do so if it is grounded in the obligation to see and understand facts as they are, and not accept any framework of contemporary mythology as a substitute for fact.

This does not mean that such a course, more than any other, should be a sterile exercise in fact-finding. On the contrary, it should provide a discipline by which the facts of commercial life can be understood. Such a discipline does not at present, to judge by the textbooks, appear to exist, at least in terms understood by junior secondary students, but it may well be developed by practising teachers applying the principle of games to the operation of the firm. In this method, the class is divided into a number of firms, which are each provided with an initial amount of capital and the necessary office stationery. Trading then proceeds between the firms, and as each transaction is completed it has to be put through the books just as in actual business practice. Thus the class becomes a prototype for the business community, and may be used both as a training machine for commercial operations and as a small model in which may be demonstrated the interrelationships of the business community.

It is normal practice to confine junior commercial teaching to those girls who intend to enter an office, but once it is seen as an instrument for developing an understanding of contemporary society the justification for this restriction disappears. Nor need the commercial courses at senior secondary levels be confined to potential secretaries, for the corollary of the idea that the stenographer is a professional colleague of the manager is that her education will be equally relevant to future managers. In fact, a common course of education for all intending to enter the business world may eventually lead to a disappearance of the notion that the only place for a woman in an office is behind the typewriter.

An indispensable element of any senior commercial course would seem to be economics, providing of course that it can break away from its earlier absorption in factual details to an understanding of the patterns which govern these facts. It may, for example, be of some interest to know the steps by which the Commonwealth Bank developed into a three-part commercial institution and a fully-fledged central bank, but it is more important to understand the role of the Reserve Bank today. This may certainly be illustrated by comparison with the days when there was no such control, but the detailed steps which have changed that situation are quite irrelevant. What is important, and what can be understood by students, is an understanding of the productive and trade cycles, and of the comparative roles of the public and private sectors of the economy.

Unfortunately, economics is still one of those new disciplines whose practitioners are so conscious of their arcane skill that they will not admit to their craft anyone who has not become fully initiated into their mysteries. They distrust the inevitable oversimplification which they observe in the schools where the models are taught as certain fact, while the professionals know that at the best they are only the beginning of wisdom. Yet a glance at the way in which public affairs are debated and conducted in this country will soon show that the problem facing us is not a simplistic approach to economic complexities but a complete ignorance of the existence of such a subject. While this chapter was in construction the Federal treasurer solemnly assured the states that their problems of deficit budgeting were no greater than his own, and not one state premier reminded him of the essential differences. The whole debate on state and federal finances goes on at a level which would be more appropriate to a family argument on whether mother should go to the pictures or father to the pub. Keynesian techniques are used quite successfully by the Commonwealth public service to keep the economy on an even keel, but until the level of public debate on economic questions can achieve some reasonable level of sophistication we will continue to see the advantages of this stability dissipated on bribes and subsidies for political advantage, while the serious economic problems remain untouched and unconsidered.

Studies designed to develop an understanding of economic reality should not, of course, be confined to students taking the commercial courses. Some of these principles can be successfully taught as part of junior history studies, which would normally be a part of every student's course. In the senior school, economics could be a compulsory part of any business course and an optional part of others.

The other vocational subjects found in secondary schools are the various forms of domestic arts. In some states the Victorian idea that a woman's place is in the home still lingers in the legislative provision, strongly supported by members of the Country Party, that all girls must be taught to cook while at school. As a consequence, a school which lacks a library or a decent science laboratory will have a four-roomed domestic block with $20,000 worth of equipment to teach the only subject which every child's own home is also equipped to teach.

In connection with the domestic arts we should also consider needlework, although this should perhaps be regarded as a branch of the visual and practical arts and crafts. Certainly, it offers invaluable vocational training for the future housewife, for whereas every girl will eventually learn to cook, if only out of a tin, the saving to the family budget which can be made by the skilled seamstress is not likely to be produced by any haphazard learning picked up after schooldays. Moreover, the needlework class offers the immediate satisfaction of producing garments which can be displayed, or used to display the owner, at the school social or local dance, and thus earns the goodwill of both the student whose social success is assured and of her father whose purse is saved. On the other hand, nothing is as productive of maternal jealousy as the different artifacts and craft marks produced by their offspring. Finally, needlework offers the opportunity to instil some elementary understanding of fashion and taste, providing the teacher has any herself. The corresponding danger is that it will merely play into the hands of the manufacturers by reinforcing the idea that the most enormous social crime is to be seen wearing last year's model.

To close the chapter, however, I must emphasize that the justification for the inclusion of any of these subjects in the school curriculum is not the eventual or even immediate practical value which will be reaped, but their advantage as providing the basis for an education which will be apparently relevant to the child's own ambitions. In the junior secondary school this advantage is gained merely by giving some time to such studies, but in the senior classes there is strong justification for planning each student's course around the vocational content, providing that this content is sufficiently widely conceived and that the resulting course does not debar the student from continuing his studies to whatever level he may eventually choose. This principle has always been observed for those following academic courses, and it is high time that the others were given the same opportunity in fact as well as in theory. Finally, we must recognize that in many cases it is only the fact that schools offer such apparently narrow vocational subjects as shorthand and typewriting which persuades many students to remain at school beyond the minimum leaving age. Some of these students eventually go on to higher studies in quite different spheres, but none of them would remain at school unless they believed that it offered them specific preparation for their careers.

7 Religion and Indoctrination

The subjects we have considered so far have all been concerned with developing understanding and skill, or with purveying facts. Any teacher is aware, however, that as well as promoting intellectual development he is inevitably inculcating various social and mental habits which may be adopted by the students without any conscious examination of the assumptions on which they rest. Without a minimum standard of behaviour, the school would be unable to operate, and unless its students accept a common attitude towards knowledge and intellectual enquiry they will not progress far in their studies. The very possibility of education in the intellectual sense depends on a belief in the existence of a truth outside the immediate experience of the individual and of various established and accepted ways of enquiring into that truth.

A school for children is not, however, merely an extension of the scholastic machinery which a community maintains to advance knowledge. It is also one of the chief agencies through which society inducts its new members into its culture, its whole way of living. It shares this responsibility with a whole range of independent institutions, from the family through the various churches and youth organizations to the local football club and the mass media, but its responsibility is the greatest in this area both because it is the largest institution designed for this specific purpose and because, unlike the family, which is essentially conservative, it has the capacity to prepare children to make the adjustments in their attitudes which will be required of them by a rapidly changing society. However, children do not come into the influence of the school until their basic personality has been formed, and at no time do they spend even half their waking hours within its environs, so that its role may be critical but can rarely be determinate. Moreover, as so much school activity seems irrelevant to the urgent issues which children find pressing on them, its importance in influencing their behaviour and beliefs is probably considerably less than either optimistic teachers or anxious parents believe.

The most important influence on a child is undoubtedly his own family. This gives him not only his fundamental standards of conduct and value, but also decides to a great extent the attitude which he will adopt to the school as an institution and to the subjects it teaches. If the parents are hostile to authority and suspicious of learning, their children are likely to be troublesome in class and indifferent towards their lessons. On the other hand, the middle class parents who place a high value on achievement are likely to have children who behave responsibly, work diligently, and learn nothing. In either case, the success of the school in promoting any particular values will probably be negligible. Its importance will be far greater in the case of the child who finds himself in rebellion against his parents, either because he seeks greater status than they have or because he finds their values restrictive, and who therefore looks to the school and its teachers for an alternative model and source of authority. It is such students who give cause for worry to those politicians who live in dread that the schools are infected by red agents vigorously proselytizing the younger generation. In fact, however, youngsters who are already mature enough to reject one source of authority are unlikely to remain bound throughout their lives to any other. It is those who discover the fallibility of their gods only after they reach adulthood who are most likely to seek the refuge of a new sanctuary.

It is the family also which decides the child's pattern of leisure activities, although these are circumscribed by the pattern of local culture, as well as by the opportunities offered by the immediate neighbourhood. The child of the completely permissive family will be allowed to do as he likes, and his spare hours of daylight will probably be spent around the streets or countryside with his mates, and his evenings before the idiot box. As a consequence, his values will derive immediately from his confreres and ultimately from the mass culture. But only the most hermetic and authoritarian of families can insulate its children from these influences, which provide the staple diet of playground gossip and activity. When the recess-time games are woven around the figures from *Thunderbirds*, the child is unlikely to sit happily through the improving offerings of the A.B.C., although the recent policy of the national channels has made their children's programs indistinguishable from the pap of the commercial networks. However, the very fact that the stereotypes of television become incorporated into the living play of children restores to them an element of humanity which prevents their viewing from having as disastrous effects as we might imagine.

Parents who are concerned about the upbringing of their children are nevertheless likely to attempt to provide a structure of leisure activities which will ensure the perpetuation of the values they themselves hold. They may insist on a certain amount of reading before the television set is turned on, or they may veto or prescribe particular programs and hours of viewing. Even if they accept the kind of values purveyed through the tube, they may still encourage such other activities as church or Sunday school, scouts, or youth club. All of these activities are distinguished from schooling by the facts that they are concerned with behaviour and morals rather than with learning, and that they make a deliberate endeavour to appear relevant to the child's immediate interests. Even the churches, which are primarily adult institutions, provide either special youth services or segments of the service, or supplementary instruction for their young people.

The most successful of youth institutions in English-speaking countries has been the Scout movement, and its feminine counterpart, Guiding, although this has suffered by the air of robust jollity which it has inherited from its origins. The success of Scouting derives in a great part from the way in which it has matched its activities to youthful imagination and social behaviour. While boys are still in the mob age, it provides them with Wolf Cubs, whose activities are built on the rich lore of Rudyard Kipling's *Jungle Books*. Through these stories, and the games based on them, the children are given a satisfying ritual, food for imagination, and a code for their conduct, founded upon a mystic reverence for the Law which fits well with their natural state of primitive savagery. These possibilities are, however, seldom achieved in practice in cub packs, which are often run either by giggling girls just out of school or by spinsterish females of more mature years, who can rarely enter into the bloodthirsty world of the boy's imagination. Nor is success necessarily any greater in packs run by male leaders, who all too often have advanced beyond childhood only as far as adolescence, and who consequently impose their own standards of rowdy athleticism and competitive sport rather than developing the patterns of ritual which are more natural to this age. The two enemies of successful work with children of any age are gentility and sophistication, and these are too often the only qualities in which youth workers excel.

Numerically the most successful part of the Scout movement is the Cub section, but in practice the best work is done in the Boy Scout Troop, which caters for boys between the ages of eleven and fourteen. The organization of a Scout troop is based on a unit of six to eight boys known as a Patrol, and the Patrol Leaders, with the Scoutmaster, constitute the Court-of-Honour, which is theoretically the governing body of the troop. The successful Scoutmaster works through his Patrol Leaders to plan and run the outdoor activities which are the staple of the Scouting program. The highlight and climax of the Scout year is the summer camp at which the year's training is both tested and justified. It is within the camp environment, where the routine activity of running a camp provides the necessary framework of order and discipline, as well as facing each boy with the responsibility of playing his part in a team whose function is real, that the ideals of the Scout movement are mostly likely to be achieved.

Scouting was in its origin an outdoor movement, and despite the Victorian fustiness of much of its founder's writings this aspect still appeals to boys. Moreover, the unit of the patrol matches the natural size of the gang to which boys of this age incline. Finally, by challenging boys to exercise responsibility in real situations, Scouting gives them both a sense of their own dignity and the opportunity to develop their own individuality, not for some hypothetical time in the future, but in the immediate world of here and now. At the time when they are leaving childhood, it gives them the chance to practise acting as adults, a chance which they are unlikely to find anywhere else until they have left school.

This potential is, however, often dissipated when Scouting becomes a weeknight activity and the troop displaces the patrol as the basic unit. Certainly, if you walk into any Scout meeting you will find the troop lined up in its patrols under their leaders, but too often these units are formed merely for competitive convenience and reflect no social or organizational structure. This development in turn comes from the decline in importance of the annual camp and the increased emphasis on the evening meeting. As the camp recedes and the patrol structure becomes irrelevant, troop and inter-troop activities grow in importance, and practical bushcraft comes to take second place to the District Swimming Carnival or the Athletics Sports. Scouting becomes just one more youth club, dressed up perhaps in a more glamorous uniform, but serving no different purpose.

For boys beyond the age of fourteen, Scouting, in common with all other adult-directed youth movements, loses its appeal. Two further sections, Senior Scouts, for ages fifteen to eighteen, and Rover Scouts, for boys from seventeen and upwards, provide more challenging and energetic activities, but they have not found either the organization or the program which will appeal to more than a small proportion of the age groups for which they cater. Reasons for this decline in the holding power of the movement have been sought in the short pants of the uniform, the authoritarian morality and the limited program, as well as attributed to the general deterioration of young people, but the truth is probably that adolescence is a time of rebellion, exploration and individuality, and that no single movement is going to cater for the increasing diversity of interests which develop during these years. Furthermore, in the process of exploring his own potential the healthy individual may not wish to persevere in any single pattern of activities for very long, and in the course of establishing his individuality he may not feel inclined to subscribe to any particular organization. Then again, the adolescent is particularly critical, and only the best of youth leaders will maintain the interest of even the minority who are interested in a particular program of activities. It is probably a sufficient success that the Scout movement does hold the interest of a considerable number of older boys who constitute a vigorous youth movement and provide a reservoir for future leaders of the junior sections.

Nevertheless, despite all the external indications of success, there is a general feeling that Scouting has somehow failed to keep abreast of the times. This may in part reflect its failure to achieve in working class localities, whose children would seem most in need of the goods it has to offer, the same success that it has achieved in the cream brick spread of new suburbs and in rural towns. Yet in an increasingly bourgeois society this middle class basis should be a source of strength rather than of weakness. The trouble is that the moral code of the Scout movement is not merely middle class, but reflects the triumphant imperialism of a British Empire which no longer exists. The movement has had its latitudinarians and revisionists who have extended the meaning of god and the queen to meet the demands of a new age, but the very vocabulary of loyalty, thrift and cleanliness has more in common with Samuel Smiles than with either the junior executives or the professional technocrats who set the pace in the world of today. The success of the movement comes from its organization and its activities, from the discipline and labour of the camp and the fellowship of the campfire, and from the example of its leaders, rather than from its ostensible moral philosophy. At its best, it prepares its members for responsible citizenship, and even at its worst it provides healthy and purposeful activitity, but those who take its teachings too much to heart are in danger of remaining perpetual adolescents, their minds blinded by outworn slogans to the shifting complexities of a changing world.

The success of the Scout movement has provoked a batch of emulators who have borrowed one part or another from the Scouting program. Some organizations, church and political, have borrowed the uniform and badge system, but outside the framework for which they were designed these become a veneer rather than a token. More commonly, the practice of camping has been adopted by a variety of youth groups which seek to give their members a holiday in the countryside, but once again the lack of a coherent purpose for the activity alters its nature. As we have seen, the Scout camp is the culmination of the year's training, and provides its own justification and its own discipline. But unless the training during the year is directed towards developing the skills needed for successful camping, adolescents will need looking after. Consequently, we find that the typical church or youth club camp has one batch of adult helpers preparing the meals and supervising the camp chores, and another organizing activities for the campers who are left with spare time on their hands. These activities range from aimless walks to organized sport, but they have in common the fact that they are planned to fill in time rather than to serve any function within the overall purpose of the camp.

Two exceptions to this rule would be the Boys' Brigade, which is older than the Scout movement and shares a similar tradition and similar problems, and the church youth conference, which uses the camp merely as a convenient opportunity to bring the participants together for a wider purpose. The first of these, however, is numerically small, and the second caters most successfully for young adults, so neither is really relevant to the purpose of this book. More relevant are the Outward Bound movement, inspired by the principles of Kurt Hahn's school at Gordonstoun, and the derivative trend among metropolitan schools to establish rural branches were their students can be brought into close contact with the realities of nature.

The Outward Bound movement attempts to give to older adolescents the kind of moral training which they have missed at school. Most of the trainees who attend its short but intensive courses are sponsored by their employers on the strength of their anticipated leadership potential. During their month-long stay at the Outward Bound centre they are organized in small groups similar to the patrols of a Scout troop, and are subject to rigid and puritanical discipline. They are trained in a variety of skills designed both to develop their courage and self-reliance and to prepare them for the journey of endurance with which the course concludes. The combination of discipline and hardship is intended to weld the participants into a team which will provide the framework of fellowship within which the students can explore and reconsider their basic moral attitudes and aspirations. The principle is not dissimilar from that employed by Percy Cerutty with his athletes on their bran and pollard diet at their training camp at Portsea, or from that which operated to strengthen and purify Scott and his fellows on their return march from the South Pole, or Mao Tse Tung and his comrades on the Long March to Yenan. The equation of hardship and virtue seems to have a particular appeal to those who fear the flabbiness of modern affluence, and the Outward Bound movement tends to attract those eccentric romantics who in an earlier age would have headed expeditions up the Nile or across the Antarctic, and who feel that the twentieth century lost something when the atom bomb put an end to the nice clean kind of war their fathers enjoyed in the past.

The heroes of the Outward Bound movement are undoubtedly excellent individuals who have had the courage to stand apart from the escalators of progress and have found their own mountains to climb instead. Yet their relevance to the problems of a modern society is not clear. The qualities which are necessary to sail a boat through a hurricane or to lead a party of skiers through a blizzard are not necessarily the same ones as those needed to manage a team of men in business or industry. In the physical situation the leader and his men need absolute confidence in each other, but the leader also needs to be able to rely on unquestioning obedience. This he can obtain because all are agreed on the immediate goal and because the exigencies of the immediate situation leave no time for the niceties of debate and consensus, but this situation is seldom reproduced in the normal circumstances of urban life. In the factory, the office or the school, the team of workers is assembled through a variety of chance factors for a few hours each day, the purpose of the operation is necessarily unclear, and the ambitions of the individuals concerned are as diverse as their separate abilities. In these circumstances the ability to produce harmony and to nourish each individual is more important than the authority to command obedience.

The very success of the Outward Bound movement in producing tough, self-reliant individuals is likely to inhibit its chances of developing those qualities of flexibility needed for leadership in an urban society, and there is indeed the danger that the movement could do for the new generation what the army and the R.S.L. did for the old, filling the boardrooms of Australian industry with venerable figures who command respect and nothing else, and who are able to maintain neither harmony nor efficiency. The noble eccentrics who climb mountains and circumnavigate the globe deserve an honoured place in our society, but not a powerful one. When their record is held up as the sole exemplar of human excellence, their example is too likely to be brutalized into a regard for toughness and endurance as ends in themselves, and a corresponding disdain for the qualities of mind and heart which are a necessary endowment for any civilized man.

The principles of the Outward Bound movement have been most extensively applied by Geelong Grammar, the school which has won fame as the host of Prince Charles and the Eton of Australia. This latter claim it owes both to the number of cabinet ministers it has provided for the Commonwealth and to their frequent lack of ability. It is distinguished from its fellow members of the Associated Public Schools by the paucity of scholars and the plenitude of eccentrics and communists who have issued from its portals. Indeed, one of its former students has claimed that it provides the best education in Australia because the system is so terrible that any man of spunk must revolt against it. It was in these circumstances that its previous headmaster, Dr Darling, decided to establish a bushland branch which would enable its students to gain in physical prowess what they lacked in intellectual distinction. For over ten years now all fourth-form scholars at Geelong Grammar have spent their year amid the mountain ash at Timbertop, beyond Mansfield, where they have added to their normal lessons practice in hiking, pathfinding, skiing, fishing and latrine cleaning. The experience will no doubt provide useful material for parliamentary oratory in the future, but its greatest immediate advantage is the absence of organized sport. For twelve months the students of one of the major institutions dedicated to Dr Arnold's worship of team games are expected to organize their own leisure hours without the stimulus of the glory to be won from competition. Yet, just as in the Outward Bound movement, the result of this freedom has been to place an emphasis not on walking or skiing or fishing enjoyed as activities worthwhile in themselves, but on the display of physical endurance by undertaking, on foot, journeys of astounding length in amazingly rapid time. The playing fields of Eton are replaced by the heroics of Marathon and an indigenous form of muscular Christianity.

Other metropolitan schools with rural branches have been less ambitious in their aims, and take their students away only for periods of two weeks or a month during their normal year. Some of these branches are plain bushland camps, others have a basis in forestry or farm enterprises. As well as the schemes run by particular schools, the various state governments operate or subsidise a number of schemes designed to take city children to the country or country children to the seaside and to give them moral training and health care as a sideline. These schemes are, however, regarded as holidays rather than as a normal part of education, and they lack both the continuity and the institutional identity of the branches attached to particular schools. Like Timbertop, these have the twin aims of bringing the students into contact with different and more natural surroundings than their usual, and providing a total environment within which the school ethos will have a greater impact. They thus can give to all the students of a school something of the sort of advantage which is normally enjoyed, or resented, only by the boarders. It is doubtful, however, whether these brief intervals outside the normal stream of school life have any great effect on the majority of the students.

Despite all these endeavours by schools and parents to reinforce their various moral codes, the main onus of moral instruction among the young still falls on the ordinary school in the course of its normal routine. In the 'Public Schools', this responsibility is recognized by the daily school assemblies, which begin with a suitable invocation of the almighty, and by the provision of weekly scripture classes. In the state schools, these ceremonies are paralleled by the 'loyal assembly', at which the headmaster couples the names of the almighty and the sovereign, and the 'religious instruction' class, during which a local clergyman gives instruction in faith and morals to those whose parents have not withdrawn them on conscientious grounds. In all states except Victoria these classes are organized on denominational lines and are supposed to be held outside the hours of normal secular instruction and conducted by a clergyman or his representative, although

South Australia now allows its teachers to volunteer for this additional duty if they have received proper clerical approval. This permission to give religious instruction was originally a sop thrown to the churches at the end of the nineteenth century, when the attempt to establish parallel national and denominational school systems had foundered on the rock of sectarian bitterness. We read that at that time difficulty was experienced from unruly classes and the shortage of competent religious teachers, and the situation has not improved markedly to this day.

The most extensive attempt to introduce effective religious education has been made in Victoria, where the Protestant churches have drawn up an agreed syllabus which can be taught during normal school hours by approved instructors. At the same time Roman Catholic or Jewish instructors may take denominational classes for their adherents, but there is neither opportunity for atheists or humanists to do likewise, nor for non-Protestant clergy to take classes unless Protestant instruction is already being provided. Under the terms of the act which has made this possible, the combined churches are now able to appoint chaplains to state schools, provided that their salaries are paid by the parents. In some twenty-two schools, where this has been done, it has proved most effective, as the chaplain is able to give his undivided attention to his task, rather than having it buried amid a host of other duties, and his position as a member of the staff gives him the opportunity to develop close relationships both with the students and with other teachers. In these circumstances, his own teaching is more effective and he is also able to engage in individual student counselling. It is, however, very doubtful whether religious instruction by visiting outsiders is of any value whatever. Although in Victoria there are now special training courses for lay instructors, and all denominations provide some advice in teaching method as a part of their ministerial training, the general standard of teaching in religious instruction classes is so bad as to be positively harmful. Even with the best of goodwill and ability, the outsider is at a disadvantage compared with the rest of the staff, as he has neither the opportunity to come to know his class nor the chance to relate his work to other parts of the curriculum. The first of these handicaps is reduced when the instruction is given on denominational lines, as the instructor will at least know those members of his faith who are also members of his flock, but this advantage is introduced at the cost of emphasizing sectarian divisions, and the very fact of division sets these classes aside from the normal life of the school.

Supporters of the Victorian system have suggested that these handicaps would be overcome if the South Australian example were to be followed and ordinary teachers allowed to take the religious classes. This would certainly raise the standard of teaching, but it could also entrench religious divisions more deeply in the life of the school by lining up teachers as well as children according to their denominational allegiance. The proposal is also viewed with deep suspicion by teachers, who rejected it at a union conference where it was suggested that, however the regulations might read to the contrary, the teacher who refused to take such instruction on conscientious grounds would henceforth be handicapped in his career. This argument provides a significant illustration of the suspicion among teachers towards both clerical and departmental authority. The proposal is, however, open to the more serious objection, at least at secondary level, that the average teacher's theological ignorance is an adequate match for the typical minister's pedagogic incapacity.

This argument, however, rests on the ground that the syllabus of study is itself a theological document, a theory which will not survive either an examination of the Victorian agreed syllabus or any observation of a normal religious instruction lesson in a state school. The syllabus is well-meaning, humane and liberal, but otherwise has little to commend it. The accompanying handbooks are slightly revised versions of a wartime series of good cheer, stuffed with banality and as dull in content as they are in format. Their idea of fitting their approach to the age of the children is to talk down in the most patronizing manner possible, while dodging all the difficult problems they imply. Men are divided, most untheologically, into the very evil (e.g., Hitler) and the saintly good. The latter category includes such dreary regulars as Schweitzer, Luther, Tyndale, Grenfell and Scott of the Antarctic, with, of course, his faithful servant and companion, Wilson. These people appear in such an inhuman fashion as to make saintliness positively repulsive. At the same time, there are bracing quotations from such exemplars of Christian love as Winston Churchill and Bernard Montgomery. The final book does devote some of its space to such social evils as slums and race hatred, and considers such social problems as work and leisure, but it could not be said to take the specifically Christian answer to these any further than a recognition that, for the believer, everything should be done for the greater glory of God. There is no attempt to consider the problem raised by the well-intentioned, dedicated and self-righteous fanatic, nor is much attention given to the proposition that Christianity is an unworldly religion which can only lose its own soul if it chases after worldly objectives. Yet precisely the opposite fault afflicts the sections on the church, which suggest that membership of this august institution is all-sufficient and raises no problems of conflicting duties or loyalties.

But the weakness of the course goes beyond presentation and style, which are matters which can be overcome by the competent teacher. It is the extent to which the style betrays the method which is most disturbing. The books have no doubt been devised and written by very well-meaning and decent people, but as books they lack any soul. Despite the occasional high-minded exhortation to the contrary, religion is seen from the outside as a veneer which can be applied to ease one's path through life. The earlier part of the course concentrates on Biblical studies, but these studies take the form of pleasant studies of Biblical heroes with moralistic applications to the present day. There is certainly no attempt to show how man's concept of God developed and changed through the Judaeo-Christian leaders and thinkers. Even such reference as is made to alternative views of God is inadequate and inaccurate. We are, for example, told that the Greek conception of a god was so lofty that the name could not be qualified by even an adjective. So much for 'bright-eyed Athena' and her rumbustious colleagues. The later part concentrates on contemporary problems, and any theology is, we are told, implicit. This approach may seem to observe the time-honoured practice of proceeding from the known to the unknown, but it has the effect that the unknown remains both unknown and unjustified. There is a fairly coherent exposition of the idea of God, but no orderly doctrine of the church, man or society emerges, and consequently the difficulties of relating these concepts to each other are never approached.

The fundamental fault in the course, however, is that it aims not at giving its students an insight into a human activity or a branch of human learning but at 'endeavouring to enable each of them to make an appropriate commitment of his life to Christ'. Such an aim is not only contrary to the proper aim of the teacher who hopes to enable his students to develop their own capacities to the point where they will be able to make their own independent judgements, but is also insulting to the basic premise of the Christian religion that God has given each man the freedom to make his own choice. No doubt every teacher is confident that the choice he himself has made has some general validity, and will hope that his students will be inclined to follow it, but to suggest that his teaching should be deliberately designed to promote this end is to be guilty at the least of the Greek fault of hubris, and probably of the ultimate Christian sin against the Holy Spirit, that is, against a trust in God's ability to order the world as He sees fit without the presumptuous intervention of mankind.

The documents produced for this syllabus all have the old-fashioned and musty air associated with nineteenth century religious controversy. They are concerned with the separate sins of greed and envy, with the quarrel of science and faith, with arguments for the existence of God. They advocate the virtues of tolerance, courage, good-humour, abstinence and chastity. Nowhere do they come to grips with the problems which agitate Christians and many non-Christians today, with the problems of freedom and authority, and the question of how far man can, or should, attempt to order his own universe. There is no attempt to consider, in relation to the population problem, Julian Huxley's observation that man now has to control his own evolution, or to come to terms with Camus' anguish that man's highest and proudest aspirations have led to his bloodiest cataclysms. There is not even any acknowledgement of the efforts which modern theology has been making to re-define God in terms which are meaningful today, but only the pious hope that a return to old and tried forms will somehow lead to a newer and juster society. There is no essential difference between this society and that which would be favoured by most humanists, except for a lesser degree of sophistication in its conception and a greater degree of self-righteousness in its advocacy.

A different approach to religion was attempted in New South Wales, where for many years 'general religious teaching' was permitted in state schools. This teaching was until 1964 provided as a special scripture course, but in that year the department withdrew the syllabus for scripture and replaced it in primary schools with a syllabus of work to be included in the social studies courses. This work was to be 'about the good life and the principles on which it is based', and was to draw these principles from a study of leaders and teachings of the great religions of the world, and not only Christianity. The proposal, however, raised immense opposition from the churches who felt that their monopoly of wisdom might be questioned, and was withdrawn and replaced by a compromise. As the present Premier of New South Wales, Mr Askin, has stated that his party believes 'the overwhelming majority of parents want only the Christian religion to be taught in schools', there is little possibility that the proposal will be revived.

It must, however, be admitted that there are severe difficulties in introducing any form of comparative religion into schools. The studies proposed for New South Wales primary children threatened to share the same superficial character which marks most social studies courses, which emphasize colourful facts and external differences at the expense of both accuracy and understanding. Even if they had been developed more rigorously, it is doubtful whether many teachers would have the training or background to take such a course satisfactorily, or whether schoolchildren are in fact capable of understanding the concept of comparative religion. It may be that the only alternative to a course of indoctrination in fear which will remain with them to the grave is a course carefully designed to allow the developing child's idea of god to grow in much the same fashion as the idea of god has grown during man's history. This would probably mean that the notion of a personal god should not be introduced until quite late, and the ideas of morality should be completely avoided until the child is old enough to discuss them in their own terms, and not as received commandments. The place of the ten commandments until then can be quite satisfactorily filled by school and parental injunctions, which are followed quite simply for reasons of expediency in the face of superior power and not because they are endowed with any supernatural sanction. As part of such a course, students could become acquainted with the myths and legends of many lands, not as 'something which some people believe', but as stories worthwhile in their own right which can be discussed by the child in their own terms. Later on, they would be ready to contrast the varying world views implicit in the mythology of, say, Genesis, Olympus and Valhalla, and eventually to compare the conceptions of a supreme being held by the main contemporary religions. Finally, by about the age of sixteen they could be introduced to such notions as humanism, existentialism and nihilism.

The aim of this course would not be to obtain a commitment to any particular faith, but to inculcate an understanding of the part played by religion in man's long confrontation with the universe, and to develop the capacity of the students to make their own free and informed choice of the faith by which they will live. This may not produce as many nominal adherents of any faith as does the present method, but it would ensure that men regarded religion as something worth serious attention, and not as something to be merely donned or doffed according to the prevailing social or intellectual fasion.

Such a course would need to be designed by theologians given the time to concentrate on the task, and including non-Christians in their numbers. Furthermore, its success would depend on training teachers to implement it. At the primary level, this would mean trainee teachers learning some basic theology as a part of their course, a practice which could lead to trouble with those enthusiasts so committed to a particular religious or irreligious viewpoint as to be unable to undertake any critical study. At secondary level, specialist teachers would need to be trained, as in other disciplines. The problem here would not be so much in finding volunteers as in finding suitable university courses for them to follow. Theological studies are excluded from most Australian universities, and from all state teachers' colleges, and the Biblical Studies which are sometimes found are too narrowly conceived to be of general value although they would certainly form an integral part of any course of theological training for prospective teachers.

As an alternative to general religious education, Victoria and Tasmania have both introduced specialist courses in Biblical Studies or Religious Knowledge for secondary schools. These subjects are in practice limited to church schools, and mainly to Roman Catholic schools, as Protestant institutions are too busy coping with the vocational subjects to have time left over for such luxuries. Both these courses are thorough but narrow. The Tasmanian course might in fact be better entitled 'Dogmatic Theology'. Its examination papers include such directions as 'Argue for the existence of God' and 'Show that (natural religion) is insufficient'. The candidates who coped successfully with this section of the paper would no doubt be able to dispose very quickly of the question which merely asks them to discuss the rise of 'Atheistic Communism'. However, as the paper requires them to answer nine questions in the three hours, they presumably have little time for more than the most pietistic simplicities. That such is the case is born out by the examiner's comment that Leo XIII's encyclical *Rerum Novarum* provides an excellent answer to the doctrines of Marx 'and others'.

The Victorian course also provides in its syllabus for the study of more general questions, but the sheer weight of knowledge required by the examination is such as to make it doubtful whether most teachers would have any time available for really effective discussion. Even in the core of the course, the emphasis would seem to be on learning rather than exegesis. Although the course leaves room for a variety of approaches and does not appear to demand religious commitment as a prerequisite to passing, it is difficult to see it being of much interest to Jew or atheist.

But as well as these explicitly value-oriented institutions and courses, the schools are constantly inculcating their own values in their schools. This process goes on through the attitudes of the teachers, the values built into the subjects and the values implicit in the schools' aims and organization. Educationists have recognized the fact for many years, and in the United States it is standard practice to incorporate in the stated aims of a course of studies such ideas as 'the encouragement of democratic citizenship' or 'an understanding of community values'. Even in Australia, it is not uncommon to read in the preamble to courses of study such aims as 'to inculcate a love of reading' or 'to raise the standard of public taste'. The educationists have now classified these aims as affective, in distinction to the cognitive aims which are concerned with the development of intellectual skills and understanding. This terminology is derived originally from the psychologists, and refers to the distinction between our conscious understanding and our affections, emotions and feelings. As used by educationists, the terms distinguish rather between the acquisition of knowledge and understanding and the less conscious acquisition of attitudes and habits of thinking and behaviour.

As all teachers, more or less deliberately, inculcate attitudes while they teach, it is argued that they should consciously and explicitly determine their affective as well as their cognitive aims when drawing up their courses of studies. This would both enable them to plan the course to achieve these aims more effectively, and give the school authorities and the community a statement of what is being done to the children. In this way, undesirable attitudes could be eliminated and more desirable ones cultivated.

There is no doubt that the individual teacher does have a great deal of power to affect the attitude of his students, by his own personality, by his selection of topics in his course, and by his manner of presentation. The 'Javas' experiment previously mentioned showed how attitudes of fear towards a mythical people could be cultivated merely by the choice of phrases used to describe this people and their habits. Thus the group who were given such information as that the 'Javas' had unusually large and powerful hands and ate the flesh of young calves whose throats had been cut acquired, not surprisingly, a strong prejudice against these people. Those who were merely told that they were like Australians, except that they had larger hands, and that they ate veal, felt no such prejudice against them.

The most surprising thing about this experiment was not the result, which merely confirmed scientifically what most teachers had realized anyway, but the attitudes which it revealed both among educationists and among the general public. The authors of the experiment had apparently not considered the possibility that children might identify 'the Javas' with the real inhabitants of Java, and so were not worried that the prejudice they were deliberately inculcating might have real effects. Even when this was pointed out to them, they were quite satisfied that they had cleared the children's minds of any prejudice by giving them a logical explanation of what had been done to them at the conclusion of the experiment. This sanguine belief rests on the assumption that once a person understands indoctrination he will resist it, an assumption which is contradicted by the whole advertising industry, which meets with as much success among the educated as among the uneducated, although it has to make slight changes in its methods for the two groups. Moreover, the experiment itself produced such evidence of unconscious learning as to give its authors reason for doubt about their ability to expunge by formal teaching what they have so effectively implanted by subliminal devices. Even if suspicion of the 'Javas' could have been eliminated, a learning experience of this nature is of a kind likely to implant a lasting prejudice against foreigners, particularly coloured foreigners.

It is this kind of generalized attitude which is the most likely result of the prejudices which teachers bring with them to the classroom, and the most amazing thing about the public controversy which followed the publication of the 'Javas' case was the pathetic belief of so many correspondents that indoctrination could be removed from the classroom. This very belief in the possibility of objective teaching is one of the results of teaching which has purported to be such, and has given the students no training in evaluating different approaches and points of view. Such teaching occurs most commonly, not where we would expect indoctrination, in the humanities, but in the sciences, where carefully constructed courses give an illusion of universal truth to what is after all only one of man's many approaches to his task of understanding and classifying his universe. The prestige conferred on scientists by their ability to deliver the goods to a materialistic generation has wrapped them in an unwarranted awe which in other ages belonged, equally erroneously, to priest, warrior or alchemist. It may be inevitable that man should always equate power with wisdom, but the belief in the exclusive wisdom of the scientists is one of the most obvious results of an allegedly objective system of education.

Yet a false belief is not necessarily a dangerous one, and it is probably better that the public should trust scientists than that they should maintain their belief in the wisdom of gods or politicians. At least the scientist, if not the science teacher, is pursuing an objective truth, even if he does not always recognize the value of other approaches to the same end. The kind of indoctrination which the public fears is that which seeks to implant a particular religious or political belief, particularly one not shared by the ordinary citizen. To protect their children against this danger, they have insisted that governments should officially forbid their teachers to express any controversial views within the hearing of their students.

Even this hope is, however, illusory. Not only is it impossible to avoid mention of politics and religion when dealing with such officially-approved topics as the reformation, the rise of the Australian Labor Party, or the phenomena of Nazism and Communism, but the very suggestion that there is a finally acceptable truth in such areas as history, economics, geography or politics is both misleading and dangerous. The teacher who tries to present both sides of a controversy with equal weight is in fact suggesting that the debate does not matter, and is inculcating that most dangerous of all perversions of democracy, the belief that 'it's a free country, everyone's entitled to his own opinion'. Such allegedly objective teaching of human affairs is not only profoundly dull, but is undermining the very substance of democracy by encouraging apathy and subservience to authority. It cannot even be said to maintain the status quo, for by its active discouragement of thought it hardens the arteries of public opinion and so reduces the capacity of society to adjust to the changes constantly being imposed upon it. Moreover, the teacher who attempts to present impartially a matter in which he is passionately committed is being intellectually dishonest in concealing part of his own analysis of the facts, and professionally irresponsible in not trusting the judgement of his own students. If they are not ready to debate a topic in full, then they are not ready to meet that subject at all.

Teaching which tries to avoid present controversy is far more likely to implant myth than fact. We are all familiar with these pleasant little myths from our own schooldays. Foreigners are quaint people who wear pretty costumes. The British Empire was the final product of man's wisdom and benevolence. The family is the model of society. Politicians are elected to express the people's will. Such ideas might have little importance if they did not continually force their way into public debate. So in the recent referendum campaign we have seen pious references to the times of the constitutional fathers, who were filled with a disinterested zeal for the people's good and untainted by the party system which has possessed the soul of their modern counterparts. Obviously, the authors of such opinions have never read of the bitter faction fighting and unseemly private accommodations which were the substance of colonial politics. Such reality has vanished under the myth of 'Australia's progress towards democracy', so assiduously propagated by generations of objective schoolteachers.

Not all the attitudes unconsciously propagated by the schools are as unfortunate as these. The teaching of nature studies in primary schools is probably partly responsible for the slightly more mature concern of the Australian public for the preservation of its native fauna and flora, although it has done nothing to lessen the silliness of the sentimental animal lovers who are able to get the newspapers more upset about the killing of brumbies for pet-food than about the destruction of whole species of Australian wild life. Similarly, the change in our national attitude to Asians and towards the White Australian Policy has possibly been influenced by a general secondary education which has included an enlightened study of our relationships with our neighbours. This is not to say that this teaching has been deliberately designed to these ends, although teachers have probably felt that such attitudes are a necessary consequence of a full understanding of the facts they present. But a teacher must accept the fact that he is moulding his students' opinions by his very choice of topics which he considers important enough to engage their attention.

What, then, are we to make of the claim that a parent has a right to have his children educated without having unacceptable opinions trust on them? In the first place, it can be argued that a parent has no such right. If he is sufficiently talented and educated to manage the education of his own family it can be conceded that he should be able to do so without state interference, but unless he has these talents there is no reason to concede him sole responsibility for the upbringing of his children. It is another of our pious myths that this was once the case, and that the state has only recently stepped in because of the increased complexity of the task and the collapse of the family. Every society has had a means of educating its new generations, and only under certain conditions has it made the family the primary institution for carrying out this task. These conditions apply in societies where the family is the primary unit, but we should not forget that most of these societies have been based on the peasantry and have had a quite different kind of family to that of a modern industrial society. At the very least, the normal family unit has included three generations, and has often been extended to include collateral relatives. These family units did not so much make individual decisions about the upbringing of the children as pass on a consistent and very conservative community code. They offer little instruction which can help us to meet the educational needs of contemporary society.

Even if it is conceded that a parent has the prior right to choose the general code of belief within which he wishes his children to be educated, this does not mean that he should exercise a detailed censorship of the beliefs held and acted upon by his children's teachers. As we have seen, the home is usually a much stronger influence than the school, and the influence of any single teacher is both limited and transient. It would certainly be desirable to offer parents a free choice of several different kinds of education, resting on different philosophies, but within anyone of these, or within the single one which the Australian states have seen fit to offer at present, it is desirable that a variety of opinions should be expressed. 'In the multitude of counsellors there is wisdom,' and this wisdom is as necessary for the child as for the state which has inscribed it on the floor of its legislature.

The most dangerous method of combating the alleged infection of subversive ideas is the authoritarian system of prescribing text-books and courses of study while proscribing any individual expression of opinion on the part of the teacher. Such a scheme may parade openly as a way of ensuring sound teaching uncorrupted by heresy, or it may masquerade under the guise of providing a rational and economic uniformity for our schools. In either guise, it destroys the essential freedom of the teacher, and so removes any possibility that the students should meet original or creative minds, and thus prevents any chance that they might receive a real education as opposed to a narrow vocational and behavioural training.

The final right of choice of topics and ideas should then belong neither to parent nor to state, but to the individual teachers, who individually lack sufficient authority and influence to do lasting harm, and can at best open new horizons to their students, not determine their final decisions. Yet to do this job effectively, the teachers need more time, more training and more freedom than they are at present granted anywhere in Australia. This will be the subject of a separate chapter.

But quite apart from the influence exercised by individual teachers, the school itself plays an important role in moulding its students' values both by its organization and by the subjects it teaches. It is impossible to teach science without inculcating some regard for factual evidence, although this regard may not be transferred to other areas. Mechanical drawing instils a concern for neatness, art for form and colour, and so on. These values will be passed on regardless of the personality or opinions of the teacher, but merely in proportion to the effectiveness of his subject teaching. Even facts are subversive of established prejudices, and understanding yet more so. But the relative time given to different activities itself depends on a value judgement, and helps to perpetuate the same judgement on which it is based. The students of a Russian ballet school who spend half of each day on eurhythmics and physical exercises can be expected to grow up with an entirely different code of values from Australian students who do seven periods a week of mathematics and one of music, one of physical education, two of art, four of cookery or woodwork and none of dancing. The fact that, in some schools, girls do cookery and art while boys do woodwork and mechanical drawing is itself an important factor in reinforcing a prevalent tendency in our national culture. Yet the limitations of school influence can be indicated by the fact that, although state schools give only from two to four periods of class time a week to sport, and the 'Public Schools' none, sport is still the most prestigious of Australian occupations both in and out of school.

Despite its scant official recognition, the typical Australian code of values has so perverted the ostensible objectives of a vast number of Australian schools that their public reputation depends on their sporting prowess and their internal organization is bent to meet the demands of this twentieth-century Procrustes. Only the sacred examination rites are less vulnerable to criticism or reason. The hoary old myths of healthy minds in healthy bodies and team spirit destroying individual pride have been handed down from Thomas Arnold of Rugby to produce a strange antipodean efflorescence in whose shade mere scholarship wanes unobserved. The gods of the school walk mighty in athletic renown, while the more studious are driven weekly to the fields to make obeisance to the holy shrine. Nor is the teacher unaffected by this frenzied cult, for when inter-school forays or special practices have decimated his class he is still required to stay with the remnant and offer them soothing substitutes until the heroes have returned and work can again have a brief spell. During the weekly festival he will have to broil in the sun by the cricket pitch, or disport himself in the unseemly garb and muddy habitat of the football umpire, while the juvenile veterans in his care mock his ignorance. If he wishes for a job in a 'Public' school he will have to prove his sporting competence, but even in the state schools he will have to do his share of coaching teams, running a house, and keeping the records. If he wishes to obtain money from the parents to supply books for the library or a projector for the geography room he is wise to first show due enthusiasm for the completion of the school oval or the provision of a new tennis-court.

Few people realize just how much time is occupied by sporting activities. In a country high school which has to travel to play its matches this is unlikely to be less than ten days, or two teaching weeks in a school year which is seldom as much as thirty weeks in effective length. Two days each for house and inter-school swimming and athletic sports, a home and an away match each for the major summer and winter sports, and a tennis carnival or a couple of special practices soon take up the ten days. If the school is in a larger association, the time lost will be greater, at least for the teams and for all the students either in their classes or in classes taught by the teachers who accompany the teams on their visits. Finally, there is the hidden loss of time and energy given by both teachers and students to organizing all these events.

If the reason for the emphasis given to these activities lies in the community's values, their origin belongs in historical conditions which no longer exist. At one time, there were few if any facilities for public recreation, and the schools provided for the need. But today there is if anything an excess of public provision, and the school's efforts are both redundant and, by comparison, mediocre. The 'Public Schools' may give too great an emphasis to sport in their code of values, but they do organize their sport well and they organize it largely outside school hours, so that academic education need not suffer. They provide for only a minority of their students, unless the school rules oblige everyone to participate, but for this minority school sport is the sport. If they are training for the school team, they receive adequate coaching and seldom feel the need to play also for a public team. But the state schools, bound by their departmental and unionized outlook, have attempted to incorporate sport in the normal school timetable. This has overbalanced the timetable without providing satisfactory sporting facilities for those inclined in that direction. So these individuals seek a place in the public teams, and if they succeed they find themselves with competing loyalties and excessive demands on their time. The pressure placed on the schoolboy football hero in a country town is tremendous, and usually it is his school work which has to suffer.

One solution would seem to be for the state schools to follow the pattern of the 'Public Schools' and organize their sport outside school hours, on a voluntary basis. In this way they could cater adequately for those who wanted to play their sport with the school, while the others could turn elsewhere and avoid the conflicting claims they are liable to encounter at present.

Yet it can be argued that there is no need today for the schools to concern themselves with sport at all. As the community is meeting this need quite adequately through other channels, the schools would be better advised to devote their resources to their peculiar functions. But the public agencies are concerned only with success, with winning at any cost, and are thus little interested in anyone other than the champion. The golf clubs are an exception to this rule, but they rarely have facilities for teaching juniors, and in the cities are open only to the affluent. The schools therefore still have a role in teaching their students the games and in providing a reasonable competition which can be tailored to the demands of the academic year.

Many enthusiasts would, of course, claim that the role of school sport is far more important than this, and that it should be regarded as a fundamental of health and a basic training in citizenship. The discipline of the team is said to teach the individual to subordinate his own desires to the good of the whole, and the need to keep physically fit is supposed to promote the education of the whole man in the Greek ideal, body and soul together. No evidence is produced to support these beliefs. The sportsman certainly needs to keep fit, but there is no reason to believe that he is any healthier for his intense sessions of training than the man who devotes a little time daily to private exercise, and even less reason to believe that his soul flourishes with his body. There is no evidence that the good sportsman is necessarily a good team man in other activities, or that the exponent of a team sport makes any better a citizen than the man who excels in such an individual skill as sprinting or skiing. Even the quality of fellowship among individual sportsmen seems no less than that among teamsters. Nor should this be a matter of surprise, for although the individual in a team must work closely with his fellows, he holds his place by his individual excellence, and will be dropped as soon as his skills are shown to be deficient. Probably only in rowing and sailing is the individual really subordinated to the team, and I know of no exponent of either who would assert his moral superiority over other sportsmen.

The quality of sportsmanship is the other value which is supposed to be derived from team games. This is no doubt quite admirable, with its emphasis on the gentlemanly code of the stiff upper lip, endurance in defeat and magnanimity in victory, but its relevance to the modern world may well be questioned. The win-at-all-costs morality of professional sport is possibly more honest and more valuable in the fiercely competitive contemporary scene than a code which reached its zenith in the days of British supremacy. Even more important would be the virtues of moral courage, humility and sympathy which are foreign to any sport. The trouble with sportsmanship is not that it is wrong, but that it is too limited, too closely identified with the outlook of a vanishing caste, and that consequently it promotes an inflexible self-righteousness and a moral myopia in fields outside its own special province.

Moral indoctrination in the schools is, however, by no means confined to the conventional academic and sporting arenas. There has been an increasing tendency in recent years to force upon the schools a whole series of subjects which have no other purpose than to promote particular forms of behaviour. These range from the on-the-spot lectures in road safety given by members of the police forces to complete courses of 'health education', and include such phenomena as examination courses in 'temperance physiology', driver-training courses, home-safety instruction, and various kinds of sex-education. Many of them result from the efforts of particular pressure groups, and all of them have in common a desire to alter behaviour rather than a concern for promoting understanding. To a certain extent, they reflect the anxiety of a society which sees its traditional values either collapsing, as in the case of sexual behaviour, or proving inadequate to new conditions, as in the case of road safety.

The most notorious of these courses is the Victorian secondary schools' health course, which is at present in a state of suspended animation following extensive opposition from teachers and their organizations. This course purports to be an extension of the primary schools' health course, which confines itself to such relatively uncontroversial matters as tooth-brushing and ear washing, although it is not altogether free from the influences of health cranks with their insistence on a 'natural' diet. It was probably of some value in an earlier generation when the principles of hygiene were less well-known and the necessary facilities less widespread, although more good might have been done by providing school meals and showers. It is not without significance that Victoria, the home of health courses, forbids its government health inspectors to enter state schools and has refused to bring these schools up to the standards laid down for private schools by the State Health Act. But although the content of the course is not very significant, its method promotes an uncritical acceptance of fashionable beliefs rather than any understanding of principles. It would probably be better if it were incorporated in the primary science courses where the emphasis could be placed where it properly belongs, on observation and study, rather than on precept and memorization with a view to practice.

These dangers are far more evident in the secondary extension of this course, where the emphasis shifts from physical to mental health, and from personal conduct to social behaviour. The course uses the methods of group discussion and self-criticism which have proved so successful in totalitarian countries, and applies that most subtle form of indoctrination—indoctrination through social pressure towards conformity rather than indoctrination by authoritarian pronouncement. The course is carefully designed to inculcate the principles of social behaviour in which its authors believed, but these principles were to be 'discovered' through discussion and analogy rather than investigated by empirical study and analytical enquiry. The thing which frightened the teachers was the proposal to engage in group therapy and to discuss publicly such issues as the proper choice of a mate and the correct conduct of parents towards their offspring, but in practice these might not have proved as dangerous as the simplistic approach to human affairs which, for example, equated the principles of family relations with those of law and justice. A further danger in such a course is that it is likely to attract those teachers who are least suited to teaching it, and who use it as a solution to their own personal problems. This danger has not been so obvious in the pilot studies, which have also attracted a number of the keener teachers who are eager to pioneer new approaches to education, but is likely to become more serious if the course ever becomes established as a normal part of the school curriculum and has to rely, as do other subjects, on the services of the untrained and incompetent. Of all possible courses in a school, this is one which should be entrusted only to fully trained experts, but at present there is not even such a course of training envisaged. The preparation offered so far has been only an indoctrination and orientation course which explains the methods of the course not one which trains teachers capable of exercising their own independent judgement.

But even if there were such a supply of properly equipped teachers, the question remains open whether the inclusion of such a subject in the curriculum is even desirable. Granted that the schools today have to cope with an enormous range of personality problems among their students, the solution would appear to lie rather in providing a proper system of student counselling than in attempting a form of mass therapy. The school in contemporary society cannot avoid taking over an increasing range of functions from older institutions, such as church and family, but to the extent that it allows these to deflect it from its primary function of intellectual training it is likely to perform all its tasks less efficiently. The new tasks are more likely to be efficiently performed by giving the school further facilities and adding ancillary experts to its teaching staff than by merely stretching existing methods and staff to cope with new responsibilities.

The nub of these problems is the extent to which we consider the school responsible for the values and social training of its students. As we have seen, it cannot escape some such responsibility, but this does not mean that it should incorporate these matters in its explicit aims. It would certainly be of value for everyone concerned with education, including parents, teachers and administrators, to reflect seriously on the values they are in fact promoting, but they should not measure their efficiency by the extent to which they succeed in implanting these values. The danger of the kind of detailed classification of affective and cognitive aims which is fashionable in educational circles is that we lose sight of the building for the sake of the bricks, and in pursuit of a multitude of detailed objectives we fragment our teaching until it has lost all value. The wisest course for both administrator and teacher is to establish his basic principles and refuse to allow incidentals to divert him from their pursuit.

For the administrator, the fundamental principle would seem to be to establish school communities within which teachers will have the widest possible freedom to develop their own subject teaching, and students will also have the freedom to develop socially as well as intellectually. But the freedom of the students will be illusory if they are merely confronted with a variety of competing claims, social and intellectual, from which they must make their own individual choices. It is the responsibility of the school to ensure that their intellectual powers are so developed that they are able to understand their world and make realistic choices on the basis of this understanding. If the development of the individual student is inhibited for social or personal reasons, the school should be able to provide assistance to him in overcoming these problems, but it should not seek to provide an environment which will prevent him ever encountering real problems, nor should it allow his social and moral training to interfere with his intellectual development. If this last is properly attended to, then he can be trusted to make his own decisions in other areas of his life.

Similarly, the individual teacher should not allow his personal values to interfere with his prime responsibility to the discipline of his subject. It is assumed that the inclusion of his subject in the curriculum is based on a reasoned judgement that an understanding in this field is a desirable part of his students' intellectual equipment. Undoubtedly his own decision to profess this particular discipline is based ultimately on a belief that it has certain valuable contributions to offer to human life, and he will assume that anyone who gains a proper understanding of its principles will share his attitude towards its practices. If students learn to read with full understanding, the English teacher, for example, hopes that they will continue to read with pleasure after they have left school. Moreover, he would be failing in his job if he made reading appear to be laborious and boring. But he is not merely a salesman of reading, nor even of English as a whole, and he has neither the right to manipulate his students into accepting his values nor the need to evaluate his success by the extent to which they do so, although he may need to re-examine both his teaching and his own mastery of his subject if he finds that none of his students grow up to share his enthusiasms. All that any teacher can do is to share his understanding of his subject with his students and by so doing to develop their understanding so that they can be trusted to make their own value judgements and choices of behaviour. It is a measure of our failure in our task that we are so often disappointed in the final response of our students, but it is no answer to this sense of frustration to deliberately meddle with their personal freedom, even for the best of motives.

8 Teachers, Teaching and Teacher Training

Of all the respectable professions, teaching has the greatest claim to antiquity and honour. In the earliest human societies it was necessary to pass on customs and techniques, and neither medicine nor law could emerge as specialized pursuits until the traditions had been codified and their transmission properly organized. Medicine has only comparatively recently started to emerge from the mists of magic and superstition, while law, fundamental as it may be to complex social organizations, has inevitably remained the province of a comparatively small number of specialists, who are called upon on great occasions and in emergency rather than used in the normal business of life.

Yet these very factors have contributed to the low esteem in which teaching is held as a profession. Practically every Australian has been to school, not occasionally, but day after day for a number of years, and it is unlikely that any professional aura or mystique could survive this constant exposure to critical attention. Moreover, this constant attendance occurs in the years of our tutelage, years which we are anxious to outgrow and to which we could not consider returning, and this atmosphere of puerility tends to cling to the teachers we knew then, whatever feelings of affection or fear may be mixed with it. The normal person's next acquaintance with the teaching profession comes when he is himself a parent, and since he quite rightly considers that he knows more about his own offspring than does any teacher he is unlikely to form any high regard for the professional skill involved in teaching, although he may admire the patience which must be exercised by anyone in charge of a whole classroom of unwilling scholars. Basically, however, his attitude is likely to be one of amused tolerance for anyone prepared to devote his career to a task so thankless and apparently irrelevant to the real affairs of life, though unfortunately increasingly necessary to endure for those who hope to reap the material rewards of a society which offers high prizes for examination success.

Moreover, there is no clear definition of the teaching profession. On the one hand, we have the scholar who is a master of his own discipline and who passes on some of his learning and skill more or less efficiently to his students. Although he is engaged in teaching, he would probably consider himself a doctor or lawyer or scientist rather than a teacher. On the other hand, we have the skilled instructor, military or civilian, who passes on the elements of a craft to his pupils. Neither of these is a trained teacher, yet they are possibly the best teachers precisely because their efficiency depends not on some technique of communication but on their mastery within their own field. Where they go astray is where they venture outside this field. The scholar is the best possible teacher for those who are able to keep up with him, but he may be useless in lecturing to hundreds of novitiates whose only interest in the subject is to gain a professional qualification. The army instructor who moves into a school will find that his techniques are less efficient because the aims of instruction are vaguer and the body of knowledge indefinite.

But as well as these people who have become engaged in teaching as an incidental consequence of their primary interests, we have a vast multitude who, lacking any apparent professional qualification, profess teaching as their chief occupation. Quite apart from the fringe dwellers in dancing academies and driving schools and similar institutions on the periphery of formal education, there are the great numbers who have been recruited from all kinds of occupations and backgrounds to fill the gaps in the classrooms. These range from people with complete or nearly complete professional training in another field to those with less academic attainment than the students they teach. They include doctors (amazingly), lawyers, architects, chiropodists, practising artists, defrocked psychotics, alcoholics, drifters and misfits of every sort except bankrupts, who are legally denied state employment, however suitable they may be in other respects.

Finally, there are those who have been formally trained and certificated as professional teachers. This formal training may have taken any form from an apprenticeship period as a student teacher, with a few formal subjects thrown in, to a double degree at a university, yet all these people, along with the others mentioned, are lumped together as members of the teaching profession. It is little wonder or worry that such an incoherent and heterogeneous mass should have earned little public esteem. Nor is it surprising that teachers have not advanced to that state of professional responsibility where they control their own affairs. This is a matter we will return to in the next chapter.

The low esteem in which teaching is currently held is, however, no new phenomenon and cannot be attributed entirely to the quality of the contemporary teaching force. As few societies have paid much regard to formal education, the professional teacher has often been outside the main social streams, isolated in a monastery where he can instruct the clerks of the future without disturbing the present by any dangerous ideas. The wisdom of this technique is shown by the example of the wandering scholars of medieval times, who escaped from their monasteries and gave the authorities a great rival religion of love. But even cultures which have valued education for its own sake have not necessarily extended their valuation to the teachers. Among European Jews the teacher has always been honoured, but he has not always been highly rewarded. The Romans also held education in high regard, but they left it mainly in the hands of Greek slaves. In more recent times, education among the upper classes has often been the province of menial governesses and tutors, and among the middle and lower of dames and ushers frequently little more literate than their pupils.

It is unfortunately this last model which has been most influential in determining the pattern of status and training enjoyed by today's teachers. When elementary education started to become fashionable during the nineteenth century, the only qualifications demanded of a schoolmaster were elementary literacy and some veneer of gentility. Alternatively, a farmer's daughter who had mastered her letters and tables might be employed to instruct the neighbouring urchins at times when they could be spared from their farm duties. Later, when it was enacted that primary education should be free, compulsory and universal, it became necessary to demand some formal qualifications, and the student teacher system was adopted. This enabled promising juniors to enter the profession by attaching themselves to an experienced schoolmaster who broke them into the routine of roll-keeping and book-marking and possibly assisted them with some coaching for the examinations which qualified them to set up business as master teachers in their own right.

Later still, it was decided to set up teachers' colleges which could give full-time instruction in matters academic and pedagogic. At first, these institutions found that they had to give their students a general education before they could proceed to their specialist training, but with the establishment of continuation schools, later to become high schools, to bridge the gap beyond elementary education, they were able to concentrate on the formal aspects of teacher training. Yet even this training, which was open only to those who had served their time as student teachers, was not regarded as an indispensable pre-requisite to teaching, and during the depression years their activities were so severely curtailed that many teachers again appeared in the classrooms with no more than apprenticeship training. The last vestiges of this system did not finally disappear until well after the second world war.

During these years state secondary education had been gradually expanding, but most of its teachers still came originally from the primary service after educating themselves with or without help to degree standard. At the same time, post-graduate courses in education were established in the Australian universities, and once education departments commenced granting studentships for full-time university training it seemed that at least secondary teaching was well on the way to obtaining a full system of professional training. However, the demand for secondary teachers soon outstripped the supply of graduates, and as well as employing unqualified temporary and emergency teachers the various state authorities introduced and extended alternative forms of training in an endeavour to expand their teaching force to cope with the sudden growth in school numbers. Although these courses were normally introduced as temporary measures to meet an emergency, the restrictions placed on university numbers and the increased demands for graduates in all spheres have resulted in these courses becoming a permanent feature of the educational scene. Meanwhile, there has been little attempt to improve the training of non-academic teachers of such subjects as art, most of whom do shorter courses which have neither the status of university education nor the practical value of technical school training, and which therefore condemn their students to a perpetual ghetto of inferiority.

The effect of this lack of any minimum standard of education as a pre-requisite for entrance to the teaching profession has not only been to lower the status of its members in the eyes of the public but also to destroy their confidence in themselves and in the ability of their profession to conduct its own affairs. The most obvious quality of teachers' college students is their docility before authority, and even those who have maintained some independence of thought or who have during their training breathed the freer air of a university quickly find themselves sunk in the mass of mediocrity which characterizes their colleagues. Such fresh ideas as they may bring with them to their first school are soon lost in the atmosphere engendered by seniors who advise them to forget all they have learnt in college and get down to the fundamentals of teaching. The most highly regarded fundamentals are discipline and examination coaching, and the young idealist soon finds that high principles are confined to speech nights and that the accepted attitude for the classroom is one of departmental subservience.

Yet the teaching services do still attract a great number of high-minded idealists who do manage to preserve their dedication in the fact of all the obstacles thrown up by the system in which they teach. The most amazing thing which confronts a visitor to the classrooms is the amount of really fine teaching which is being done despite all handicaps. At the same time, he will be appalled by the amount of completely useless class teaching—teaching which is factually wrong, teaching which is irrelevant, above all teaching which is utterly boring. If Australian man is born free, nothing puts him into chains more effectively than the classrooms of the nation. Young animals are essentially active and high-spirited, yet every school day a large proportion of the two and a half million students in our schools are condemned to some hours of boredom. Fortunately, the possibilities of boredom are probably least in the earliest school years where it might matter most, but they are at their highest in the other critical period, the early years of secondary school. It is here that the pressure of numbers is greatest and the shortage of teachers most acute, and in many, if not most, cases, the damage done in these years is never repaired.

The statistics which governments continually produce to show that the number of qualified teachers has increased or that the average size of classes has diminished conceal the essential fact that a child is only in one class at a time. If twenty per cent of teachers are unqualified, then he is likely to spend the equivalent of more than one year of his secondary schooling being taught by these unqualified teachers. This year may be long enough for him to lose touch with one subject, or with schooling altogether. We have noted the survey by Melbourne University School of Education which found that approximately half of the students who possessed the ability to profit from university studies failed to stay at school long enough to matriculate. This proportion may since have improved, and we cannot assume that poor teaching was the cause of any particular proportion of this loss. However, we can be sure that poor teaching would be partly responsible in many cases, and we can be equally certain that poor teaching would prevent a great number of students developing their potential sufficiently to even appear in these figures.

There is no mystic proportion of students capable of undertaking tertiary studies, nor is there any completely reliable means of assessing those students who will profit by our present tertiary courses. The community provides a certain number of places in universities and senior colleges, and these institutions then devise various arbitrary tests to select students to fill these places. More efficient testing would select different students, and more efficient teaching would enable different students again to develop their interests and abilities to meet these selection standards. At the very least, the weaknesses of our schools at present are reducing the size of the pool from which we eventually draw our highly trained experts. At the worst, these weaknesses are depriving the community of a great number of talents of which no one has ever become aware.

The point which must be remembered is that a great number of school subjects are cumulative, and that if a child misses one stage of the process he may never have the opportunity to recover. If he fails to understand simple mathematics in first form he will have little chance of repairing the deficiency in third form, by which time he and his teachers will be convinced that he has no ability in mathematics. The same problem will confront the child who fails to learn to read in the primary grade where it is taught, or who misses one of the crucial steps in his earlier years of a foreign language. Even a comparatively small misunderstanding in the elementary stages of a subject may lead to a complete failure to cope with more complex developments, yet by this stage it may be quite impossible for the most experienced teacher to diagnose the fault without special training and facilities.

Although this problem would appear to be most serious in cumulative subjects where each successive stage demands a mastery, not merely a competence, in the skills learnt in the previous step, difficulties similar in kind if not in degree appear in any school subject which is not adequately taught in every year. Historical misconceptions planted in early years recur to plague the examiners years later; a wrong emphasis in English teaching permanently stifles fluency, clarity and imagination; an emphasis on memorization in any subject cripples the students' confidence in their own judgement and hence their capacity to undertake the critical analysis which is the basis of any higher learning.

These handicaps are not so formidable to those students whose home environment enables them to develop their ability despite the school. These students often have the desire for success which drives them to score high marks for even the least competent teacher, so that they reach the higher forms and better teachers with confidence in their own abilities and with a school record which guarantees them continued esteem and attention. Their ambition makes them pliable material in the teachers' hands, and their later years make good the loss of the earlier. On the other hand, the more independent student who has made trouble through his earlier years responds to work which stretches his abilities and to teachers whose ability is not markedly inferior to his own, and he too appears to overcome the difficulties of the lower forms. Heartened by this evidence of success, we persuade ourselves that our system is not so bad after all, and that success eventually attends all who deserve it. We may even preen ourselves on the excellent remedial work which has salvaged so many of the scamps of junior forms to become ornaments of scholastic success in their final examinations.

But at least two groups of students suffer beyond all hope of rescue under these conditions. In the first place, there are those earnest plodders who conscientiously do everything the teacher tells them and consequently achieve high marks in the lower forms. However, when they come to the upper school they find that they cannot understand the work and sooner or later they bow graciously out. We nod our heads sagely and remark that they have reached their limits, forgetting that in many cases these limits have been imposed by the type of teaching they have had imposed on them in junior forms. We are not so happy or so worried about the other category of students whose needs the school fails to meet. These are those who give both academic and behavioural problems. Their school careers are short and unruly, and they depart with few regrets on either side. We are as sure as they are that school had nothing to offer them, and their departure enables us to concentrate on the students whom we can assist. Under present circumstances we are possibly correct, although too often the difficulty of the problem is used as an excuse for doing nothing to meet it. But it should be realized that however little success we may have in practice in meeting the problem posed by those we regard as ineducable, the problem itself is not inherently necessary, but is to a great extent a product of social circumstances, among which school methods, unduly large class sizes, and incompetent teachers loom large. Until these factors are eliminated, there is no possibility of determining how much of the problem is avoidable. In the meantime, the community suffers through the loss of many of the talents possessed by these individuals, and by the general loss of efficiency in an education system which has to divert a proportion of its meagre resources to preventing these students from causing trouble without giving them any compensating advantages for their loss of the only enjoyable activity open to them.

The sad truth about our schools, or at least our secondary schools, is that most of the teachers in them are devoting their attention to those who need them least. This is partly because the better teachers cannot be spared from the examination forms, where they are engaged in the constant task of repairing the ravages inflicted by their forerunners in the lower form. It is a vicious circle, for to remove these teachers to lower forms would prepare the next cycle of students more effectively for their vital examinations only at the cost of the success of the present cycle. These students have reached the higher forms in many cases without any proper understanding of the subject, and although the classes are too big to give each the individual attention he needs if all the harm is to be undone, and although there is no time to take the whole class back to fundamentals, a great deal can be achieved for those students with the right aptitudes. Moreover, by efficient drilling in the techniques of answering examination questions a great proportion of amenable students can be coached to conceal their ignorance well enough to pass the examinations, and in the process some will learn a little of lasting value. But at the best he will only help those who, because of their environment, have had sufficient aptitude to survive the lower forms without any permanent damage. Either he will not see the others at all, because they leave before they reach him, or they will come to him already persuaded of their inability, and so beyond his reach. Moreover, among those whom he has to drill remorselessly to reach examination standard will be a considerable number who would be able to make significant advances in understanding if he could afford to adopt different methods, but who cannot advance fast enough to acquire real facility in time for the annual examination fiesta. For these there is no alternative but the pseudo-education which will give them their certificate at the price of their learning.

The problem of examinations is that there is a constant battle between those who set them and those who seek to pass them, and that this in turn leads to a very real conflict of professional duty for the teacher. Most examinations propose a series of tasks which any person completely educated to the appropriate standard could carry out with ease. For example, the precis test required in many senior English expression examinations is probably one of the best single indicators of a person's general accomplishment in the English language. To pass on precis, he has to be able to read with understanding and express his understanding clearly, concisely and correctly. If I were employing someone to act as private secretary, or in any other position which required literacy and intelligence, I can think of no simpler test to eliminate those without the requisite talents.

Unfortunately, the precis test is not administered in similar circumstances to these, nor is it used to eliminate all those who cannot do a perfect precis. Instead, the perfect precis, itself an indefinable product, is used as the ultimate standard for a test on which about two-fifths will be failed. The fail mark is determined by constructing a scale running from one hundred per cent for perfection to forty per cent for just better than dreadful, and spacing out all the samples provided along this line. Those which fall below fifty are then said to have failed.

The imprecision of this test stems from the same qualities which make it suitable as an indication of accomplished all-round ability. The person who is able to precis a range of material at a consistently high standard obviously possesses a number of separate abilities. But a person who fails to make a coherent precis of a particular passage may be lacking in only one of these talents, or may even possess a further talent, such as literary appreciation, which inhibits him from displaying his ability for litteracide. For example, the specimen passage may contain a single key passage which the candidate fails to comprehend, with the result that his precis becomes meaningless. Now it may be that the key passage is of such a kind that anyone who failed to understand it should be failed in his examination, but it may also be that candidates fail to appreciate its significance because of carelessness, lack of time, or just plain nerves. The test gives us no opportunity to discriminate between these cases. Nor does it really enable us to grade candidates. We can say that one person has written a successful precis, but once we have said that another has failed to attain complete success there is no valid way of assessing the degree to which he has approached success. A grossly inadequate precis may be such because the candidate, while appreciating the meaning, lacks fluency in his own composition, while one which appears to be close to success may be produced by a candidate who in fact has learnt nothing from the original passage but has been able to string together phrases from it with sufficient facility to simulate an understanding.

I have spent this time on precis because I feel that what has happened in this case is symptomatic of what goes wrong with examinations. There are other faults in the precis test, faults associated with the reliability of the marking, and there are also tests in common use with both greater and lesser degrees of validity and reliability. However, all these tests suffer from the same fault as the precis once they are embodied in an examination which is used to determine a student's success in completing a given body of work. The examiner must of necessity determine those elements of a course which are assessable by his particular techniques, and his tests are constructed on this basis. But the external signs which the examination measures are only the symptoms which will be displayed by the person who has in fact learnt his subject thoroughly. On the other hand, they can be counterfeited by the person who really knows nothing of the subject. The teacher is therefore confronted by the dilemma of whether his responsibility is to his students, to instruct them how to forge their passport to higher positions, or to his subject, to encourage his students to learn it thoroughly and hope that sufficient of them will do so to maintain his average number of passes in the final examinations. The private coaching colleges exist because most teachers choose a path somewhere between these two extremes.

This mistaking of the appearance for the substance is what distinguishes the quack from the expert. There are plenty of medical quacks around Australia who will cure the symptoms of disease and develop the appearance of health, but the reputable doctor insists on discovering the true cause of a complaint and treating this. Not only does he attend to his patients individually, rather than thirty at a time in mass consulting rooms, but he treats them at his own pace, and not in accord with the edict of an external authority which allots to them a period of his time, examines their health at the end of it, and determines his professional competence of the results of this examination. Yet a teacher is in an even more invidious position, for the final examination not only terminates his course of treatment but also provides a certificate by which his client's intellectual health may be determined for the rest of that client's life.

The tremendous value which the Australian community places on examinations is both a measure of its distrust of teachers' professional competence and a reason for the continued low standards of this competence. It is easier to coach for examinations than to teach, and many teachers, being human, taken the easy way out, just as many doctors prefer prescribing proprietary drugs to curing patients. The crucial importance of examinations in the career of the individual students distracts the attention of even the teacher who is most aware of his responsibility to his subject, and mere subject teaching and learning for its own sake become forgotten. Moreover, the people in the positions of crucial responsibility in our schools, the heads of subject departments who determine the academic content and quality of the various school courses, are the people who are most involved with the examination system and who are therefore the least likely to understand the difficulties and needs of the majority of their students. For although the nature of the secondary school population has changed entirely in both its origins and its daily environment, the nature of examinations has remained the same. Consequently, the senior teachers are most likely to perceive the problem as merely one of declining standards which can be remedied only by providing more sound teachers and by manning the barricades against those pernicious innovators who are trying to introduce new methods for new times, but who are in the process destroying all the old-fashioned fundamentals of drill and discipline.

But if the influence of conservatism still reigns firmly among the older classroom teachers, it is not they alone who must accept the blame. The general tone of a school and its staff is determined by the headmaster. If he is alive to new ideas, or even concerned with real problems, then his staff is likely to be lively and interested in experiment. If he is a knowledgeable and critical educationist, then the experiments are likely to bear sound fruit. But if he has a mind and attitude which has long since been hardened by departmental routine, his staff are likely to divide into the crusty old reactionaries who are quite content to teach as they have always done and relieve their feelings by grumbling at the decadence of today's youth, and the angry and frustrated young men who serve out the time of their bond and get out of the profession as soon as possible afterwards.

Unfortunately most state headmasters fall into the second category. As the chief qualification demanded of them is seniority, only those who have had the endurance to stay a depressing course become eligible for appointment. Even if they had ideas in their earlier days, these are likely to have been long since crushed out of them, not by active resistance from the authorities, but merely from departmental inertia. If they retain ideas, they lack the energy to implement them, for they do not reach the top of the ladder until they are within a few years of retiring age.

This picture has changed very slightly in recent years, for the vast expansion of secondary education has enabled numbers of younger men to become headmasters while still in the prime of life. However, these happy few still have to combat the established traditions and the well-entrenched disapproval of their senior colleagues if they do anything revolutionary. Even to take sides with the staff rather than the administration during a teaching strike is virtually impossible, while it is unknown for government headmasters' organizations in any state to have sponsored any major reforms or even to have taken measures to acquaint parents and politicians with the relevant facts about their schools.

One of the effects of the seniority system is to prevent the appointment of men with specific abilities to the particular posts where these abilities can be used, or even to allow them to stay in positions where they are already performing valuable services. Consequently they are more likely to identify themselves with the department they belong to rather than with the school they administer. Appointments to more prestigious schools are sought not because they provide any opportunity to carry out any particular tasks but rather because they are badges of honour behind which the incumbents can retire to premature senescence. Because these positions are so highly prized, it is normal for them to be held for brief terms by a succession of headmasters who have reached the pinnacle of their career with only three or four years left. Yet, as these schools often share the twin advantages of established staffs and specially selected students, their lack of permanent leadership is not as serious a handicap as it is in some of the smaller country schools or the depressed inner metropolitan establishments where permanency of both staff and headmaster would be an indispensable prerequisite to progress.

These schools are far too often treated merely as stepping stones for their incumbents' careers. The small country high school usually has so many problems of staffing and money that the headmaster is left with no time to serve his proper function, and it is possibly fortunate that such schools usually fall to younger men who still have the energy and ambition to accomplish something despite the handicaps. But by the time they have settled down in their position, either they are due for promotion or the school has advanced sufficiently to be given a higher classification, and in either case the reigning head is forced to move on. He may have to go back for a term as a classroom teacher, or he may be able to go on to an immediate appointment as head of a larger school. Meanwhile, the school can have as many as three heads in three years. The first one arrives while it is still in a low classification, but after he has had twelve months there he finds that he is eligible for promotion. Not to take promotion when eligible is not merely to miss out on a job and extra pay for one year, but to lose a year's seniority for the remainder of a teaching career, and so the opportunity cannot be lightly passed over by anyone who still has further ambition. But the new man stays no longer, for at the end of his first year the school can be raised in classification, and even if he is due for promotion he must also be the most senior applicant for this particular school if he is to remain there. So a third man comes, and if the school is not by now classified in the highest class the process can begin again.

The insecurity of tenure and the inability of the authorities to appoint particular headmasters to the posts for which they are most suited brings about the situation where the major emphasis is placed on the lowest common denominator of success—administrative efficiency. The educational problems of each school are unique, but the administrative difficulties are practically identical, and by concentrating on these both the headmaster and the inspectors obtain a ready measure of comparative virtue and are able to conceal from themselves the critical issues which they are paid to face. It would be at least a step towards meeting these issues if headmasters could be selected according to the needs of particular schools. Thus a strong disciplinarian could be chosen for a school which had got out of hand, while another school in the same area might be given a leader with some imaginative sympathy with the students and a readiness to experiment with new ways of meeting their needs. A school which is serving a useful function in a particular environment by offering a purely academic course might be best served by a head with some pretensions to scholarship, and the good fund-raiser could do his most valuable work in a depressed area. The present system, however, expects every headmaster to be able to produce any of these qualities on demand, and as few of them are paragons of all human virtues they opt for the easier solution of retreating from their difficulties behind a barrier of administrivia.

The consequence of this system has been to breed a generation of state headmasters who would be unlikely to understand responsibility even if it were thrust upon them. The few independent characters who have reached the position of head have in fact been able to free themselves from a great deal of departmental interference and regulation, just by the force of their own personalities, even though they have not been able to obtain that indispensable prerequisite of autonomy, a voice over the appointment of at least their senior staff. Yet even this concession would be more likely to follow if there was more evidence that heads were prepared to use the power they have at present. Instead, they exercise their authority in such trivial and irritating matters as insisting that all mail coming into the school should be addressed through them and not directly to the teachers concerned, or laying down directions on how teachers should use their time in spare periods, while at the same time showing their pusillanimity by referring to the departmental authorities decisions on such vital matters as whether competitors might be dismissed early on the day of the swimming sports.

The insecurity of so many headmasters and principals in state schools is indicated not only by their subservience to constituted authority and fear of controversy and parental opinion, but also by their resentment of any interference by bodies outside the official hierarchy and their inability to consult with their own staff on matters of school policy. Although the alternative to the autocratic head is not necessarily the democrat who gives away the authority he is paid to exercise, the headmaster who wishes to run an effective school must realize that his efforts depend on the co-operation of his team of professional teachers. Unless he is prepared to seek and give due weight to their opinions, and to treat them as colleagues rather than as subordinates, he may receive but he will not deserve their loyal support. The difference between the headmaster and his staff should not be that he commands and they obey, but that each respects the other's sphere of responsibility. It is the final responsibility of the head to make the decisions of school policy, but they should be made openly and after full consideration of all relevant factors, including the opinions of the teachers and of such outside bodies as subject associations which may have relevant specialist knowledge to offer. Furthermore, the head should not take it upon himself to make decisions which intrude on the professional competence of his teachers, providing that they can show that they are carrying out their work within the broad framework of the school policy. Finally, the individual teacher should have the right to seek transfer if he cannot agree with the way in which the school is run.

These suggestions are based on the assumption that the individual headmaster should be the supreme educational authority. The role of the central department should be limited to providing him with the facilities of staff, buildings and equipment needed to do his job. This would mean that each school would need to be regarded as an autonomous unit, with a head selected by a specially constituted appointment committee with knowledge of the particular needs of the school. This committee could have representatives from the state department, teachers' bodies, and local parents and school committeemen. Once it had appointed the head, it could then work out with him the general lines of school policy. Further staff appointments would be made by this same committee in consultation with the head. The grounds for appointing the head or the members of staff would include experience, although not seniority, and at the end of the term of appointment the person concerned could seek a renewal, look for a similar position elsewhere, or try for a different position elsewhere. Normally, appointments would be for a minimum of five years, although there could be provision for releasing staff going to more responsible positions before their term was completed. Rather than considering the position of headmaster as the culminating glory of a teaching career, it could be regarded as merely one of the possibilities open to an experienced teacher, and even after serving a term as headmaster there is no reason why a man past the prime of his life should not move on to a position as subject head, inspector, or teachers' adviser, where he could use the benefits of his experience without suffering the constant strain of responsibility.

The difficulties of such a scheme are obvious. The idea of a man attaining the peak of his career in the prime of his life is contrary to all the principles of seniority, and would be bitterly opposed by teachers' organizations. Moreover, under our present way of thinking it is hard to imagine someone willingly abdicating the seat of responsibility to step down to a lesser post. This objection is, however, only an indication of the poverty of the esteem we extend to ordinary teachers today. If the senior teacher is accepted as a professional equal, entitled to be kept informed and to be heard on matters of school policy, then there is no reason why his position should be less highly regarded than that of the headmaster.

Finally, there is the objection that such a system would contradict the principle of equality which is supposed to be enshrined in state systems. The wealthiest and most popular areas would get the best heads, the best teachers, and the best schools, and the rest would be left lamenting.

In the first place, this objection supposes that the best areas do not get the best schools now. It is true that education departments direct teachers to areas where they might not go voluntarily, but this applies on the whole only to the more junior appointments. The senior teachers ensconce themselves comfortably away from problems in the affluent areas. That these schools are not in fact better than they are is due only to the malfunctioning of seniority as a means of choosing the best teachers, but those left in the less endowed areas are engaged in such a busy merry-go-round of appointments to work their way into the better schools that they are not able to give the schools in which they actually teach the best benefits of their ability. Even if they wish to stay longer to cope with a particular problem, the system will push them on again. It is a poor system which can only ensure equality by thus depressing all schools towards a minimum common standard.

Seniority, headmasterly incompetence, brevity of appointment and departmental impersonality combine to reduce the ordinary classroom teacher to a mere cipher who goes through the routines of teaching in the time he can spare from his more pressing clerical duties. Non-teaching duties performed by teachers include maintenance of records and equipment, running book-stores and canteens, organizing fetes and conducting charity appeals. In addition, routine tasks associated with teaching include examination vigilance, playground supervision, and the correction of their students' work. Any of these tasks which involves money has to be conducted according to the rules imposed by civil service auditors who guard against the loss of cents at the cost of many dollars' worth of professional time. The headmaster is responsible for all the routine school administration, but as he is denied sufficient clerical and professional assistance he has both to hand out extra tasks to his teachers and divert his own energies from educational matters. The cost of employing people at professional salaries to carry out tasks which could be performed more efficiently and at lower cost by clerical staff has not been ascertained, but it is unlikely to be nearly as great as the cost in terms of lost efficiency which is incurred by diverting people from the jobs of teaching for which they have been trained. It costs the state between four and six thousand dollars to train one teacher, yet we are content to employ him at something like half his professional efficiency in order to make an apparent saving of a few thousand dollars on administrative expenses. This would be quite crazy economics even if we had sufficient trained teachers to meet the demand, but in a time of critical shortage it is nothing less than criminal incompetence.

The constant frustration of being unable to do the job as well as they believe they could is one of the main factors in driving so many of our best teachers into other employment, and for demoralizing those who, for one reason or another, choose to remain in the state schools. The problems of providing universal secondary education are immense and inescapable. Our society is changing so rapidly that its demand for trained minds and our need for flexible responses can be met only by raising the standards of education of the whole population. Even a universal and effective system of education for the new generation may not prove to be sufficient, and we may well have to embark on a vast program of adult education, but this will take far more human resources than we can provide at present. The old methods which were designed for educating an elite to fill the key positions in our society are no longer adequate, and the challenge of the future affects every teacher from kindergarten to university. It will be met only by giving these teachers the training and the opportunity they require. But while teachers are still restricted by departmental routines and the cramping burden of clerical and administrative responsibilities they cannot begin to meet the new situation.

The prime barrier which prevents any real improvement of teaching conditions is the myth that the present situation is a temporary product of a post-war bulge in the birth-rate, and that once the new generation starts to enter the schools as teachers all will be well. This has proved partially true in the primary schools, although they face a new bulge in their numbers from the early nineteen-seventies. However, secondary schools are faced by an increased proportionate as well as absolute level of demand, due to the increasing length of the average time for which students remain at school. Moreover, all sections of the teaching profession are faced with increasing competition from other fields for graduate and tertiary-trained staff. Not only does an affluent society have a greater demand for doctors, dentists and lawyers, but a growing society has a greater need for engineers, a sophisticated society has greater employment for the various ancillary professions, such as social work and various kinds of therapy, and a technological society has a constantly growing need for more and more trained specialists. These demands not only place an increased strain on the schools to educate enough students to meet the need, but also compete with the schools for the staff to carry out their functions. Finally, an affluent society makes many more opportunities available to the young, so that teaching can no longer count on a supply of young men who see it as the only way open for them to higher education, security and respectability.

To sum up, state school teachers are working under a system which robs them of freedom and responsibility, their training is in many cases inadequate and they lack the degree of public esteem which would give them the confidence to act in a professional manner. There are not sufficient of them to do the job according to present ideas, and this shortage is likely to grow worse. Instead of sharing the feeling of an older generation that they have bettered their position in the world, many of the younger teachers feel that, compared with their contemporaries of similar or less ability and training, they are worse off both financially and professionally. Yet this low state of morale, with its consequent retreat to positions of authority and tradition, or despair and resignation, comes on the eve of a change in the nature of the resources available to teachers which could alter the role of the teacher and his relationships to his students beyond recognition.

The same technological developments which have changed the task of teaching from that of training an elite to that of educating a nation are now creating the facilities either to make this possibility a reality or to destroy the idea of education for a generation. These alternatives are posed by the introduction of the computer, the teaching program, and the mass-produced text-book. The last of these is in one sense nothing new, and has in fact plagued education at least as far back as the Bell-Lancaster monitorial systems of mass education. But the new textbooks are produced by committees rather than individuals, and by committees backed by the tremendous financial resources and prestige of scientific and charitable foundations and by governments. To parents and administrators they offer the welcome prospect of a teacher-proof education which can be guaranteed to function whatever the defects of the individual standing in front of the class. To the hard-pressed teacher they offer a magnificent way of keeping abreast of the knowledge explosion by receiving it in this predigested form. To the thoughtful, they threaten a dreadful prospect of nation-wide mental standardization.

The excuses offered for standardized texts are that they enable the understanding of the top men in each field to be brought to bear on the problem of school learning, and that the results of their deliberations can then be shared with all students, by means of the textbook. The parent enjoys the incidental further economy of size, because the numbers of books produced enable the individual copies to be sold cheaply. Finally, true equality of opportunity is given because every student is able to study the very best book in his field. Under the present haphazard form of textbook production, individual authors have their work marketed through various publishers who then attempt to get the books known and accepted in the schools. A new book may take three years from conception to prescription, and by this time it is partly outdated. Its author, moreover, has probably been able to work on it only during such time as he has been able to spare from direct teaching duties, and this part-time form of production does not lead to the highest quality of product. Nor does the individual teacher have an adequate opportunity to assess the comparative merits of the various books competing for his attention. Either he can rely on the recommendation of a subject committee whose individual members have little more opportunity than he does to assess each book, or he can trust to his own judgement, but in either case the validity of the judgement will not be known until he has used the book in the classroom for at least twelve months. If he then decides it is unsatisfactory he has to change his prescription and face the wrath of parents who believe in their divine right to be able to sell off their children's used texts on the second-hand market to the next year's students.

The standardized text can avoid these problems. If it is adequately planned from the first, it should not become quickly outdated, or else annual supplements can be issued to cope with new discoveries. As it can draw on the assistance of scholars working on the frontiers of knowledge it enjoys an inherent advantage over any book produced by a schoolteacher, who must wait until material is published, possibly in book form, and possibly even then only in secondary sources, before he is aware of its existence. If it is financed by a government or foundation, it can use the services of full-time writers who can thus do both a better and a speedier job than can teacher-authors. Finally, it can be thoroughly evaluated before publication, so that teachers can have confidence in its value as a source of learning. Textbooks of this kind already in use in Australia are those produced for the new P.S.S.C. science courses, and a similar text for the biological sciences, *Web of Life*, is now also on its way into the schools. Although the producers of these texts have not shared all the advantages of time and money which have been enjoyed by their American counterparts, their work has already contributed to a revolution in the attitude adopted by teachers in these subjects.

However, the very advantage which these books appear to offer of making teaching easy is the source of their greatest danger. The textbook has always been a dangerous weapon in the hands of the teacher who uses it as a substitute for his own thinking, but the great weight of prestige attached to these new works is likely to lead even good teachers who would otherwise have something of their own to offer to abandon their own competence in favour of the pre-packaged educational substitute.

A further danger lies in the fact that, although these books present a revolutionary approach to their subjects, the teachers who use them have been trained in the old ways and have had little opportunity or inclination to think about fundamental principles since they finished their own course. When they are confronted with a gleaming new course, their response will be anything from horror to ecstasy, but only the rare few will see beyond the surface. Consequently, all the external appearances of the new learning are applied, and soon revolution becomes orthodoxy. Where once the students had to learn their tables, now they have to discover the rules for themselves. But unless the teacher has himself imaginatively discovered the principles of the subject he is teaching, the educational value of the new methods will be illusory. For the individual child obviously cannot during his own education repeat the whole course of man's intellectual history, and must in fact be guided through the highlights so that he gains the understanding for himself. The principle of allowing him to discover for himself is important only insofar as it allows him to gain real understanding. His mind should imaginatively grasp the principle not as something which he has been told but as something real in itself. But when the teaching merely emphasizes the physical techniques of discovery, the external apparatus of scientific method, then the principles may in fact be hidden beneath the litter of method, and not learnt even as working techniques. It is an acquaintance with this kind of teaching which underlies much of the criticism that the new methods are abandoning fundamentals for frills. In fact, those who have designed the new approaches have tried to get beneath the traditional manipulative techniques to the fundamental principles, but the teachers who have followed them have changed their courses into a new series of routines, and in doing so have cast out the best of the old without gaining any good from the new.

The dangers and opportunities present in the standardized textbooks are present to an even greater degree in teaching programs and such mechanical aids to learning as language laboratories. These aids purport to do the teacher's job for him by allowing each student to progress at his own speed towards a predetermined goal of knowledge or skill. The simplest programs merely provide a series of carefully graded exercises which develop the students' skill by infinitesimal stages. More complex courses provide what are called branching programs, so that if the student gives the right answer to a question he goes straight on to the next step, but if he gives a wrong response he is directed to supplementary exercises to correct his weaknesses. The most sophisticated programs provide for what is called in the jargon divergent thinking, and there are probably now even programs to develop creativity.

The strength of a program of learning is that, like the standard textbook, it brings to the student the work of the most advanced scholars in the field, but unlike the textbook it takes the student from his existing stage of development and allows him to proceed at his natural pace. This contrasts with the normal classroom situation where the fastest students have to mark time while the slowest are lost in a maze of bewilderment. Furthermore, the program provides an instant check on each student's comprehension. If he does not understand, he cannot move on. The most glamorous programs are those which have been promoted as teaching machines, wherein the successive questions and answers are produced by some mechanical means in a small screen, but the same techniques can be applied equally effectively in book form. The S.R.A. Reading Laboratories are probably the commonest teaching programs found in Australian schools at present. These laboratories provide a series of graduated exercises designed to promote reading speed and power. Each exercise is on a separate card, and whole kit is contained in a box which is readily accessible to the students. Each student works on exercises appropriate to his present level of development, and it is the teacher's responsibility to promote his to each further stage as soon as he is ready for it.

The other dramatically new aids available to teachers are the vastly increased range of visual aids and material now on the market. These include the well-established slide, film-strip and movie-film projectors, overhead projectors, and, above all, television. These enable the teacher to bring into his classroom a whole range of experience which would otherwise be either com-

in science, history, economics and geography could well raise the average level of learning in these subjects, but only at the cost of reducing the total of knowledge available to the nation in each of these fields. The uniformity of approach would apply not only to the essential core of learning but also to the incidental periphery, and this in itself would tend to lessen the amount of public debate in these fields except possibly among specialists. Yet all of these matters impinge closely on the fields of national decision in politics, business and social matters. Such decisions are most commonly made by people who are not expert in the various fields, and the level of public debate on these issues certainly depends on the understanding of the amateurs involved. If all of these people have been conditioned by a common body of learning to adopt a common approach the chances of an objective perception of the real issues will be seriously reduced. This problem may at present appear most urgent in the human studies, but scientific issues will in the future occupy an increasingly important part of the field of public and private decision, and it is as necessary that there should be a wide variety of approaches in this field as in any other.

Yet the possible dangers of uniformity of approach and sterility of ideas should not allow us to be deterred from pressing ahead with plans for the wide introduction of learning programs and technical aids at every level. The ideas generated in the creation of such courses are themselves one of the most potent sources of new educational ideas, and only through the application of new ideas is there any possibility of our schools meeting the challenge of contemporary society. But if the new ideas are to achieve their full potential our initial enthusiasm should be tempered with critical understanding of their limits, and with a recognition that the role of the teacher in this new environment is more rather than less important. The textbooks and teaching programs he uses can neither offer him an encapsulated course nor compensate for his own deficiencies, but they can be a valuable source of new ideas which he can adopt to his own purposes, and they can provide him with techniques for coping with specific problems among his students.

Yet the fact is that today's teachers are not capable of dealing with the new situation. Their habits of thought are conditioned by the departmental outlook, by examination-oriented courses, and by an outdated tradition of teaching and learning. Despite their pleas for professional status, few teachers would be prepared to accept professional responsibilities or work professional hours. This does not mean that teachers do not work long hours at present, despite public belief to the contrary, but a great deal of their work is routine preparation and correction, and they have little conception of the kind of reading, study and planning which would be required of them if they were to be given true professional responsibility. This has become most obvious in those Victorian technical schools which are being raised to degree status, where it has been found that not only are many of their staff unqualified for taking higher studies but few of them are prepared to forgo the security of guaranteed hours and holidays. The union tradition of extra pay for extra duties is well entrenched, and most would prefer to work under these restrictive conditions rather than accept the freedom and obligation entailed in the university tradition. Moreover, even where the individual teachers are prepared to accept these conditions, they more often than not find that their principals and the departmental administrators are not willing to concede the freedom which must accompany the responsibility. As far as the administrators are concerned, teachers are public servants, and it is more important to ensure that they fulfil the prescribed minimum duties than to see that they are given the opportunity to use their abilities to the limit. Even in present circumstances, a teacher's duties may require him to work back night after night, but woe betide him if he arrives a quarter of an hour late in the morning, even if he has no class at that time, or if he seeks a day off to pursue his private research. This attitude is so effective that after a few years in the service a teacher begins to feel guilty if he is caught reading a book during a spare period.

The introduction of new techniques and the recognition that the shortage of teachers is a permanent phenomenon are going to force a reappraisal of the teacher's role and responsibilities.

The fully-trained subject teacher will no longer be able to regard himself as an individual in charge of a certain number of classes, taking each one independently, but rather as the leader of a team of junior teachers and specialist ancillaries. If we are to break the vicious circle of pseudo-teaching by the incompetent in junior secondary forms and salvage work for the few by the competent in senior forms, the fully-trained teachers of proven ability will have to accept responsibility for the education within their specialties of all the students in the school. As these numbers are and will remain too large for such teachers to take on their own, they will need to learn to apply the techniques of team teaching, and to use the facilities provided by the new forms of teaching aids, so that they can concentrate on the overall design and implementation of courses of studies suited to the local environment and to overseeing the progress of the individual students. To assist them in this task they will have not only the younger teachers who are still learning the trade, but also the services of specialists in the techniques associated with the various aids and programs available.

One of the chief obstacles to any reconstruction of education to meet contemporary needs is the present examination system. While it may be worthwhile having some form of final examination to give a candidate the opportunity to display his command of a discipline at the end of his tertiary education, there is little point in the kind of all-purpose annual examinations which characterize our secondary and even parts of our primary education. These examinations purport to measure by some arbitrary standard the success which students have achieved during twelve months' work, and on their results scholarships are awarded, promotions determined, and jobs allotted. Yet the methods of sampling used in compiling the papers are invalid, the techniques of marking statistically unreliable, and the final aggregate percentages obtained meaningless. If a child obtains fifty per cent in English expression, it means no more than that the teacher has awarded him half the possible marks on a particular selection of his work, usually performed under conditions which reduce his level of performance to the minimum. Even if the examination has been a purely objective test of knowledge and skills, a mark of fifty per cent means no more than that he has been able to perform half the tasks set. Equally, he has failed to perform the other half, and so the reliability of his knowledge in the subject is highly suspect. Yet this mark is counted as a pass, and he is judged by the school and the business world accordingly.

The public examinations conducted in each state attempt to reduce the element of chance by predetermining the percentage of candidates who will pass each year. This is a built-in safeguard against alterations in the difficulty of the question-paper. If in one year the questions are harder, then automatically the pass-mark, or the standard of work required for a pass-mark, is lowered. Conversely, if the question-paper is easier, a higher standard of answer is required for a pass. Under this system, a pass means that the candidate has attended school for whatever number of years is needed to qualify for examination, and that he is probably in the upper two-thirds of those who have done so. The method is probably accurate enough to ensure that those who have done no work or lack all ability will fail, and that those with well-developed ability will pass, but in between these two extremes chance plays the major role.

One of the weaknesses of this system is that it assumes that the standard of the candidates remains invariable. If this assumption is not accurate, the standard of the examination will change. If the quality of teaching improves, it will require greater ability to obtain a pass, but if the quality of candidates falls, as many claim it has done, then the standard of the examination must also fall. As the background of students has changed during the last twenty years, and the quality of teaching has declined, it is possible that the pessimists are correct, and that the standard of public examinations has fallen. On the other hand, the nature of the courses prescribed for examination purposes has risen and both the amount of work required and the competition for success have increased, so that it is probable that there is little real difference in the quality of, say, a matriculant of today and one of twenty years ago. However, there have undoubtedly been variations in the comparative quality of passes in different subjects during this time.

The question of examination standards is, however, of little significance in comparison with the effects of the once-for-all nature of the examinations. In every state the regulations require, in order to qualify for a certificate, the passing of certain basic subjects, usually English, and of certain groups of subjects. Even where this requirement has been relaxed for the lower certificates, it is still required as a pre-requisite for matriculation. The educational principle behind this requirement is undoubtedly sound, for it prevents undue specialization and guarantees a minimum study in the basic disciplines. What is to be questioned is the wisdom of the universities and public examination boards in imposing courses on the schools in the first place, rather than granting them the same autonomy which they themselves demand to conduct their own business, and the use of the regulation as part of an examination system anyway. The true function of examinations should not be to determine courses but to assess the standard which the candidates have reached in their studies. It is bad enough that this assessment should take the form of an arbitrary pass or fail at a mythical standard rather than of a measure of actual achievement; it is worse that this pass or fail should finally be a lump aggregate of quite different tests rather than a detailed assessment of the student's attainment in each part of the examination. If it is believed that skill in related fields is needed for future success in any particular subject, then surely the examining authority should require evidence of these skills in the examinations in these particular subjects instead of relying on a pass mark in a quite different examination. There might, for example, be less concern about the literacy of scientists if they were required to display this quality in their own work instead of merely being coached to pass an English examination before they are allowed to commence their science courses.

The proper functions of examinations are to diagnose strengths and weaknesses, to assess progress, and to provide a report of attainments for parents, employers of other interested persons. The pass-fail kind of test is of limited value for any of these purposes. Diagnostic tests provide the information needed to plan the individual's studies, and are best drawn up in standard form by experts, not by classroom teachers. Progress reports, on the other hand, are largely subjective, and should be made by the individual teachers concerned, with the help of such normative tests as may be available and applicable. However, all formal tests carry with them the inherent danger that they will determine the nature of the course by limiting the teaching to those aspects which can be most easily tested, and the teacher must be careful to use them only as aids and not as masters. Finally, any assessment of attainment is a matter for experts in mensuration, and should be drawn up to meet the needs of a specific situation. The tests devised for the Commonwealth Scholarships illustrate this principle, for they are designed not to measure how effectively a particular course has been learnt, but to assess the degree to which the students have developed those abilities considered to be relevant to the purposes of the scholarship. They do not determine the design of the course followed by the students, but throw on the teachers the obligation to construct those courses which will best develop the abilities of their students. As with any other kind of examination, the performance of the students can be improved by specific coaching, but in this case such coaching can fill only a marginal role and cannot displace the general education which is the prerequisite of success.

If educational, university and employing authorities could be persuaded to adopt this view of examinations, there would be a fundamental change in the role of the teacher. He would no longer be seen as a coach engaged in training his pupils to qualify for a meal-ticket, but as a professional concerned with the whole intellectual development of his students. Similarly, the outlook of the students would have to undergo a fundamental change, for they would no longer be engaged in a contest with the examiners but would have to learn to strive for mastery in the various subject fields they were engaged in. The tests need not even be conducted annually, but could be administered as the occasion arose. Where the test was one to determine the award of scholarships or admission to universities, it would no doubt be necessary to conduct it at a given time throughout the state, but where it was a question of choosing candidates for particular jobs the tests would, at the request of the employer, be administered by the school to those interested. If, for example, a local business-man wanted to take on another junior, he could come to the school and discuss with the vocational counsellor the nature of the job, the skills required, and the general level of education he felt desirable. The school staff could then select the appropriate tests and invite interested students to compete. As a result of these tests, the most suitable candidates could be recommended and the employer could take his pick. On the other hand, the big national employers, banks, insurance companies, and so on, might like to devise their own tests to be administered by the schools. In none of these tests would there be any question of passing or failing, but rather of making a comparative assessment of particular abilities. Even in the case of university entrance, there would be no need for a single examination. Instead, each faculty would design tests for the knowledge and skills they felt to be desirable prerequisites for their students and select the given quota of applicants on the results obtained.

The introduction of such a system would mean that education would no longer be seen as a series of annual trials of increasing difficulty, but as a continuing process at which the student could continue until he felt ready to seek a job. But to be successful it would mean that each school staff would need to include, as well as classroom teachers, experts in counselling, vocational guidance and measurement. According to the size of the staff, these people, who should be fully-trained teachers, might also be engaged in classroom teaching, and they might undertake two of these special functions. However, it would be essential that they have proper training in these particular duties and that they be given sufficient time to carry them out effectively.

Once teachers could be freed from their traditional role of coaching and examining, other changes in their role would become simpler. Instead of functioning as independent units in charge of separate classes, they could come to see themselves as specialist members of a team. On the one hand, the various subject teams would work under their department heads at the task of developing learning in their particular disciplines. On the other, the same teachers would have specific responsibility for the counselling and oversight of groups of students, which they would carry out under the general supervision of the school counsellor. In each of these tasks they would be helped by a number of sub-professional auxiliaries. In their academic work, they would be able to call on the services of a trained teacher-librarian with a team of assistants to provide both reference services and such supplementary teaching material as charts and maps. Other auxiliaries might assist with correction. The school would have sufficient clerical staff to relieve them of administrative duties and to assist them with keeping their own records. Laboratory assistants, projectionists and other specially trained staff would free them from routine preparation and cleaning up in order to allow them to concentrate on their proper professional duties. The school's measurement and testing expert would assist them in both their academic and their counselling functions. Finally, the senior members of all departments would constitute a school council which would work with the headmaster and parents' bodies to formulate and co-ordinate school policy.

To many people, this scheme would no doubt seem a piece of utopian fancy, yet there is no part of it which is not already being implemented in some part of Australia already. It certainly requires a non-teaching staff of such dimensions as to make any treasury official shudder, enough periods free of all teaching duties for the professional staff as to give the horrors to anyone who has compiled a timetable, a concept of shared responsibility which would drive the traditionalists into dementia, and a recognition of the need for sub-professionals which will send the teaching unions into a frenzy of repudiation. Yet if we admit the inadequacy of our present system, and recognize that the shortage of fully-trained classroom teachers is not a transient stage in our development, then an eventual reorganization of such magnitude becomes inevitable. It need not be implemented overnight, nor would it be desirable that it should. Gradualism is not only a valuable political tactic, but also a useful means of easing the shock of change and ensuring that the pursuit of novelty for its own sake does not lead us into irrevocable error. It would, however, be welcome if such changes as are being brought about by the various authorities could be seen as a part of a general strategy, instead of being merely conceived as ad hoc measures, which bring quite unforeseen consequences in their train. Even apparently small changes, such as the Commonwealth scholarship scheme, cause gradual readjustments in the whole educational structure, and it is a pity that we do not choose to plan these changes in advance instead of waiting until we are confronted with the further problems they bring in their wake.

Yet the apparent cost of major changes is probably greater than the actual. The inefficiency of the present system, in terms of wasted man hours, in terms of the cost of employing people at professional rates on unskilled jobs, and in terms of employing unskilled people at professional rates on professional jobs, is so well camouflaged that its economic cost is forgotten. If our present numbers of fully-trained professional teachers were given proper professional conditions, including at least one free day a week for study and sufficient clerical, administrative and auxiliary assistance, they could effectively educate a greater number of students than they can at present. A classroom teacher on thirty periods a week of forty minutes each, with classes of thirty, theoretically provides six hundred man-hours of learning a week for forty-four weeks a year. In classes of this size, the top and the lowest third of the students are wasting some or all of their time, so this reduces the learning he provides by half. A further third of the possible time is lost to examinations and school administration. A proportion of the remaining three hundred hours is wasted because he has not had sufficient time to prepare and plan. The same teacher with a teaching auxiliary could take forty students for the same number of periods and with similar efficiency—an increase of one-third in learning hours to offset the salary of the assistant. A team of three teachers with three auxiliaries could take their day a week off for study and so increase the effectiveness of their courses without further cost. If, in addition, they were to be freed of clerical and administrative duties, they could give greater thought and assistance to the faster and slower members of the classes and also reduce the number of weeks lost to school administration—a further improvement to the numbers of learning-hours per staff member. The aim of the administration should be to increase the number of learning hours until it equals the number of student-hours actually spent in the classrooms.

These calculations are based on a subjective estimate of a teacher's capacity, and it is quite possible that in fact the economic gains of some such system would be even greater than I have suggested. It could be a profitable project for the new Commonwealth Department of Education and Science to sponsor some research into the economic efficiency of present schools and into various ways of improving it. Such studies as have been made overseas suggest that the average student is attending to his work for less than half his time even in normal conditions, so that any avoidable additional loss of learning time represents an enormous wastage of national resources.

It is in this context that the use of teaching programs, standard textbooks and similar materials should be considered. These devices can neither replace the teacher nor offer complete courses, but they can replace the formal class lesson and provide sources of ideas and activities, and be of use in developing specific skills, With their assistance, the teacher can supervise the education of a much greater number of students, but to do so he must have the kind of professional conditions we have been discussing in order to familiarize himself with the material available and to plan a course which will integrate this material with work designed to meet the specific needs of the pupils. Under these circumstances we can envisage the single teacher with the assistance of two or three auxiliaries supervising as many as three times his present number of students, but beyond this limit the effectiveness of the education would almost certainly collapse.

It would, however, be a misconception to regard this change as a way of saving money. A total staff as large as, or larger than, the present would be required. However, instead of all being regarded as general practitioners of teaching, they would be divided between teachers and specialist assistants, and would work under the leadership of the experts. In this way, the limited numbers of qualified staff would be so employed as to place every child's education under professional supervision, and the less experienced teachers would have an opportunity to learn their skills before being placed in sole charge of students. The economic advantage would come not from any saving of expenditure on salaries, but from an elimination of wastage. If the responsible authorities are not prepared to make this provision for auxiliary staff, then they should be prepared to admit their inability to provide universal education and should introduce quotas in secondary education. This would be unpopular, because it would make the truth obvious, but it would be more just than the present system where the numbers who actually receive an adequate education are determined largely by chance.

Changes in the role and responsibilities of the teacher, which are inevitable whether any major reorganization is undertaken or not, will demand great changes in the nature and length of teacher training. The first requirement of any teacher, primary or secondary, is a thorough grounding in one or more academic disciplines. This is necessary both because of the enormous increase in knowledge in all fields and because of the changes in our understanding of the principles underlying these fields. It is difficult to conceive such an understanding being given in less than three years of tertiary education, and so it would seem that the minimum acceptable length of basic teacher training is four years. This would allow for a complete academic education and an introduction to teaching method and to the history, sociology and philosophy of education. Specialist training in such fields as measurement, psychology and guidance or counselling requires still further time.

The outlook and control of teacher education also needs to be revised. At present most of it is conducted by the state departments which are also the employing authorities, a situation which leads to the perpetuation of the old apprenticeship traditions, the separation of teachers from the rest of the professional and academic community, and a narrow indoctrination into the departmental outlook. A separation of teacher training institutions from the various education departments would at least free the students from the constant surveillance of big brother and would allow staff to be recruited by open competition without regard for seniority. This last condition is not, however, one which should be confined to teacher education. One of the most stifling conditions of education is the bondage which for most practical purposes ties teachers to a single employing authority. Once they leave the department with which they started their career, whether to go abroad, interstate, or merely to an independent school, they can return only at the cost of all their seniority. Moreover, every such transfer involves a corresponding increase in the cost of superannuation. This constricting atmosphere would best be destroyed from the very start by encouraging students to move interstate to do their initial training. Later on, it could be hoped that the same freedom of movement would be extended to teachers. Such a move would in itself do much to remove the feelings of frustration which are the present lot of so many teachers who have no wish to abandon their career but who would dearly like to cut free of the classroom and their present employer for a time.

Finally, there is the question of the internal structure of courses of teacher training. At present, the majority of teachers' colleges offer integrated courses of academic and teaching studies, while the universities offer end-on courses in which the education studies occupy a year after the completion of a first year, although three universities now also offer integrated undergratuate courses in education and academic subjects. The objection to the integrated course is that it enforces specialization at too early a stage, that it separates teachers from other students, and that it confers on its students a second-rate degree which is acceptable only for teaching. These objections would seem to embody a low opinion of teaching as a profession, for in no other fields do the practitioners consider that a specific course of training makes them inferior or remote from those who have undertaken more general studies. However, the root of this objection is not so much in a concern for academic standards as in a distrust for the employing authorities and a belief that the bargaining position of teachers is irrevocably weakened when they do not have a qualification which could be accepted by employers in industry and commerce. However, this objection would lose its force if teachers were granted freedom of movement, for they would then be in a position of bargaining not with one, but with a number of employers.

The great advantage of the integrated form of teacher training is that it can enable the student to explore the relationship between the two branches of his activities, with consequent benefit to both. Teaching is the introduction of students to the principles of the various academic disciplines, but such an introduction is impossible unless the teacher has himself mastered the principles. On the other hand, the consideration of practical problems in teaching is itself an excellent way of gaining an understanding of the academic principles involved. If, for example, a teacher finds that his students gain nothing from a particular poem he has taken with them, he is forced to re-examine his own interpretation of the poem. Even more seriously, if he is unable to develop their ability in reading and writing, it is possible that his understanding of language is at fault. Only by considering classroom experience will he perceive these problems, but only on the basis of a deep understanding of his subject will he be able to solve them.

The danger of the academic courses in teachers' colleges is that they become too superficially practical, with a consequent loss of the necessary scholarly depth. The practical approach assumes that the student needs to know only the facts that he will teach, and the means of passing them on. This conception can be seen in the design of courses, which require that students study three or even four 'teaching subjects'. These studies may continue for only one year, but it is then assumed that the teacher is qualified to teach this subject for the rest of his life. But while in the general courses, such as primary training, the emphasis is on this wide spread of courses, in special courses, such as those for art teaching, the emphasis appears to be reversed, and the student is given no opportunity to take subjects which lie outside his immediate sphere. Yet this apparent difference masks an actual similarity, for in both cases the assumption is that the teacher has to learn everything he will teach and nothing more. The student art teacher is not encouraged to become an artist or a scholar of the arts, but is required to dabble in every little skill he may ever be called upon to demonstrate.

A further consequence of this narrow approach is the fragmentation of teachers' courses between academic and practical, a factor which destroys much of the potential of the integrated course. The consequence is that many students graduate from their colleges with admirably developed classroom skills and nothing to teach. Yet such is the docility induced among departmental students that, far from rebelling against the narrow training to which they are subjected, their most common complaint is that they have to waste too much time on academic nonsense before being allowed to get on with the job which will be their bread and butter.

There is little hope of these conditions changing as long as teachers' colleges remain separated from the rest of the academic world. There is no chance that universities as at present constituted will ever be able to assume responsibility for training all secondary teachers, let alone all others as well, but there is a possibility of the colleges coming in under the university umbrella. This would give their courses a certain prestige, but more importantly it would subject their standards to academic scrutiny. Moreover, it would enable their staffs to work alongside colleagues accustomed to a freer environment, and so assist them to break clear of the deadly departmental mentality.

Once teachers' colleges achieved independence of the employing authorities, they could change their function from places where students are trained to carry out specific teaching duties to places where they receive an opportunity to develop their abilities in their chosen fields until they are fitted to be teachers. Teaching techniques would become an extension of academic studies, while basic studies in education would be pursued not in order to obtain certain hints for better teaching but because they are fundamental disciplines with which teachers should have some acquaintance, if only in order to become aware of their own limitations. During this education, students should be encouraged or required to undertake a thorough study of the disciplines they will eventually teach. Primary students will inevitably have to study in at least two fields, language and mathematics, but should also be given the opportunity to pursue their interest in one another. Secondary students, on the other hand, should be regarded as subject specialists, studying in a single major teaching field and in such other areas as attract their interest. Apart from this, there is no reason why there should be any major difference between primary and secondary training.

The qualities we need in our teachers are scholarship, independence of mind, and technical teaching ability. These can be fostered by the programs of training, but they will only be retained if teachers are given full professional conditions of employment. These must include as a minimum freedom of movement, responsibility, and time for study. Otherwise, our best teachers will either resign or retreat into despair. But to give them the conditions to do their best work we will need to adopt a far more flexible approach to both employment and organization. Human characters are not susceptible to regulation, yet we attempt to run our schools as if every teacher and every student was merely a statistic in a book. But just as each student needs individual attention if he is to realize his potential, so each teacher should be treated individually if he is to achieve his best. Some will be best on pure teaching, some on experimentation; some will need more time for study and research, others may be best spending time on administration. But this flexibility will come only when our individual schools are granted autonomy to make their own arrangements.

Finally, we should remember that academic qualifications can themselves be erected into matter for exclusive rules which defeat their own purpose. It is an unfortunate fact about teaching that no clear correlation exists between formal training and classroom success. The main ingredients for the latter would seem to be maturity, personality, and an understanding of the subject which can come equally well from years of reading and thought as from institutional study. If we are to make the best use of our teaching resources our schools must be completely open to those who have developed their abilities away from universities and colleges, and at the same time we should be prepared to sack those who, whatever their nominal qualifications, prove themselves incompetent or unreliable. The value of formal education does not lie in the certificates awarded at its conclusion but in the abilities which it develops and trains, and the test of a teacher should finally rest not on the qualifications he brings to the classroom but on the use he makes of them once he gets there.

9 Schools and Society

Despite advances in teaching techniques, changes in organization, or developments in our body of learning, the ultimate factor determining the nature of our schools is the community in which they function. This community provides the body of tradition which the schools hand on, it allocates their economic support and decides upon the role which they are to perform. Yet no society is a static organization, and the schools it supports will in their turn change its own nature, not only by the ideas which they put into circulation, but also by the changes which the fact of education makes to the social structure. In short, society determines the kind of schools we will have, but these schools play a major role in deciding who will obtain power and what sort of values will be current in society.

In Australian society, although responsibility rests with the states, the critical influence is exercised by the Commonwealth, which not only intervenes directly, although still peripherally, in the business of education, but also makes the major decisions affecting the proportion of the national income which will be available for public purposes and the amount of this which will be at the disposal of the states. This situation has applied at least since the uniform taxation agreement of 1942, but it is only recently that the Commonwealth has shown significant signs of recognizing its responsibilities below university level, although it has of course financed schools in its own territories. In 1945, by the same act which established in permanent form the Universities Commission, it established a Commonwealth Office of Education, and in 1967 the office became one of the foundation stones of a fully-fledged Department of Education and Science. The present educational responsibilities of this department include the administration of Commonwealth secondary and tertiary scholarships, of research grants, and of grants for science laboratories and technical education, including tertiary technical courses, and for teacher training. In addition, it conducts certain liaison services and distributes information.

The most important of these functions in the immediate future is likely to be its research activities. As well as administering, through a committee, grants for post-graduate research in a wide variety of fields, it is considering sponsoring specific projects of educational research. These projects are likely to be established schemes which show promise for further development, or attempts to find solutions to particular problems which are troubling the authorities. Into the latter category come such matters as the university failure rate, or the difficulties caused by a lack of uniform standards between the various states.

The most obvious characteristic of Commonwealth involvement in education, outside the universities, has been the lack of any general planning. Solutions have been devised only when public clamour has made it impossible to avoid the problems any longer or when there have been immediate political dividends to be reaped. Yet although the measures the Commonwealth has taken in secondary and technical education have been intended only to deal with symptoms rather than to alter the basis structure, they have in fact started a cycle of change which cannot but affect every aspect of education. The choice confronting the Commonwealth is not whether it will change what has traditionally been a state province, but whether it will plan these changes.

The most important Commonwealth activities in secondary education at present are the Commonwealth scholarship scheme, the system of grants for school science laboratories, and assistance to technical education. The professed aim of all of these schemes was to reduce the economic disabilities which had previously prevented many students from outaining the education which would best develop their talents.

The scholarship scheme is the most direct means to this end, and has possibly been the target of the most direct criticism from teachers' organizations, for it interferes most directly with the internal functions of the school. Although it was at first intended that these scholarships should be awarded on the basis of existing examinations, the varying nature of public examinations from state to state and the absence in Victoria of any single external examination at the required level has led to the introduction of a special scholarship examination which is now used in every state. This examination was designed for the Commonwealth by the Australian Council for Educational Research, and is a measure of developed ability in mathematics, science, expression and the humanities. In order to allow for the criticism that chance sometimes led to the less deserving students obtaining the award, in some states teachers' recommendations are now also taken into account in determining the final allocation of scholarships. However, as this subjective assessment is used to take scholarships from those who have won them on the objective test and award them to those who have not, it is doubtful whether it leads to any greater degree of justice. A better scheme would be to make the initial awards solely on the basis of the tests, and then to grant further scholarships to a limited number recommended by the schools. There is also a strong case for giving a few special awards to students who do not qualify on the general tests but who have exceptional ability in some particular sphere such as music.

Such amendments are, however, merely tinkering with the principle, and do nothing to overcome the most serious criticisms of the scheme. The first of these is that the nature of the scholarship examination is such that the wrong students are selected, and subsequently fail in the higher studies for which the award has been made. This criticism goes further than the idea that the final allocation should be amended in accordance with teachers' recommendations, for it suggests not just that there are other factors than the examinable to be taken into account, but that the abilities measured by the tests are not in fact those most relevant to the purposes of the scholarship. A modification of this criticism which sometimes appears is that the tests give an undue advantage to science students, because everyone has studied expression and some humanities, but only the specialists have continued to this level with their sciences and mathematics. This criticism can, however, be answered by the principle that those who intend to continue to higher education should not have been allowed to drop their studies in these vital areas at such an early stage. The few exceptions to this rule would be catered for by special purpose scholarships. As for the major issue, that these tests measure the wrong things, this would seem to imply that our traditional examinations measure the right things. The factual basis of this claim could only be assessed by collating figures which would show the reliability of the scholarship tests as a predictor of future examination success, but even if such reliability proved to be low this would not invalidate the tests as a device for selecting those most likely to profit from further education, but would merely reinforce doubts about the value of the traditional examinations which the scholarship holders are required to sit for as they proceed through their higher education.

The most serious objection to the Commonwealth scholarship scheme is not that its criteria of selecting the best are wrong, but that such selection is irrelevant to the avowed purpose of opening the pathway to higher education. The author of the scheme, Sir Robert Menzies, was himself a scholarship student at a time when the universities were largely the preserves of the wealthy, and scholarships were a very real factor in enabling those of exceptional talent to obtain a suitable education. It was no doubt with his own experience in mind that he conceived a scheme which would multiply such opportunities. However, in contemporary Australia poverty curtails the education of only a tiny proportion of those who get within two years of university, the stage at which they become eligible for Commonwealth scholarships. Certainly, these last two years are also the most expensive, and the government grant has no doubt been both welcome and useful to most of its recipients, but the majority of them would have been able to manage without. The truly poor in today's society come from conditions which rarely enable them to obtain any measure of scholastic success, and so remain outside the orbit of this scheme. Moreover, as only ten thousand scholarships are awarded annually for the one hundred and fifty thousand students eligible to enter, the chances of the proportion of really needy students qualifying for assistance are remote. The scheme, then, is welcome to those who benefit by it, but of little relevance to either the problem of increasing the numbers proceeding to higher education or the problem of hardship. In fact, the first of these problems may have increased, for students who have failed to obtain an award have in some cases equated this with failure to achieve a respectable standard, and have left school although they have undoubtedly possessed the qualities which would enable them to benefit from further education.

The two alternatives which have been proposed to the present scheme are that a smaller amount of money be given to all eligible students, and that the awards be made on the basis of need instead of ability. If the first of these ideas were adopted, the present maximum sum allotted to the scholarships would enable a grant of about $24 to be made to each student in his penultimate secondary year. This would not be enough to pay the book bill for most of them. On the other hand, the introduction of a means test would cause political difficulties from the complaints of those who found themselves just ineligible, but it could be a real means of avoiding cases of genuine hardship. Its effect on the total numbers going on to higher education would not be great, but if the Commonwealth is genuinely concerned to remove economic handicaps at this stage of education it should seriously consider adding such a scheme to its present measures. There is something reprehensible about a scheme which gives the most assistance to those who are already well off, and which thereby enables them to further improve their economic position at the expense of the general taxpayer.

The scheme of subsidizing science blocks in schools has probably done much to remove the economic handicaps which have beset science teaching in the poorly endowed Roman Catholic schools, but it has done nothing to reduce the overall range of inequality between different schools. At the same time as it has raised some Catholic schools towards state school standards it has enabled the wealthy colleges, Catholic and Protestant, to further improve the material advantages they already enjoyed over the rest of the education system. The assistance it has given to state schools has been largely dissipated on providing oddly assorted supplementary equipment to all schools, regardless of their particular needs. It is now possible to go into a high school and find a lavish refrigerator storing a single dead rat for the biology class, and somewhere else there may be a telescope for the use of such astronomers as may care to come back at night to use it, but you will not necessarily discover such essentials as a sink with running water or an efficient stink-cupboard for isolating the rotten egg gases whose production seems to constitute such an enormous proportion of junior chemistry courses. The best that could be said of the measure is that it has established a principle of Commonwealth intervention and that it has enabled some of the Catholic schools to hang on a little longer in a desperate situation. The claim by the responsible minister that these grants will eventually provide every school with adequate science facilities has been supported by no figures showing the existing or future need, or even the present deficiencies which it is hoped to overcome.

The same criticism can be made of the grants to technical education. The sum made available was apparently determined by administrative convenience rather than by any estimate of the amount necessary or of the goal intended. This sum has been made available to the states to spend as they determine. In at least one state the offer had to be deferred while the state authorities got themselves sufficiently organized to decide how they wished to use their windfall. As yet, it is impossible to discern any significant improvements in technical education which could be attributed to this Commonwealth generosity.

It is to be hoped that the same casual and arbitrary approach does not characterize Commonwealth intervention in educational research, although the vague mutterings which have been overheard about standard textbooks and syllabi suggest that it may. A Commonwealth initiative to establish the significant problems in various fields of education, followed by a study of possible solutions to these problems, would be a most valuable move towards improving the quality of Australian education. Such work could be done, for example, in the field of science teaching, where projects could be sponsored to discover the most valuable methods of teaching and the resources needed to implement these methods. Alternatively, the factors involved in literacy could be studied, and programs produced to develop specific skills. Such action would eventually provide a much better range of knowledge and resources for teachers, and so enable them to teach more students more effectively. But projects based on a priori assumptions about the desirability of standardization or the value of uniform programs can only succeed in stifling individual initiative and cramping a new straightjacket on education which will destroy that flexibility which is essential to its very nature.

The approach of the present Commonwealth government to education is determined by its respect for the constitutional principles of the founding fathers and by its policy, enunciated by the Minister for Social Services[1], that government expenditure in these fields is determined not by the need but by the funds available. The first of these beliefs is encouraged by state parliamentarians who, jealous of their own preserves, expect the Commonwealth government to provide them with more money without interfering with the details of their activities. The Commonwealth is quite happy to encourage this illusion of independence because it enables it to escape the consequences of its own actions. The decisions of the Commonwealth Treasury, expressed through budgets and banking policy, finally determine what proportion of the nation's production will be available for public purposes and what will be left in private hands. The greater amount of public funds is raised by the Commonwealth through the various forms of taxation available to it. In 1964-65, total Commonwealth and state expenditure, after subtracting state expenditure on railways and business undertakings, which would largely be covered by receipts, was approximately $4,500 million. Of this, $756 million was paid by the Commonwealth to the states, and they raised only a further $600 million from their own resources[2]. This means that, of the total funds available for expenditure on all state responsibilities, including education, less than half were raised by the states themselves.

However, a more serious limitation on state expenditure as compared with federal arises from the fact that the Commonwealth government can virtually print its own money, whereas the states are restricted to the exact sums they can raise by the ordinary means available to them. Certainly, a federal government which tried to finance any great proportion of its expenditure from

[1] Australian Resources and Living Standards Convention, Melbourne, 1967.
[2] Commonwealth Year Book, 1966, pp. 757, 758, 787, 789.

new money issues would create the kind of galloping inflation which destroyed the Weimar republic in Germany, but the flexibility conferred by the ability to create new money frees federal agencies from the type of penny-pinching economies which constantly beset state instrumentalities.

These facts mean that the states cannot be held completely responsible for their conduct of education, or for that matter of any other of their functions. The effect of the Commonwealth financial stranglehold has been to impose a uniformity of mediocrity, not only in education, but in all state services. If one state decided, as a matter of social policy, to move into a new field with, say, the provision of universal free kindergartens, or the provision of special school facilities in under-privileged areas, it could do so only at the expense of its other services. A prime illustration of this occurred when the New South Wales government won the 1965 elections on a policy of financial grants for independent schools, and followed the elections by slashing some millions of dollars off the building program for state schools. The consequence of this situation is that the individual states can make only marginal changes in administration or in the order of priorities, but that the overall standard of provision is fixed for them by the Commonwealth.

The answer of the states' righters to this problem is that the Commonwealth should return its taxing powers to the states so that they can exercise responsibility as well as nominal authority. Such a solution might be to the apparent advantage of Victoria or New South Wales, but it flies in the face of economic reality. There is a certain demand for state and Commonwealth government services, and there is a certain national income from which to provide the goods and services needed to meet this demand. It is a public and political decision what proportion of the available goods and services should be directed towards public purposes, and argument about whether the levy should be made by state or federal authorities can only distract attention from the central issues.

The case for the return of taxing powers to the states depends on the assumption that the Commonwealth is taking more than its fair share of the available revenue. To prove such a case it would be necessary to show that the Commonwealth, as well as vacating certain taxing fields, intended to vacate certain fields of expenditure. If it does not do so, then any return of powers to the states could only be illusory, because the total amount of money available would still remain the same, and the change in taxing authorities would only mean that the states would have to bear the onus for any increase in the total amount of taxation collected, for in fact such an increase is the only possible way in which education can be properly financed. On the other hand, if the Commonwealth were to vacate entirely the field of state finance, such a state as Western Australia, small in population but large in responsibilities, would necessarily suffer in comparison with Victoria, which has the advantage of a large population concentrated in a relatively small area.

But although the demand for the return of state taxing rights misses the main issue of a shortage of funds for education, it does arise from a justifiable resentment of the way by which the amount of money available to the states is determined. This is officially decided at a meeting between the Prime Minister and the various state premiers, but in fact the Commonwealth has determined both its projected level of expenditure and the total amount of Commonwealth revenue beforehand. With both the size of the cake and the size of the federal slice determined beforehand, the states can do little but make loud noises and then prune their spending accordingly. If they protest bitterly enough, the Commonwealth may reveal that it had another piece of cake hidden up its sleeve all the time, but in fact they can make no real difference to a decision which is taken both without consultation and without any consideration of the need and demand for the state services which are pruned in this arbitrary fashion.

One solution of this problem might be for the states to follow the lead of federal departments which have dealings with the Treasury, and employ sufficient economists to present their case reasonably instead of in the accounting terms in which it appears at present. A further step would be for the Premiers' conference to accept responsibility for determining the total level of public taxation, instead of merely trying to get their own share of this sum increased. This could be politically difficult, but it would put an end to the present position whereby Commonwealth departments are able to operate more or less according to their own forecast needs, provided that these needs are approved by Treasury and Parliament, whereas state departments suffer from a constant poverty because their level of operations is determined by a Commonwealth Treasury decision which is made at best on purely economic grounds and takes no account of the detailed situation. If total government expenditure was fixed by a joint Commonwealth-state body, at least all government departments would suffer equally from a political decision to limit public spending. At present, the Commonwealth departments remain sublimely unaffected by the vicissitudes of economic and political fortune, or of budgetary policy, while the state departments are left to stagger along with whatever scraps are left over from the federal table.

Yet this picture of total Commonwealth responsibility must be qualified by two major considerations. In the first place, the states have shown a marked reluctance to expand those sources of revenue which are available to them. They are quite prepared to heap on stamp duty or to increase railway fares, for these charges are passed on to the public and affect the small men most seriously. But of two major possible sources of state revenue, one, payroll tax, has been totally ignored, and the other, land tax, has been steadily eroded in the interests of feather-bedded primary producers.

A form of state payroll tax would be one of the most effective sources of further revenue, for the section of the constitution which guarantees freedom of trade would ensure that increased costs resulting from the new tax could not be passed on to the consumer beyond the limit set by the natural protection of distance and transport costs. It would be a means of ensuring that industry, which causes new strains on state resources, would meet its share of the cost of meeting these strains. If the tax led to the diversion of new industry from states with this charge to those without, this would be of advantage to the country by encouraging more balanced development. The same advantage could be enjoyed within a state by exempting, for example, all industries outside a certain radius of the metropolis. Finally, the tax would ensure a certain automatic balance between private and public development.

The second objection to the theory of Commonwealth responsibility is the total ineptness of state administration, which is a model of waste and inefficiency. This situation is partly a product of the low calibre of state administrators, and partly of the gross centralization of the state systems. These two factors are interlocked, for whereas centralization removes responsibility from the individual teacher and headmaster, the seniority system locates it in the hands of men who have done the long crawl up from the classroom through the inspectorial ranks to the remote atmosphere of the administration, and who now have neither the time nor the recent experience to judge the results of their actions in terms of the classroom situation. In the few cases where they have retained a few ideas during their weary pilgrimage, they have done so defensively and eccentrically, so that when they encounter opposition to the execution of these ideas they react hostilely, and so jeopardize the success of their projects by their authoritarian inability to lead rather than command. But such individuals are rare—the more typical administrator is so overwhelmed by the tremendous pressures of his office that he hopes for nothing more than the good fortune to endure each day as it comes, and thinks of nothing else than the ignorance of those who criticize him from outside. These men forget that, although they may understand the reasons for their actions, it is the critics who see the results. What is most needed in education in Australia is an administrator who will look at these results and demand that his subordinates do something to avoid them. The energy which is at present devoted to concocting excuses for the inexcusable would be sufficient to work an educational revolution if it were turned for a time to avoiding the avoidable.

One of the cruellest aspects of the present centralization of state administration is the way in which it destroys the ideas men who rise through it. The case of the Wyndham scheme in New South Wales is illustrative of this phenomenon. This scheme, which was discussed in more detail in an earlier chapter, is probably the most visionary plan ever conceived for state secondary education in Australia, yet it has largely failed in its major aims, partly because of political factors, but more particularly because of the lesser capabilities of men in the lower echelons of the administration. But these men would not have had any obstructive importance if their role had been purely administrative. Instead, they were charged with the responsibility for executing the scheme, a responsibility which should have rested solely with the teachers. As a consequence, the teachers who should have been given the time to study and absorb the scheme until they were ready to go forward on their own initiative have been driven into it with varying degrees of resentment and understanding, and as is usual under such circumstances the details are being implemented at the expense of the spirit.

If the tragedy of New South Wales has been that a system unfitted for ideas is unable to handle those that do arise, the tragedy of the other states is that the ideas so seldom arise. The seniority system is to a great extent responsible for this. In the Commonwealth service, it is customary to appoint younger men as departmental heads, and to pay them according to the ability which is regarded as a prerequisite of the office. In the states, it is customary to appoint as head of the education department the senior eligible inspector, and to pay him a salary commensurate with the mediocrity which has enabled its recipient to survive the departmental rat-race long enough to reach the summit. Once there, he becomes the apologist for his ministerial head, without either the energy or the opportunity to carry out any measures of reform before he reaches retiring age and makes way for the next body thrown up by the seniority escalator.

When all the senior positions in a department are filled in this fashion, a general intellectual torpor ensues. This is not because these administrators are lazy men—far from it, for they are often possessed by a stern morality of duty which drives them on to perform ever-more fantastic prodigies of sheer hard work. The worse the situation in the schools, the harder the administrators work, dealing with complaints, shuffling their few available teachers around on an everlasting merry-go-round to satisfy whichever headmaster is grizzling loudest, holding conferences, preparing plans, never resting from a ceaseless illusion of activity. The one thing which they never have time to do is to think.

The first step towards rationalizing this craziness would be for administrators to realize that it is not their function to organize education, but only to provide the wherewithal by which education may be carried on. This wherewithal includes teachers, but once they have been found they should be left to do their task in their own way. If they prove unable to do this, then they should be removed as incompetent. On the other hand, if they are unable to do the job properly because they lack proper supplies, or because they are expected to act also as clerks and school cleaners, or because the school itself is unsuitable, then the person responsible for this state of affairs should be removed. When the whole education system is failing, as it is anywhere in Australia today, then the Minister should either demand the dismissal of the head of his department or resign himself. Certainly, when the whole system is in chaos there is no place for senior administrators who fill their days considering how to dispose of surplus desks or worrying whether every teacher has signed the time-book correctly.

The business of education is carried out at the level of the local community, and it is here that the final professional responsibility should lie. This is not possible while the schools are hamstrung for lack of money, but neither is it possible while the state administrations concentrate power and prestige at their respective centres. The ideal system would probably be one by which the Commonwealth accepts responsibility for finance and for the standard of material provision, the states for administration, and the schools and teachers for the actual education of their students. Such schools would be autonomous institutions within a national framework. Their courses and internal organization would be their own responsibility, and their facilities, such as sportsgrounds, classrooms, halls and libraries, could be shared by the communities to which they belonged. Their function need not be restricted to daytime courses for full-time students, but could embrace the whole range of adult education as well. The teachers would be appointed to the individual school on the basis of their own abilities and the needs of the particular area, but they could shop for further jobs on a nation-wide market. The combination of a breadth of interests and responsibilities within the school itself, tenure of position, and free movement of teachers throughout the nation would go a long way to breaking down the narrow provincialism and departmental rigidity which is at present one of the more depressing features of Australian education.

Within this pattern there would be room for considerable variation both between different states and between different schools and areas within each state. There is no reason why we should be committed to the present rigid primary-secondary-tertiary divisions, or the split between technical and general or professional education. Some schools could experiment with the senior high school proposal adopted in Tasmania and under consideration in Victoria. This proposal enables the immediate needs of senior students to be met more adequately, but this could occur at the cost of junior students and may well lead to a reduction in the proportions going on to further education, as well as to an increased emphasis on examinations. Other divisions, such as the four-four-four system of infant, middle and senior schools, each providing four years of schooling, might prove more satisfactory in enabling each school to be organized according to the needs of a developmentally homogeneous group. On the other hand, the concept of a single school from kindergarten to adult, with flexible groupings within it, might prove more successful. Such schemes could be tried in suitable areas, but there is no reason why any one should ever be adopted universally. With a number of such arrangements, parents could be given a real choice about the kind of education they wanted for their children, a choice which is denied by the present state-wide uniformity. Further choice could be given by organizing different schools according to different scales of priorities, academic, social, creative. The onus would be on the individual school to prove that its system worked.

Fundamental to any such schemes is the principle that the teacher must be educated sufficiently to meet the challenges of contemporary society, which demands a broad and thorough education of all its children to enable them to cope with the changes of a constantly growing technology and a constantly developing complexity in its own organization. As teaching is not an easily definable skill, we also need a system for recognizing those who have proved their capabilities despite their lack of formal qualifications, and for allowing entrance to the profession to those who have manifest ability but unorthodox training. As the total of all such teachers will always be short of the demand, we must equip these teachers with all possible mechanical and human aids, and then give them the responsibility to carry out their job as they best see fit. Only then will we have started to come to terms with the problems which beset our troubled schools.

Although the states could make a start towards implementing such changes, we have seen that their financial resources, even if they were to be exploited to the full, are not sufficient to make changes of the magnitude needed. Furthermore, their departmental hierarchies contain such solidly entrenched ineptitude that any scheme sufficiently radical to make an appreciable impact on the present situation is doomed to failure if it relies on the present administrators for its implementation. Finally, any such scheme would necessarily affect the advancement prospects of teachers who are quite comfortably moving up the existing ladders, and would run into stiff opposition from teachers' organizations, which are dedicated to the preservation of mediocrity. Consequently the only real hope for the future lies in the icy corridors of Canberra.

The first step which the Commonwealth government could take to get education moving would be to take control of its own schools in the Capital Territory. At present these are paid for from Commonwealth funds, and are consequently the most lavishly designed and equipped in the country, almost up to the standard of the latest British schools. But they are staffed from the New South Wales department, and their teachers remain under the supervision of the state authorities, so there is little chance or incentive to try out new ideas, and no chance to recruit teachers from other parts of the Commonwealth.

If the Commonwealth Department of Education and Science were to take full responsibility for these schools it would enable it to make them laboratories for the nation as well as keeping its own officials in immediate touch with the practical problems of the classroom. It could recruit teachers on short-term contracts from all over the nation, give them the facilities to develop and evaluate new ideas, and then allow them to return to the states to put into practice the results of their experiments. The schools would be pace-setters not only in appointments but in ideas.

A system of short-term contracts, with transferable superannuation rights, once pioneered by the Commonwealth, could be extended to the states and thus free teachers from their present servitude to single monolithic departments. At present, it is normal for a teacher to go from his local school to university or college, finish his training, and return to the same system in which he was educated. He may once in his life be able to travel overseas, but the schools across his state borders remain as foreign as if they were in the remotest provinces of Central Asia. If he does resign to gain experience in another place or another occupation, he can return only at the bottom of the ladder, with little chance for years of putting his ideas into practice. At last, Victoria is showing interest in changing its system so that a new teacher can be appointed at a level of salary and responsibility commensurate with his experience, as opposed to his seniority, but education in Australia will not have come of age until this practice is accepted as normal throughout the country. Only then will teachers be free to act as professional individuals, seeking employment on at least a nation-wide market according to where their interests and qualifications can be best used.

It should not need to be said that short-term contracts should not be such as to jeopardize the security of the individual teacher or to place him at the mercy of a local board of laymen or administrators, as happens in the United States. Normally, it should guarantee tenure of office unless he is convicted of a professional misdemeanour, and reasonable prospects of advancement in the position. But if he wishes to seek higher or different responsibilities, he should compete against all comers on an open market, and experience should be only one of the qualifications taken into consideration. On the other hand, teachers and administrators should face up to the problem of removing the incompetent and the irresponsible who at present clutter so many classrooms. This could be done by instituting a professional board of registration, consisting of practising teachers, which could periodically require evidence of continuing professional standards of performance, either from the headmaster or, upon appeal, from specially appointed school visitors. This move, too, could be taken on Commonwealth initiative by the Commonwealth making it a condition of education grants to the states.

The question of the employment of women is also relevant to the professional status of teachers. As long as women are debarred from holding any positions of responsibility, or paid at lower rates, the entire teaching profession suffers. Not only is the shortage of qualified teachers increased, but the profession is demeaned by having to take into account extraneous circumstances in making appointments. The only consideration in making any appointment should be the competence of the people applying, and it is belittling to men to have artificial rules protecting them from the competition of women. It should be possible for any woman teacher, married or otherwise, to apply for and be appointed to any professional position and to fill it under exactly the same conditions as would a man. Similarly, it should be possible for any teacher, man or woman, who wishes to work only part-time, to be appointed as a permanent professional officer at proportional rates of pay. At present, the various states have different rules governing these circumstances, but they are alike in discouraging the employment of married women and in employing part-time staff at inferior salaries and conditions. No other professional tolerates such sub-standard conditions, but again it is probably only Commonwealth initiative which can remedy the situation.

The Commonwealth, then, can play a role in education by acting as a pace-setter in its own schools and by using conditional grants to the states to establish the outlines of a national teaching profession. But if further action is to be properly guided, and if anomalies are to be spotted and corrected, some form of continuing public audit of education is needed. This could take a similar form to the present Parliamentary accounts committee, or it could be entrusted to a statutory body of disinterested outsiders, such as the Australian Universities Commission or the Commonwealth Advisory Committee on Advanced Education. The essential conditions for such a body are that it have its own staff, that it have complete access to all educational institutions, that it have complete power to initiate its own investigations, that it make periodic public reports, and that it be free of public service control. In its duties, it would resemble the Parliamentary Accounts Committee rather than the other bodies mentioned, for its responsibility would be to keep a detailed check on the actual operation of education rather than to recommend how the Commonwealth should spend its money. However, it should also make periodic general surveys of needs and recommendations for planned developments of the total pattern of education.

The most important structural change needed in Australian education is the promotion of autonomy for individual schools. The Commonwealth could do this by setting up its own schools, each independently run, alongside the existing state schools, or by providing money for churches and private bodies to establish and operate non-fee-charging independent schools to serve particular areas rather than particular groups in the community. These schools could be most beneficially established in presently depressed areas of the inner suburbs where the students need additional facilities merely to give them an equal opportunity. They would provide an alternative avenue of employment for teachers and a real choice for parents. At the same time, the states could endeavour to develop their own schools to a stage where they could be given local autonomy. By such measures, the problems of the wealthy independent schools would gradually be overcome, as they would eventually take their place as equals in an educational community rather than as isolated islands of privilege. However, a condition of such an eventuality would be that these new schools should accept all applicants from their district, for any form of selection merely replaces economic privilege with some other form, and removes the need for the state schools to compete.

More direct Commonwealth intervention in education could

take the form of providing ancillary services for the schools. These would include libraries, school counsellors, vocational guidance, the evaluation of educational equipment and teaching programs, and testing services to provide teachers with materials and advice for testing the progress and achievement of their students. Some of these services could be provided by direct subsidy, others by the provision of qualified staff who could either be attached permanently to existing schools or be given an itinerant commission, and others by setting up new institutions within the Commonwealth Department of Education. Together, they would provide the classroom teacher with the range of specialized assistance which he needs if he is to carry out his job properly. They could be considered as analogous to the kinds of services the Commonwealth Department of Health provides for state hospitals and for individual doctors.

An urgent need in Australia is a body to sponsor, finance and co-ordinate research in education, and to make the results of the research available to teachers. This task could be entrusted to the present Australian Council for Educational Research, which operates on a minimum subsidy and on the profits it makes from selling testing materials to the schools, or an entirely new body could be constituted. Present research in Australian education tends to merely scratch the surface of isolated and easily manageable problems, and there is a need for a body analogous to the CSIRO which could embark on more ambitious projects involving not only the collection of data and the application of the techniques of statistical measurement and behavioural psychology, but all the resources of the social sciences as well as of the specific disciplines concerned. Problems such as the teaching of languages to migrant children can be handled by the present universities, if they are given the funds, but larger topics such as an investigation of the aims and methods of a particular subject, or a study of alternative curriculum patterns, need to enlist the talents of scholars across the nation.

A major reason for the time-lag between even such research as has been carried out and its application in the schools is that we at present rely almost entirely on the printed word for the dissemination of new ideas. Here we can learn from the State Departments of Agriculture, which not only maintain research stations but train and pay their staff to work with the local farmers to spread and apply their ideas. A major function of a Commonwealth educational research body would be to employ extension officers who would both conduct training courses for practising teachers and go out themselves into the schools to work on the application of new ideas.

The worst possible way for the Commonwealth to conduct its research activities is for it to imagine that it can sponsor narrowly-conceived projects which will yield immediate practical results in the form of standard techniques or courses which can be applied across the nation. The answer to any problem in education opens up a dozen new problems, and research must always be a continuing process. Nor is any answer the right one, but merely the one thrown up by the particular techniques and circumstances of the experiment. Moreover, the discipline of education is itself uncertain of its methods, and still at the stage of classifying its material and developing its instruments. Research in education is far too important to be left to the professional educationists, but must involve the whole community of learning, if only to keep in check the brash arrogance which it uses to camouflage its insecurity. Any research project, therefore, should be carried out by several teams operating simultaneously but independently, and representing different traditions and backgrounds, and all the answers discovered should be made available to teachers to adapt to their own requirements.

Finally, education should be accepted as the business of the whole community. Schools should open their doors to all-comers, and no one should feel that he is too old to continue formal education. The school in each locality should be both a community centre and a centre of learning, and the community in its turn should be a part of the school. This development can arise only as a product of a change of attitude on the part of teachers themselves and of the community at large, and not as a direct result of any government action. When it does occur our schools' troubles will be over, and a new lot will have begun.

Appendix A

Independent Schools and a Power Elite:
See:
C. Wright Mills, *The Power Elite*, Oxford University Press, New York, 1956.
S. Encel, 'The Old School Tie in Business', *Nation* (Sydney), 10 October 1959.
S. Encel, 'The Political Elite in Australia', *Political Studies*, 1961, pp. 16 et seq.

Wright Mills' book is the basic study of the social and biographical characteristics of the body of decision makers in the United States whom he christened the 'power elite'. Encel, in the two articles cited, analyses some of the characteristics of Australians in positions of power, and also investigates the methods by which they are selected and the environment in which they work.

Encel remarks in 'The Political Elite' that 'it is one thing to establish that the large organized hierarchies of government, industry, finance and military power throw up small directing groups whose members exhibit well-defined social characteristics. It is a rather different undertaking to investigate the setting within which these 'power holders' or 'decision makers' operate. . . .'

Encel's figures show that 28 out of 47 non-Labor Federal and State ministers in his survey went to private secondary schools, and that 18 of these attended member-schools of the Headmasters' Conference. These schools could be considered the equivalent of the English Public Schools. On these figures, therefore, it would seem that, although independent schools contribute an undue proportion of non-labor leaders, there is every opportunity for students from other schools to reach as high a rank in our political hierarchy. The success of ex-independent school students may in fact be due not to any improper privilege, but merely to a coincidence between the money needed to pay for independent schooling and the factors which would lead one to join the non-Labor parties.

However, we need to make two qualifications to this sanguine picture of opportunity for all. Firstly, the proportion of independent school students would seem large enough to determine the total outlook of the group. It is more likely that the state school minority would conform to the standards of the established majority as a sign of their success than that they should retain a breadth of sympathy from their origins.

Secondly, Encel's groups covered the whole federal period and included both state and federal ministers. In modern Australia, state parliaments no longer attract as many individuals of high calibre or ambition. Nor do they now have a power of decision making to compare with that exercised by the federal government. Moreover, in the federal sphere politicians in both parties are becoming more sophisticated and, as a group, more highly educated. (Encel points to the increased proportion of white-collar workers among Labor members.) In the non-Labor parties, these factors might be expected to lead to an increase in the proportion of members with independent school backgrounds, and a decline in the number of 'self-made men'.

If we look at the last Menzies Ministry, as listed in the *Commonwealth Parliamentary Handbook*, 1965, we find that of the 20 who list their schools in *Who's Who in Australia* 11, or over 50 per cent (cf. 35 per cent in Encel's sample), attended independent schools.* Only one of these attended a Roman Catholic school, Aquinas College, W.A., a member-school of the Headmasters' Conference, and therefore not a typical Catholic school.

Only three Liberal Party ministers fail to list their school background, and two of these, who did, I believe, attend independent schools, list prestigious tertiary institutions instead (Duntroon and Cambridge). However, only two of the six Country Party ministers bother to mention their schools, and one of these lists Horsham High School.

These figures would suggest that at least in the top ranks of the Liberal Party the old school tie is a powerful aid to success, but that the Country Party is more concerned with more apparent qualifications.

Encel's survey of business executives revealed a similar advantage towards the independent schools. 55 per cent of his sample attended private schools, and 28 per cent had both their primary and secondary schooling free from the taint of state school influences. Of the 180 who attended private schools, 31 went to Melbourne Grammar School and 26 to Scotch College, Melbourne. After these schools came Wesley College, Melbourne, Sydney Grammar School, and St. Peter's, Adelaide. These numbers should be compared with the number of graduates in the sample—96 from universities, 18 from other tertiary institutions (see Appendix C, Employment and Education).

In considering the advantages conferred by a Public School education, we must avoid imagining any nefarious plot behind this advancement of a small section of the community. As the guidance and careers master at Wesley College, Melbourne, explained, he has a network of contacts through old boys and parents, and when he wishes to place a boy he knows both the boy's own record and the employer's attitude and requirements, and so he has an excellent chance of wedding the candidate to the right opportunity. In other words, the school only has to do its job conscientiously and efficiently, and the

* Two of the other nine attended Fort Street High School, Sydney.

built-in advantages of the school will automatically be transferred to the student.

The harmful effects of this process are three-fold. In the first place, the 'Public School ethic', a minority if respectable code, comes to determine the attitudes of the community. In this connection, it would be interesting to see a survey of the school to which successful politicians and businessmen from state schools send their own children. Secondly, it represents a waste of potential talent among those who have not enjoyed these advantages. Thirdly, it can lead to the promotion of mediocrities to positions of power for no better reason than their social background.

Appendix B

Language, Ability and Educational Prospects:
See:

Basil Bernstein, 'Some Sociological Determinants of Perception—An Enquiry into Sub-Cultural Differences', *British Journal of Sociology*, 1958.

Basil Bernstein, 'A Public Language—Some Sociological Implications of a Linguistic Form', *British Journal of Sociology*, 1959.

Basil Bernstein, 'Language and Social Class', *British Journal of Sociology*, 1960.

In these articles, Bernstein analyses the differences between the use of language of working class and of middle class children in England, and the implications of these differences, particularly in relation to their educational prospects.

Bernstein argues, on the basis of his research findings, that the middle and working classes are differentiated by their differing ways of perceiving the world—in the case of the middle classes, with an emphasis on relationships between objects, which develops in them the ability of analytical thinking, and in the case of the working classes, with an emphasis on content, which leads to a use of language for descriptive rather than analytic purposes.

The language of the working classes he calls a public language, for it analyses experience in social rather than in personal terms. An example of this language can be found in the Opies' collection of *The Lore and Language of Schoolchildren*, which Bernstein has reviewed (*B.J. Soc.*, 1960). This language gives children socially acceptable, often tough-minded, terms in which to explain their own experience. However, it does not encourage them to analyse this experience, or to express their personal feelings. Where personal emotion is expressed, it is expressed bluntly, with a reliance on gesture and tone rather than on words. It does not take much imagination to realize the handicaps children used to this form of expression will suffer from when they are asked to embark on highly formal tasks of writing in the schoolroom.

The middle-class child, on the other hand, is encouraged from his earliest years to develop a more flexible, logical and analytical use of language. Parents talk at greater length to their children, using quite complex grammatical forms, and discussing their feelings and thoughts rather than just issuing commands or uttering conventional phrases of approval and disapproval.

Bernstein also claims that the different forms of these language uses account for the readier orientation of middle-class children to long-term goals of the kind required for success in formal education.

Bernstein's comparative study of the scores of middle and working class children on verbal and non-verbal tests of ability confirms the results of his language studies. The two groups show comparable ability on the non-verbal tests, but no member of his working class group obtained a score in the higher levels of the verbal test of ability.

His interpretation of this result is that the range of operations required in the verbal test was outside the capacity of the working class group. This could be due to innate factors, but there is no reason to suppose this. We are left therefore with the conclusion that the result is due to cultural factors which have inhibited the development of ability in the working class group. These factors would include linguistic deprivation.

The score on the non-verbal test may suggest that the working class group is of comparable development in particular directions, but Bernstein warns us that it probably means no more than that the manipulative operations it requires are within the experience of both groups.

Bernstein concludes from his work that the extension of the same sort of education to all parts of the community may merely serve to exaggerate and justify social differences. 'The middle-class child is capable of responding to, manipulating and understanding a public language, expressive symbolism and a formal language . . . structured . . . as a result of his class environment . . . As a result of the close relationship between education and occupation, a situation may soon be reached when the educational institutions legitimize social inequality by individualizing failure . . . [through] a loss of self-confidence [by the person who, because of his social background, has failed at a socially-approved trial].'[1]

It is important to realize that this language difference is not merely a matter of two different sub-cultures, each with its own value. The middle-class child learns the public language, but he simultaneously develops a formal, analytical language. The working-class child, on the other hand, has only his own direct, possibly colourful, but limited language. This handicap will become greater the further he goes with his schooling. He may show no trouble in coping, for example, with the simple, concrete operations of arithmetic manipulation in his earlier school years, but he will be in trouble in passing to the more abstract field of algebra. In all subjects there is a similar progression through the school towards more abstract thinking, and the child who has not learnt to handle abstract language from his earliest years will find steadily increasing difficulty. It may, incidentally, be some such phenomenon as this which lies behind the favourite excuse of teachers that a certain student 'has reached his limits' when they mean that they are unable to teach him any more.

[1] *Sociological Determinants.*

Bernstein's findings would seem to require us to make some qualifications to the educational theories which have flowed from Piaget's work (see Further Reading list). These suggest that the child's success in handling abstractions later in its schooling will depend to a great extent on a rich experience of concrete operations during its earlier years. It appears, however, that this experience must be accompanied by a constant encouragement to talk about experience, so that the necessary language skills are developed to explore the nature of experience. This conclusion is also supported by the experience of the 'Head-start' program among American negroes.

This work of Bernstein should not be taken as necessarily endorsing the values of the middle-class sub-culture. He is concerned with the handicaps encountered by working-class children in schools which are dominated by middle-class values, and consequently he has not attempted, in these studies, to investigate the positive values of working-class language within its own community. The direct apprehension of experience, without the mediating influence of a highly cerebral language, and the security of an organic community transmitting its values through language, are qualities which might well be of advantage at all levels in a modern society. However, it would be pure romanticism to suggest that such working-class values are in themselves any nobler or more generous than those of any other part of society, or that the working-class sub-culture is adequate to contemporary demands. Education cannot succeed if it attempts to keep each class imprisoned within its own sub-culture—it should rather attempt to make the best parts of each available to all members of society.

To do this, however, it must recognize that each individual brings with him to the school different strengths and different handicaps from his social environment as well as from his personal characteristics. It is, therefore, the task of the teacher to ensure that each receives the kind of education which will use his strengths and compensate for his handicaps. This will require not only a different treatment for each child, but also a different kind of educational program for each individual school, according to its locality. Those children who come to school with the more limited 'public language' should not be brought up immediately against the demands of formal abstract learning, which they will inevitably find difficult, and which therefore will start to destroy their confidence, but rather encouraged to spend their time on the more directly sensuous activities of painting, music and playacting, at which they will probably perform better than their more inhibited middle-class confreres. Having thus gained a deserved confidence, they can be led to talk about their activities, and so develop the formal language powers which must precede any success in formal written and analytical work.

However, we cannot easily transfer Bernstein's findings to Australian society, with its different class structure and class values. Nor can we assume that the middle-classes habitually use analytic and formal language to approach all the problems of life. It is more likely that the child learns that there are certain areas of life to which such responses are appropriate, and others to which he must respond with the same kind of glib social formulae as the working-classes habitually use. Thus, he may learn that the formal and analytic approach is necessary in the more remote fields normally discussed in school, but he is unlikely to be encouraged to talk in any meaningful way about personal behaviour and family relationships. Later on, this same pattern of acceptance will be transferred to the political, religious and moral fields, which are similarly outside the range of school.

While writing this appendix, I have encountered a striking illustration of the inability of the Australian middle-classes to analyse their own motives and behaviour, or their political attitudes. An A.B.C. radio program broadcast interviews with strike-breakers during a postal strike. The people interviewed included one who gave his occupation as teacher, and all spoke in a form of 'educated Australian' which would suggest a middle-class background. Yet all of them explained their actions in glib political cliches which revealed not only a lack of any understanding of the situation but, more alarmingly, a lack of any curiosity about it.

Research into the language patterns of Australian children, the language demands of formal education, and the relationship of language and school success could well be one of the most valuable projects which an Australian government interested in promoting education could sponsor. Its results could not only lead to changes in curriculum patterns to ensure greater equality of opportunity, but could well tell us a great deal about the nature of education itself.

Appendix C

Leaving School This Year? Blank Insurance Society invites enquiries from BOYS*—of at least Leaving Standard.* GIRLS*—Leaving Standard preferred—satisfactory Intermediate Subjects essential.*
Executives and specialists appointed from those who join as juniors.
Girls—Clerical, Typing and Machine positions. Marriage Bonus—uniforms provided.

These extracts from an advertisement which appeared in the Melbourne *Age* alongside the public examination results this year can tell us a lot about the attitudes of Australian employers. In the first place, they seem to believe that males and females have quite different abilities, and so should be offered different jobs and asked for different qualifications. This attitude is one of the factors which determines the kind of education offered to and sought by girls.

But more importantly, from our point of view, is the attitude it reveals to qualifications. First, there is the assumption that someone with a Leaving Certificate will want a clerical job—there are no advertisements for manual workers in the same pages. But more importantly, there is the assumption that such a qualification is necessary for such a job. Once, bank and insurance officers were recruited with Merit Certificate (eighth year). Now Leaving Certificate is required (thirteenth year).

There are undoubtedly some good reasons for this. Insurance and banking, like the world in which they operate, are more complex than they were forty years ago when today's executives entered with their merit certificates, and the new employees must start where their predecessors finished—they cannot afford to spend a lifetime merely reaching the same place. But there is little evidence that the possession of a particular school certificate is either a sufficient or a necessary qualification for embarking on the task of mastering insurance, banking, or any other line of business.

Certainly, the Psychology and Guidance branch of the Victorian Education Department claims, on the basis of its experience, that the girl with Leaving Certificate is likely to perform better in an office than the one with only Intermediate. The additional year at school gives her a poise and maturity so that she will be able to act on her own initiative, to compose letters as well as type them, and generally behave as a secretary rather than just as a typist. But this is just a general comment about the average student. Some have this maturity at Intermediate level, others can obtain Matriculation level without acquiring it.

What I suggest has happened is that employers have merely pushed their entrance levels up as the market will allow—partly as a way of ensuring, by rule of thumb, that the average standard of their recruits will remain constant as the average leaving age increases, and partly as a way of enhancing the reputation of their particular callings, and seeking for them that elusive 'professional status' which seems to have become the goal of all Australian middle-class occupational groups.

On the other hand, the smaller businessman, who has probably come up the hard way himself and can see no need for any schooling beyond the 'university of hard knocks', often laments the passing of the older, lower-level certificates. He not only has to wait longer for his employees to leave school, and pay them more when they do so, but he may well find that the work he has to offer them is not sufficiently demanding intellectually, so that they become restless and discontented. This he will no doubt attribute to the current fashion for over-educating everybody.

Yet the interest of larger firms in education is strictly limited. In the same week *The Australian* twice carried an advertisement from a team of rural scientists who were urgently seeking employment. Presumably their previous employers had suddenly discontinued the project on which they had been employed, and they had been thrown out cold onto the labour market. Yet the capital value of an established team of trained and experienced research workers would be considerably higher than most other disposable assets which the normal firm would possess. However, a news report at about the same time suggested that in America they are now starting to reckon the capital value of established staff, so we may hope that these methods will eventually reach Australia and finish the need for advertisements of this kind.

When this does occur, we may also hope that businesses will spend time and money investigating the actual qualifications they require of new junior staff, instead of relying on such arbitrary, external and misleading criteria as public examinations.

Appendix D

Science and the Economy:

See:

S. Encel, 'Science, Education and the Economy', *Australian University*, 1965.

Frederick White, 'The Strategy of Australian Science', *Australian Journal of Science*, Vol. 26, No. 7, 1964.

These two articles both suggest that science and technology have a direct and critical part to play in the future economic growth of Australia.

Encel argues that science and technology have played the crucial role in the expansion of industry and production around the world during this century. However, their influence in industry has grown only under great difficulties.

Although Great Britain was the first country to pass through an industrial revolution, its early lead was overtaken by Europe and the United States largely because of the emphasis they placed on higher technical education. In England, on the other hand, science was undervalued, and consequently Britain still suffers from a gulf between pure and applied science, a lack of appreciation of the value of a general training in scientific principles as opposed to the apprenticeship method of training in techniques, a belief that management and administration are not fit disciplines for formal study, and a 'development gap' between discovery and industrial application.

The Australian manufacturing industry produces largely for local markets, and therefore has not needed to develop new skills and techniques so much as to adapt existing ones. In fact, Encel argues, Australia 'may actually be over-supplied with skilled manpower, a large number of whom find their skills under-utilized by a derivative industrial structure'. On the other hand, our technical education has, after a good start, been relegated to a second-rate status, and our arbitration system has tended to freeze our ideas of the use of trained manpower in an out-dated mould, although he suggests that the outcome of the Professional Engineers' Case may lead to a re-thinking of our attitudes towards professional skills.

The consequence of our industrial history and traditions is that it has been left to government institutions to encourage the development of scientific and technical skills. The largest proportion of Australian scientists are employed by government bodies, and many of those employed in private firms are not in fact engaged on scientific work. Nor is there any indication that industry would employ more scientists if they were available.

The situation Encel reveals, therefore, is that, although there is a need for more scientists in industry, particularly in development, there is no evidence of an effective demand for them. Moreover, the number of Australian university engineering graduates, who might be expected to provide the need for development as opposed to research, has not grown in the years since the war at the same pace as the numbers graduating from other faculties.

Encel concludes that 'because the demand from the private sector is so relatively weak, the *total* pressure of demand is affected so that certain crucial areas of the public sector are in short supply'. Sir Frederick White, however, does not foresee any significant change in this pattern whereby government provides the greater part of the support for scientific endeavour, which he sees as characteristic of all scientific growth during this century.

Sir Frederick's theme is that, while pure science is merely the pursuit of knowledge for the sake of knowledge, with no other motive in view, science can also make a significant contribution to the welfare of society, and that in order to do so it must plan its efforts so as to concentrate on those fields which are likely to prove of the greatest benefit to the community.

In Australia, he sees the first of these fields as the agricultural and biological sciences, where our reputation is already high. However, we need both a better co-ordination of research in these fields, an expansion of purely biological studies, particularly at post-graduate level, and a greater concentration on purely local agricultural research so that the major findings can be more effectively and speedily applied in particular localities.

In industry, Sir Frederick sees a challenge to our scientific endeavours from our increased involvement as an industrial trading nation, and from the threat to our traditional exports posed by new products developed by overseas scientists. We need scientific work to improve our traditional products, and scientific effort in our manufacturing industry both to devise new products and to develop new methods which will make our production more efficient. To accomplish this, we need both the 'frontier' efforts of the pure scientists, both to develop talent and to create a favourable intellectual climate to the growth of science, and applied science to encourage the development of those new processes which will enable us to take the initiative on world markets instead of merely emulating our competitors.

Sir Frederick argues very strongly that this scientific effort must be controlled by the scientists themselves, who are best able to see what new areas of research are likely to yield profitable results, and who will work better in this fashion than if they are merely employed to tell the executives how they can produce what they have already decided to produce. Similarly, technological development will come from the employment within industry of scientists and technologists who understand the immediate problems and weaknesses of their particular industries and who also have the impulse to work from general principles to devise entirely new systems. But such a policy can only eventuate if the government takes the lead in supporting the research and encouraging industry to follow in its wake.

The immediate implications of these arguments for the schools would seem to be that we should continue the policy of expanding our science teaching so that we can produce these increasing numbers of pure and applied scientists who will be needed by government and industry if we are to continue our economic growth. However, this is not necessarily so. Manpower is still the cheapest of assets to buy, far cheaper to buy than to train, and there is no reason why we cannot import any number of scientists and technologists we may need to meet any future deficit of supply below demand. The very smallness of our industry can be an advantage, for we can afford to buy the scientists we need whereas the American and European giants need huge teams, and would have to raise the ante for all of them to withstand our bids. On the other hand, there is at present some evidence of over-supply, and an acknowledged drain of our scientists overseas, so it is doubtful whether the economic justification for increasing science training in the schools is very strong.

The strongest argument for improving the quality of science teaching in our schools is still purely educational. Science is of fundamental importance to our daily lives, not so much because of its contribution to our way of life as because of the explanation it offers of the world around us. It has become an indispensable part of the intellectual equipment of modern man. Yet its practical potential remains to a great extent inadequately utilized precisely because the average modern man does not understand enough about it. He regards it as some sort of magical god which will provide him with the wealth of Croesus, and precisely because he does regard it in this way he is unable to utilize its achievements to bring the results he so ardently desires.

An improvement in the quality of scientific education will probably lead incidentally to an increase in the numbers of trained scientists, although we should be planning for this to happen anyway as a product of an improvement in the quality and amount of general education. However, its most direct contribution to our economic well-being would be in the enhanced possibility it would bring of the community adopting the kind of program for the utilization of scientists which Sir Frederick envisages. Then it would not matter whether these scientists were home-grown or imported, for the general climate of the community would ensure a sufficient supply of the specialists we might need from time to time.

See also:
Lord James of Rusholme, 'The Education of the Scientist in the Modern World', *Technology,* the journal of the University of New South Wales, December 1967.

This lecture is not concerned with the supply of scientists to the economy, but with the education of men, not only scientists, for a scientific world. Lord James considers, among other matters, the moral and social relevance of science, its power as a humanizing discipline, and the essential role of the teacher. He also has some pertinent comments on the heresy of the two cultures, the false concern about the dangers of specialization, and the exaggerated deference paid to pure research.

J. A. J. Caine, 'The Employment of Scientists and Engineers', *Australian Journal of Education*, 1957. A straightforward statistical argument that demand will increase, together with suggestions for increasing the supply.

Further Reading

A. BOOKS

School and financial statistics, and some facts, have been taken from the *Official Year Book* of the Commonwealth of Australia, no. 52, 1966 and the *Review of Education in Australia*, 1955-62, A.C.E.R.

History:

A. G. Austin, *Australian Education 1788-1900*, Pitman, 1961. Church, State and Public Education in Colonial Australia.
A. G. Austin (ed.), *Selected Documents in Australian Education, 1788-1900*, Pitman, 1963.
Gwyneth M. Dow, *George Higinbotham: Church and State*, Pitman, 1964.
C. E. W. Bean, *Here, My Son*, Angus and Robertson, 1950. An account of the independent and other corporate boys' schools in Australia.

Society:

A. F. Davies and S. Encel (eds.), *Australian Society: A Sociological Introduction*. F. W. Cheshire, 1965. See also R. W. Connell, 'Class, School and Behaviour', *Politics*, November 1967.
W. J. Campbell, *Growing Up in Karribee*, A.C.E.R., 1962. A study of child growth with development in an Australian rural community.
W. F. Connell et al., *Growing Up in an Australian City*, A.C.E.R., 1959. A study of adolescents in Sydney.
O. A. Oeser and S. B. Hammond (eds.), *Social Structure and Personality in a City*, Routledge and Kegan Paul, 1954.
O. A. Oeser and F. E. Emery, *Social Structure and Personality in a Rural Community*, Routledge and Kegan Paul, 1954.
Craig McGregor, *Profile of Australia*, Hodder and Stoughton, 1966. A popular and personal account of modern Australian society.

The School:

Gwyneth M. Dow et al., *Parent, Pupil and School*, Cassell Australia, 1966. Victoria's education system.
P. J. McKeown and B. W. Hone (eds.), *The Independent School*, Oxford University Press, Melbourne, 1967. Papers presented to the Headmasters' Conference.

Language, Literature and Education:

Kornei Chukovsky, *From Two to Five*, translated and edited by Miriam Morton, Jacaranda Press, 1963, Australian edition.

Ernest Roe, *Teachers, Librarians and Children: A study of libraries in education*, F. W. Cheshire, 1965.
F. D. Flower, *Language and Education*, Longmans, 1966. An application of linguistic principles to English teaching, based on experience with further education classes in England.
David Holbrook, *English for Maturity*, Cambridge University Press, 1961. English in the secondary school.
David Holbrook, *The Secret Places*, Methuen, 1964. Essays on imaginative work in English teaching and on the culture of the child.
Brian Thompson (collector and editor), *Once Around the Sun: An anthology of poetry by Australian children,* Oxford University Press, Melbourne, 1966.
H. P. Schoenheimer (ed.), *Education through English*, F. W. Cheshire, 1967.
Iona and Peter Opie, *The Lore and Language of Schoolchildren*, Oxford, at the Clarendon Press, Paperback edition, 1967.
Charles D. Gaitskell, *Art, Education and Adolescence,* The Ryerson Press, Toronto, 1954.
Herbert Read, *Art and Education*, F. W. Cheshire, 1964.

General:

R. W. T. Cowan (ed.), *Education for Australians*, F. W. Cheshire, 1964.
W. F. Connell, *The Foundations of Secondary Education*, A.C.E.R., 1961.
Martin Mayer, *The Schools*, Bodley Head, 1961. A discussion of American schooling, with comparisons with practice in England and Europe. Mayer's observations are most pertinent to Australia.
John Wilkes (ed.), *Tertiary Education in Australia*, Australian Institute of Political Science (proceedings of 31st Summer School), Angus and Robertson, 1965.
J. A. Richardson and James Bowen (eds.), *The Preparation of Teachers in Australia*, F. W. Cheshire, 1967.
Jerome S. Bruner, *The Process of Education*, Vintage. An account of the deliberations which preceded the development of the new American science courses, and a summary of Piaget's theories of child development and their relevance for curriculum development.

Pamphlets:

Australian Labor Party, (Victoria), *Looking to the Future.* A plan for education in Victoria. Second edition, 1967.
Race Mathews, *Meeting the Crisis*, Victorian Fabian Society, 1967. Federal Aid for Education.

Novels:

Dan Reidy, *It's This Way*, Heinemann. Australian primary school.
Brian James, *The Advancement of Spencer Button*, Angus and Robertson. Australian education department.
G. W. Target, *The Teachers*, Penguin Books. An English school.
Bel Kaufman, *Up the Down Staircase*, Prentice-Hall. An American school.

B. ARTICLES

Note: Although the entries in this section are grouped under chapter headings, these should not be taken as definitive, as many topics occur in several chapters. Where possible, I have grouped all articles relating to a single topic under the same chapter, although some references may be more relevant to other parts of the book. For example, all references to examinations, selection and streaming are included under Chapter 1, although this topic is also considered in Chapters 8 and 9.

Chapter 1

G. W. Bassett, 'The Social Role of the Secondary School in Australia,' *Australian Journal of Education*, 1957.

The writer argues that the present state of professional opinion is such that our knowledge of adolescent behaviour is used to promote non-educational as much as educational objectives. 'Opposed to education is exploitation, the use of another person for personal or group advantage. Irrelevant to it are social prestige, and some forms of vocational training . . .' 'It is suggested that the dominant role of the secondary school in our society is that of an agent of social selection, and that our psychological knowledge of the adolescent, particularly of individual differences, has been used rather more to assist this role than to advance the education of this age group.'

James B. Conant, 'The Role of Education after the High School in Moving Freedom Forward', *Australian Journal of Education*, 1957.

Conant argues that education is a prime liberating force in the community and should be extended as widely as possible. As not all the population are interested in or suited to formal tertiary studies, and as the social disciplines are best handled by mature students, he advocates four-year liberal arts community colleges alongside the universities.

Alice Hoy, 'Present Trends and Problems in Secondary Education', *Australian Journal of Education*, 1957.

Joyce F. Wylie, 'Education and Planning for Freedom: A Discussion of the Views of Karl Mannheim', *Australian Journal of Education*, 1957.

Mannheim believed that a modern democracy must deliberately plan for freedom, and that education had a crucial role to play, as an integrative force in the community, as a means of nourishing a creative intelligentsia, and as a means of spreading culture without diluting it.

Hugh Campbell, 'Tension in Planning: Karl Mannheim', *Australian Journal of Education*, 1958.

Campbell offers a conservative critique of the paradox inherent in Mannheim's doctrine of 'planning for freedom'.

E. R. Wyeth, 'The Case for the Junior College', *Australian Journal of Education,* 1958.

This essay argues, mainly on the basis of the phenomenon of university failure rates, in favour of a two-year, pre-university college which would serve both to free schools from university control and to ensure a better preparation for university studies. It is of relevance both to the Tasmanian matriculation-college experiment and to the Victorian controversy over senior high schools.

M. Balson, 'The Philosophical Vacuum in Australian Education', *Australian Journal of Education*, 1960.

This essay offers an introductory account of the educational relevance of the philosophical schools of pragmatism, idealism and realism.

Salvatore D'Urso, 'Mass Society and Educational Goals', *Australian Journal of Education*, 1967.

In this article, D'Urso uses some of the concepts of Mannheim, Wright Mills, Dewey, Mumford and Brameld in his consideration of the nature of modern society and the proper role of education within it. He agrees with Mannheim that the cultivation of the individual personality is an inadequate statement for the aims of modern education, which must endeavour to cultivate the wholeness of man within society, to equip him to overcome social and personal alienation by recovering the social role which enables him to control his environment instead of being controlled by it. 'Our time of cultural confusion demands the widest understanding, particularly among those entrusted with the education of adolescents, of the inextricable connection between private aspirations of happiness and the great issues of the day; . . . purposeful work in education serving the quest for the individuality of learners is bound to be frustrated so long as we refuse to acknowledge the ethos and forces of the mass society within which our work is increasingly conducted; . . . educators should not fear to become . . . "the unacknowledged legislators of the world", at a time when the future of man is being seriously questioned.'

D'Urso argues that education can fulfil its role by adopting the 'core curriculum' approach (see W. E. Connell, *Foundations of Secondary Education*, A.C.E.R., 1961, Chapter 5), and by ensuring that courses of teacher education are integrated and inspired by a philosophy which confronts the critical issues of our age. With the latter of these ideas I would agree, but I remain suspicious of the core-curriculum as a necessary approach to the problem of providing a meaningful education. I believe that it is likely to lead to a concentration on the educational structure instead of a grappling with the educational problems. Properly educated teachers should be able to approach these problems through their individual disciplines in a manner which is more likely to be meaningful than an approach worked out by a team of people with different backgrounds and different degrees of commitment.

A. M. Badcock, 'The Vocational Fallacy in State Secondary Education in Victoria, 1900-1925', in E. L. French (ed.), *Melbourne Studies in Education, 1965*, Melbourne University Press.

Badcock provides a salutary account of a misdirected attempt to relate secondary education to local vocational interests, and incidentally reveals a good deal of the attitude towards public secondary education when it was established at the turn of the century.

J. J. Pratt, 'The General Pattern and Development of Australian Education Since World War II', W. D. Neal, 'Developments in Secondary Education', W. Wood, 'Education for Exceptional Children', P. Hughes, 'Curriculum Development in Primary Schools', H. S. Williams, 'Technical Education', *Australian Journal of Education*, Decennial Issue, 1966.

Each of these five articles gives a factual survey of current developments and issues in its particular field. Incidentally, 'exceptional children' is the current euphonism for children who are in any way handicapped.

Sol Encel, 'Policy and Politics', S. Murray-Smith, 'Dead End: Outlook for Youth in the Sixties', Joyce Wylie, 'Education and Social Class', J. R. McLeod and C. R. Brown, 'The Origins of Literacy', *Outlook*, February 1962.

These four articles, together with editorial comment, form a special survey of 'Crisis and Opportunity in the Schools' in which the practical educational implications of a socialist philosophy are examined.

C. Sanders, 'University Selection: Its Theory, History and Psychology', *Australian Journal of Education*, 1957.

Sanders provides a comprehensive study of the methods used for selecting university students in Australia, and their success in comparison with methods used overseas. Sanders concludes that the present forms of selection are superior to psychological and attainment tests at present available, and that in combination with first-year university results they provide a reasonable correlation with eventual success. He points out, however, that there is too much variation for them to be regarded as adequate predictors of final academic results in regard to the individual, except in the case of a few outstanding students. It should be noted that this study was written before university quotas were widely imposed.

L. C. D. Kemp, 'Ability and Attainment', *Australian Journal of Education*, 1958.

Kemp examines the concepts of general intelligence, or IQ, and the validity and variation of scores.

F. J. Olsen, 'Failure in First Year University Examinations', *Australian Journal of Education*, 1957.

Two of the three major reasons for failure which Kemp discusses lie in inadequate preparation at school. However, Kemp does not consider whether this inadequacy is not due to the kind of demands which are made on schools by university examinations.

J. A. Keats, 'The Development of Abilities', *Australian Journal of Education*, 1957.

Keats compares two approaches to the way in which children's abilities develop. One approach suggests a progressive differentiation or specialization of abilities, while the other, based on Piaget, suggests that there is a progressive development of the kind of operations the child can handle. Both theories emphasize the danger of specializing too early.

F. N. Cox and S. B. Hammond, 'Educational Streaming and Test Anxiety in Children', *Australian Journal of Education*, 1964.

This study presents evidence based on a Melbourne study that there is an increase in test anxiety among children in the lowest stream in their public examination (fourth secondary) year. On the other hand, there is some indication of a diminution of test anxiety among students in the upper streams.

D. M. Toomey, 'Styles of Thinking and Learning in Education', *Australian Journal of Education*, 1964.

Basing his work on the theories developed by Bernstein and others about linguistic deprivation, Toomey argues for school reform to meet the needs of children whose home and language background does not fit them for formal education. He questions the automatic value of raising the school leaving age.

F. N. Cox, 'A survey of streaming in two Australian schools (*Child Development*, Vol. 3, No. 2)', reported in *New Society*, 4 October 1962.

'Streaming produced higher levels of anxiety . . . in . . . B stream than in A stream.' General anxiety (drive) was not affected, but anxiety related to classroom situations was markedly increased, particularly among older children.

Derek Miller, 'Seven Ages of Man (III)—Adolescence', *New Society*, 19 November 1964.

S. S. Dunn, 'Examinations', in R. W. T. Cowan (ed.), *Education for Australians*, F. W. Cheshire, 1964.

A survey of the theory and value of examinations and testing.

J. W. B. Douglas, 'Streaming by Ability', *New Society*, 6 February 1964.

This study suggests that at present streaming improves overall school results, but that this is because the better students improve while the students in the lower streams actually regress. The author draws attention to the class bias in streaming.

D. F. Swift, 'Who Passes the Eleven Plus', *New Society*, 5 March 1964.

Swift claims that the best way of ensuring your child's success in an English primary school is to be a pessimistic lower middle class clerk.

Brian Stanfield, 'The Argument Against a Catholic School System: a Summary', *Dialogue*, Vol. I, No. 2.

Stanfield marshals the arguments, from overseas and local sources, which state the Catholic position against a church school system. The arguments are historical—that the needs of a modern society are different from those of the society for which church schools were established, theological, that the schools are not serving the mission of the church, and educational, that the schools are not serving their general or religious educational purpose.

Gregory Meere, 'The Arguments Against a Catholic School System Re-assessed', Kieran Geaney, 'The Catholic School in Our Times', Peter Fensham, 'On First Looking into Father Ryan's Thesis', *Dialogue*, Vol. II, No. 1.

The first two of these essays state a case for a church school system, in reply to Stansfield and his sources. Both seem to me to depend on the assumption that secular humanist ideas must prevail in a state school system, an assumption of doubtful validity in the present context, if it is taken to mean that students at a state school are influenced, consciously or unconsciously, to adopt this outlook, and one which ignores a point made explicit by Fensham in his essay, that a massive Catholic involvement in state education would qualitatively change that education.

Fensham's essay is a comment on a detailed study of the actuality of Catholic schools—N. J. Ryan, 'Catholic Higher Education in Victoria', unpublished Ph.D. thesis, Melbourne University, 1966. This thesis forms part of an as yet incomplete study of the scholastic and general performance of students from Catholic schools who matriculated during the years 1950-58. The published thesis refers only to matriculation and university results. The findings include that Catholics as a whole do as well as others at matriculation, but that this masks a poorer performance by Catholic girls, particularly in science, than Catholic boys or than girls from other schools. Students from Catholic schools have a difficult first university year, but after that they more than hold their own as a group.

Helen G. Palmer, 'Free, Compulsory and Protestant', *Outlook*, June 1961.

In this article Helen Palmer traces the weakening of the secular nature of state schools and the steady intrusion of Protestant teaching in the form of religious instruction, chaplains, and religious studies in the syllabus. The generally sound argument is slightly weakened by the repetition of the fallacy that the secular clause was introduced into the original educational acts as a matter of principle. Certainly, the more enlightened thinkers of the time believed in the principles of liberty for the individual conscience, but secularism was adopted by the majority as a necessary expedient to get any form of public education.

Helen G. Palmer, 'Free, Compulsory and Tolerant', *Outlook*, October 1964.

A discussion of the attempt to introduce general and comparative religious studies into the N.S.W. social studies syllabus, and of the reactions of the churches to this move towards tolerance.

Alan Barcan, 'The Terms of State Aid', *Outlook*, August 1965.

Barcan considers overseas experience of aid to church schools, in Scotland, France, Holland, England and 'new lands'. Useful for reference.

J. R. Lawry, 'Third Choice?' *Outlook*, August 1965.

After a brief examination of the competing positions in the Catholic church, Lawry puts forward an argument for providing a sufficient subsidy for private schools to bring them up to minimum acceptable standard.

Alan Barcan, 'State Aid in Retrospect', *Dissent*, Spring 1964.

This article traces the history of state aid, direct and indirect, in Australia, and concludes with a plea for a policy of aid for independently but democratically controlled schools. He argues that these need not be elitist schools if they provide scholarships, but this seems just another form of combining an elite of wealth with an elite of ability.

Ronald King, 'Grammar School Values', *New Society*, 1 July 1965.

King presents evidence that the effect of the school on the students' cultural and moral values was nil, but that they 'rapidly learn the ways of the world of work and the attributes and conditions of success in it'.

D. P. Derham, 'Problems of University Selection: the Story of a Quota', *Ormond Papers*, 1967.

In this account of the design and working of a selection system for the Melbourne University Law School, Professor Derham reports discouragingly on the predictive value of a specially prepared admission test of ability, and encouragingly on the reliability of matriculation examination results. It should, however, be pointed out that the best selective test merely limits the amount of injustice by ensuring that those with the best statistical chance are admitted. It will always exclude numbers who would in fact have proved most successful if they had been given a chance. However, Professor Derham shows that first-year university results can give a strong indication of the likelihood of eventual success.

Chapter 2

J. B. Mays, 'Education and the Urban Child', reviewed in *New Society*, 18 October 1962.

This review quotes some of the conclusions of a book which examined the question of why some students lose all interest in school after the age of about thirteen. A survey of the inner Liverpool area suggested that the reasons were buildings, irrelevant subjects, but, above all, uninterested parents. It cites the case of one headmaster who was able to enlist the co-operation of parents and largely overcome the problem. 'The distrust and timidity which at present characterize the attitude of many teachers towards collaboration with the home are major obstacles in the way of progress.' (Mays.)

Jerome S. Bruner, 'The Growth of Mind', and 'Learning and Thinking', republished in Judy F. Rosenblith and Wesley Allinsmith (eds.), *The Causes of Behavior*, II, 2nd edition, Allyn and Bacon, Boston.

In the first of these articles, Bruner examines how man thinks both as an individual and as a member of a society, and traces the educational implications. In the second, he starts from the idea that we learn in order to think, i.e., that we discover generic principles as a basis for future action. He then considers in some detail how classroom teaching can be organized to this end, concluding with the idea that it depends on so organizing educational resources that the maximum use is made of the experienced teachers who alone can do this.

Ronald King, 'Grammar School Values', *New Society*, 1 July 1965. See further reading notes for Chapter I.

Ezra Robert Wyeth, Wastage—Interim Report. Melbourne University School of Education, unpublished pamphlet, 1955.

J. C. Neild, 'The School Community and Child Development—Notes Towards the Development of a Theory of Educational Relations', *Australian Journal of Education*, 1960 and 1961.

This essay commences with a depressing survey of the social climate of secondary schools. Nield portrays an 'affectional desert' of inhumanity, negative discipline and formal teaching which produces on the part of the pupils a general resistance to learning and within the school an environment hostile to child growth. He argues that the school must be deliberately designed as a 'transitional community' which will accept the fact that childhood is a time of conflict, and will provide the child, through its syllabus and authority, with support as he grapples with his conflicts. ' . . . a full organization of the community aspects of schooling will provide a varied pattern of relationships that can support maturation at each of a number of levels.' He indicates how this could be done in terms of the teacher's role towards the students, the students' function in the conduct of the school, and the symbolic patterning of school activities.

D. K. Wheeler, 'The Adolescent at School in Western Australia', *Australian Journal of Education*, 1962.

This study surveys the attitudes of High School students to school and study, and is slightly more encouraging than Nield's remarks, although it is not dealing with precisely the same question.

Chapter 3

Lord James of Rusholme, 'The Education of the Scientist in the Modern World', *Technology*, the Journal of the University of New South Wales, December 1967.

This article comprises the second Wallace Wurth Memorial Lecture given at the University of New South Wales in the year of its publication. Its author is Vice-Chancellor of the University of York. His concern is with the education of men, not just scientists, for a world in which science is shaping, not only the material environment, but our way of understanding ourselves and our surroundings. He considers, among other matters, the moral and social relevance of science, its power as a humanizing discipline, and the necessary role of the teacher. He also has some pertinent comments on the misleading heresy of the two cultures, the false concern about the dangers of specialization, and the exaggerated deference paid to pure research. He notes that the idea of a special scientific method of thinking is itself dangerous. The mind of the physicist works in just the same way as the mind of the historian or the economist. He claims that the gap between the disciplines will not be overcome by merely teaching each specialist a smattering of other fields, but by extending his knowledge of his own field to understand its relevance to others.

Lord James is, of course, talking about university education, including the education of science teachers, but to a great extent his principles apply also in secondary schools. At this level, the students may not have specialized to the extent that they will have in a university, but this in no way removes the obligation of the teacher to show them the furthest implications of his subject.

Lord James, however, does perhaps lean rather too far in the direction of claiming that science is just another of the many forms that the activity of the human mind has taken. Although probably all intellectual and artistic endeavour includes the element of finding patterns in our experience, there is an essential difference between the generalizing activity of science, which seeks to explain in terms of principles the concrete facts of what has happened (and possibly to predict what will happen, although philosophers differ on the role of prediction in science) and the activity of the artist who seeks to convey in its uniqueness the wholeness of a particular moment of experience.

G. C. Morris, 'The Development of Science Subjects in Australian Secondary Education', *Australian Journal of Education*, 1964.

P. W. Hughes, 'The Changing Face of Mathematics', *Australian Journal of Education*, 1960.

C. E. Moorhouse, 'Technical and Technological Education in Australia', *Australian Journal of Education*, 1960.

G. R. Meyer, 'Factors Accompanying the Scientific Interest of a Selected Group of English Secondary Pupils', *Australian Journal of Education*, 1961.

Meyer finds that home factors are most important in the development of a scientific interest. Among girls, however, the attitudes of society about the proper role of women seem to be the crucial factor in inhibiting the growth of such an interest. He finds no relationship between interest and ability at science, but he does find significant relationships between the interest in science and an interest in mathematics and in English/history type subjects. He suggests that an interest in science is best promoted in the school by encouraging students to solve problems independently, by using books, experimentation, or consulting experts, rather than by too readily answering their questions.

G. R. Meyer, 'Factors Related to Scientific Attitudes Within the Secondary Schools of an Australian City', *Australian Journal of Education*, 1963.

This Australian study comes to much the same conclusions as his English study. However, he finds less resistance to science among Australian girls. The rank order of preferences for scientific subjects is chemistry, zoology, physics, biology, botany, geology, physiology.

The girls in this sample chose zoology first, the boys chemistry. The reasons given for the choices were less vocational than in the London sample. More frequently, the Australian students chose the subject for its intrinsic interest.

G. R. Meyer, 'New Concepts in Science Education in Secondary Schools', *Australian Journal of Education*, 1965.

Meyer acknowledges the advances made by the new science programs in the United Kingdom (Nuffield project) and the United States (National Science Foundation—P.S.S.C., etc., see Bruner, *Process of Education*, C.U.P.), which have stripped away trivia and concentrated on generalizations and principles. However, he considers that they are still at fault in keeping the individual sciences separate. He then discusses the New South Wales general science course, introduced under the Wyndham scheme. He believes this integrated approach meets the needs of cultivating scientific principles and of catering for the individual differences among students. He concludes with a discussion of examination and evaluation methods which will be in keeping with the aims of the syllabus.

Appointments Board of the University of Sydney, *Annual Report to June 30, 1967*.

This report gives a detailed statistical survey of courses and employment of first degree graduates of the University of Sydney. Among the more alarming features it reveals are the lack of interest among private employers in university graduates, apart from specialists, and a continuing shortfall of engineers.

Sir Fred Schonell, 'Higher Education and National Progress', *University Gazette* (Melbourne), February, 1967.

Chapter 4

E. J. Tapp, 'Some Thoughts on the Teaching of History', *Australian Journal of Education*, 1962.

Tapp considers the reasons for teaching history, and some ways of giving it more bite and depth.

Alec Allinson, 'We Starve Our Pupils of Literature', *Outlook*, April 1965.

Allinson outlines the inhumanizing and inefficient methods in vogue for cultivating literacy, and indicates an alternative. A fuller account of his methods and ideas can be found in *The Secondary Teacher*, 1964, and in H. Schoenheimer (ed.), *Education Through English*.

Ernest Roe, 'Education in 1990', *Outlook*, April 1965.

In this article, Roe answers the question 'Beyond literacy, what?' in terms of the technological changes which will have transformed our ideas of learning, working and leisure by 1990.

M. Balson, 'The Acquisition of Prejudice Through Programmed Learning', *The Programmed Instruction Bulletin*, May 1967.

In this article Balson gives an account of the 'Javas' experiment which I refer to in this chapter and again, in more detail, in Chapter 7.

Chapter 5

W. J. Campbell, 'Impact of Television on the Primary School Child', *Australian Journal of Education*, 1965.

Although Campbell's survey of the research evidence does not disclose any harmful effects arising from children's television viewing, he recognizes that there could well be incipient trends not yet discernible. He does not consider possible effects on children's language, mythology, or method of thinking, which could well be more important than the more easily measurable behaviour patterns he notices. Nevertheless, he feels that the fact that so many programs are merely time-wasting, and that they do contain positively harmful elements, presents a problem which teachers have a professional responsibility to confront, both by taking direct action to influence the content of programs, and by including television in their teaching programs, not as a teaching medium, but as a topic for study. He makes a very good distinction between the elements of television which are conventionally criticised, such as violence, which cannot be shown to be harmful, and the significantly dangerous feature of television programs, tension and anxiety, and points out that constructive measures will depend on a sophisticated analysis of the medium and its effects.

Chapter 6

N. F. Dufty, 'Vocational Choices of 13-14 Year Old Males in Relation to Intelligence and Reasons for Job Choice', *Australian Journal of Education*, 1960.

This Western Australian study found that a greater proportion of the students choosing science and medicine do so because of the intrinsic nature of the job than do students choosing other professional careers. The only professional career to attract a greater number for this reason is teaching. However, science and medicine considered separately rank low among professional careers. Public service and selling attract the least able of those wishing to enter clerical occupations, and banking the most able. Pay and security are the most important reasons for choosing clerical occupations, but pay alone is important to those who choose unskilled occupations, who do not consider security important. Mechanical and electrical technicians are the most popular skilled trades, and a considerable number chose 'adventure occupations' such as aviation, the police force and the services. The level of aspiration is considerably above the likely level of occupational attainment, and Dufty considers that the professional occupations are over-selected from the standpoint of the likely needs of the market. However, this may be a valuable portent for a society in which the service industries are likely to expand most rapidly during the next decades. The survey reveals that, when the group is considered as a whole, the nature of the work is the most important reason for choice. Dufty finds that the less-well-known trades attract less candidates than they need, while the best-known are over-supplied. He suggests that more information of these trades would serve a useful purpose. For a discussion of how this might be done, see Connell's discussion of the 'Core Curriculum' in *The Foundations of Secondary Education*, A.C.E.R., 1961, Chapter 5.

N. F. Dufty, 'The Characteristics of 13-14 Year Old Males Choosing Skilled Trades as Occupations', *Australian Journal of Education*, 1966.

This follow-up study compares a sample of those choosing skilled trades with a sample of all the others. Again, work type is the most important single factor for both groups, with pay and security next. Security was, however, slightly less important to the trades group than to the others.

Gwyneth M. Dow, *Parent, Pupil and School,* Cassell, Australia, 1966, pp. 168-177.

In these pages, a very concise summary is presented of the changes in employment demand and opportunity in Australia and overseas, and the educational implications of these changes.

S. Murray-Smith, *A History of Technical Education in Australia: with special reference to the period before 1914*. Unpublished Ph.D. thesis, University of Melbourne, 1966.

Chapter 7

K. C. Dempsey and J. Pandey, 'School and Religion', *Australian Journal of Education*, 1967.

This study of students entering the University of New England in 1965 shows that students from Catholic schools show a significantly higher degree of religious observance than those from Protestant and State schools, while the only significant difference between the latter groups is that more of the former state school students attend church weekly. However, the authors point out that these differences cannot be directly attributed to school influence, as the Catholic church puts a higher value than the Protestant churches upon formal religious observation. Nor can any conclusions be drawn from these results about the influence of religious belief or school training on general behaviour and moral standards.

A. W. Anderson, 'Personality Scores of Western Australian University Students Entering from State and Private Schools', *Australian Journal of Education*, 1960.

This study also suggested certain personality differences between students from Catholic, non-Catholic independent, and government schools. Among the findings were that entrants from Roman Catholic schools were, as a whole, more radical than those from church schools; that male entrants from government schools were of higher intelligence, more radical, and more self-sufficient, and lower in sensitivity and guilt-awareness than entrants from the other two groups of schools; that female entrants were higher in intelligence, radicalism, sensitivity and adventurousness and lower in paranoid tendencies. The males from government schools were less adventurous than those from independent schools. Anderson suggests that, although the differences may be attributable to differences in secondary school environments, his study involved no measures of home background and social and cultural differences which could equally well account for the personality differences. However, it would at least be reasonable to assume, on the basis of these two studies, that, whatever the prime cause, there are slight personality differences between the groups of students in different kinds of schools, and that the schools would at least reinforce these differences.

R. W. Connell, 'The Origins of Political Attitudes', *Politics*, November 1967.

In this article Connell surveys the theories of the origin of political attitudes, and then sketches the development of such attitudes in Australian adolescents. The role of the school would seem to be fairly minor, and limited to inculcating simplistic reverence for the nation and hero figures in early years, and later providing the data from which attitudes are formed. On the evidence, it would seem that Australian teachers could afford to be a lot more active in promoting political thinking without running into any danger of being responsible for mass indoctrination.

J. D. McCaughey, 'Tradition and Freedom in Education', in E. L. French (ed.), *Melbourne Studies in Education*, 1963, Melbourne University Press.

McCaughey bases an argument for the proper inclusion of religion in the normal school curriculum on three recognitions: that education furthers traditional disciplines, and that religion is one of these traditions; that there is a need to maintain the autonomy of each tradition; and that neutrality is the enemy of true freedom.

This study is one of five lectures printed in this volume on the problem of 'Objectivity and Neutrality in Public Education'. All are worth reading, but McCaughey gives the most cogent arguments in favour of pure religion within the curriculum.

Mary Raphael Leavey, 'The Relevance of St. Thomas Aquinas for Australian Education', in E. L. French (ed.), *Melbourne Studies in Education*, 1963, Melbourne University Press.

Sister Mary Leavey presents a detailed critique of liberalism as a foundation for an educational philosophy, and contrasts it with the philosophy of St. Thomas Aquinas. Her essay concludes with a criticism of Catholic schools in Australia for failing to institutionalize the 'Catholic Idea'. 'There is no community of scholarship . . . to present the Idea, there is no Institute of Catholic education, there is no national Catholic journal of education.' Since Sister Mary Leavey wrote this, the last deficiency at least has been remedied with the foundation of *Dialogue*, although this journal serves more than the Catholic community.

Kenneth Orr, 'Moral Training in the Boy Scout Movement', in E. L. French (ed.), *Melbourne Studies in Education*, 1963, Melbourne University Press.

Kenneth Orr, 'Social Training in the Boy Scout Movement', in E. L. French (ed.), *Melbourne Studies in Education*, 1965, Melbourne University Press.

Chapter 8

C. Sanders, 'The Profession of Education', *Australian Journal of Education*, 1959.

W. B. O'Connell, 'Profession of Education and the Primary Schools', *Australian Journal of Education*, 1959.

W. C. Radford, 'The Purpose and Aim of a Primary Teachers' College'.

These three papers discuss the function of teacher education on the basis of the actual task of a teacher, and Radford adds some interesting data on the limitations of people entering teachers' Colleges. They are concerned with the problems of general and technical (or professional) training in teacher education, and with the need to give the future teacher an understanding of his subject matter, of the psychology of his students and the dynamics of the classroom, of scholarship, and of the values and life of his society, for nothing less is sufficient for the task he has to undertake.

R. D. Goodman, 'The Will-o'-the Wisp of Professional Status', *Australian Journal of Education*, 1960.

By the criteria of training, code of ethics, professional organization and income, teachers are not and cannot become members of a profession in the traditional sense. One insuperable obstacle is their usual status as public service employees. However, the older professions are in a condition of change, and teachers may aspire to emulate the new models.

Goodman's discussion would have been more valuable if he had made comparisons with other professions whose members are usually employees, such as social work, nursing, or engineering.

L. C. D. Kemp, 'Research on Teaching Competence', *Australian Journal of Education*, 1958.

This essay shows a change in the interests of researchers from pedagogy to group dynamics, but reveals no useful results. A study of teaching incompetence might prove more fruitful.

Robert Nelson Bush, 'The Teacher-Pupil Relationships in Australian Secondary Schools', *Australian Journal of Education*, 1958.

N. R. Anderson, 'Training as a Factor in Raising the Status of Teachers', *Australian Journal of Education*, 1958.

This paper discusses some of the reasons for raising the level of teacher training, and the kind of training which would result.

G. W. Bassett, 'The Occupational Background of Teachers', *Australian Journal of Education*, 1958.

G. W. Bassett, 'Teachers and their Children', *Australian Journal of Education*, 1961.

These studies suggest that teaching is usually chosen as an avenue of upward social movement, and is not favoured as an occupation by many children from homes in the higher occupational groups such as professional, business and administrative. They show some family continuity in teaching, but this could conceal a three-generation movement from unskilled to primary teaching to secondary teaching to a higher profession.

H. H. Penny, 'Trends and Problems in Teacher Training', *Australian Journal of Education*, 1958.

L. W. Shears, 'The Training of Teachers for Primary Schools', *Australian Journal of Education*, 1958.

The first of these articles discusses the problem of teacher training from a historical and philosophic point of view, although in rather general terms; the second proceeds from the problems of bricks and mortar by way of administration to a consideration of the aims and control of teacher training. Both authors wrote as Principals of Teachers' Colleges, and neither examines many fundamental assumptions. However, they represent practical approaches to the problem.

J. C. Greenhalgh, 'Problems in Curriculum Development', *Australian Journal of Education*, 1957.

This account of the revision of a primary school curriculum in Queensland illustrates the normal departmental procedure. The most interesting aspect is the way in which professional responsibility is interpreted in a kind of pseudo-democratic fashion which results in a union representative on the revising committee and in the response to a questionnaire seeking teachers' opinions being used as prime data for the revision. The only principles used in the revision appear to have been the kind of idealistic generalizations which pass in Australia for a statement of aims, and there is no evidence that the revising committee felt under any obligation to employ the services of academic experts in the field they were planning.

D. F. Miller, Review of *Parent, Pupil and School, Dialogue*, Winter 1967.

This review is particularly valuable for its remarks on departmental committees which represent the power structure rather than the experts.

W. F. Connell, 'Portrait of a Teacher', *Australian Journal of Education*, 1966.

This is a discussion of a report on 'The Teaching Profession in Australia', which was presented to the College of Education. Connell discusses the problems revealed in the report and suggests action which could be taken to remedy them.

G. F. Berkeley, 'What the Statistical Survey Reveals', A. W. Jones, 'From Secondary Student to Secondary Teacher', in P. H. Partridge and others (eds.), *Teachers in Australia*, F. W. Cheshire for A.C.E.R. Melbourne, 1966.

The first of these essays examines some of the more significant findings of the College of Education report referred to above. The points he raises include that the average age of all teachers is 35.2, but of educational administrators it is 55.3, that approximately one-third of teachers have four or less years experience, another third between five and fourteen years, and the remainder from fourteen to upwards of twenty-five. Forty-one per cent of all teachers have one year or less of training, and about as many have only two years.

Jones discusses a small group of students who went through teacher training in the middle 'fifties. He discusses the criteria of selection, college and university performance and teaching career. The group as a whole showed a three-fold improvement in the number of credits obtained at university as opposed to public examinations, but Jones remains doubtful of the wisdom of encouraging honours students to enter teaching. He feels they are too narrowly specialist, and prefers the all-rounder. He cites as evidence the unsatisfactory records of honors students at school as students and as teachers. This record may of course be due to the schools rather than to the honors men.

Tyrrell Burgess, 'Not Enough Teachers', *New Society*, 19 July 1964.

Burgess suggests that forecasts of a solution to the teacher shortage are fallacious, and suggests ways of starting from the existing supply and fitting it to meet the demand.

Chapter 9

P. J. Fensham, 'The Distribution of Commonwealth Scholarships in Victoria', *Australian Journal of Education*, 1965.

The following table, extracted from Fensham's tables, shows the scholarship winners from each class of school as a percentage of the total number of students in the form from which the winners came.

Commonwealth Scholarship—1964. Winners as % of all students in form.

	Fourth Form	*Fifth Form*	*Sixth Form*
Government schools			
Metropolitan	8.5%	13.0%	14.5%
Country	5.0%	9.0%	10.0%
Total government	7.0%	11.5%	13.0%
Roman Catholic schools	10.0%	15.0%	16.0%
Independent schools, non-Catholic	16.5%	18.5%	18.0%
All schools	9.0%	13.5%	15.0%

Distribution of pupils and of tertiary scholarships—1964. Percentage of total in each category.

	Victoria		*New South Wales*	
	Pupils	*Scholarships*	*Pupils*	*Scholarships*
Government schools	54.5%	47.5%	64.0%	63.0%
Roman Catholic schools	19.0%	20.0%	22.5%	23.0%
Non-R.C. independent schools	26.5%	32.0%	13.5%	14.0%

(Tables quoted by permission of the author.)

The Fourth and Fifth Form scholarships were awarded to students in these forms on the basis of a special external examination. The Sixth Form scholarship is the Commonwealth Tertiary Scholarship, awarded on the basis of the marks obtained by each student in his best three subjects at the Matriculation examination.

Professor Fensham examines a number of factors which could influence these figures, and it is difficult to draw firm conclusions. Factors which could influence these figures would include transfer of brighter students to independent schools, the time the schools have been operating at public examination level, the home background and ambitions of the students. However, after making due allowance for these possibilities, it would still seem that the student at the independent school has a significantly better chance of winning one of these awards, and that his chances would be considerably decreased if he should attend a Catholic school, a metropolitan high school, or, worst of all, a country high school. The comparison with New South Wales is perhaps the most revealing feature of these figures, for there is no reason to assume that independent schools in that state are of a lower standard than those in Victoria, and thus we must assume that the government schools are far better north than south of the Murray.

Father N. J. Ryan's thesis (see Further Reading List, Ch. 1) reaches similar conclusions regarding the relative performance of Catholics and others at sixth form level.

It should be noted that Fensham makes more detailed analyses of the results than I have indicated here.

D. F. Miller, 'The Culture of Social Quiescence', *Dissent*, Winter 1966.

Miller argues that political and social apathy in Australia is due to various features of our educational system.

Ronald Deadman, 'Parents Unite', *New Statesman*, 20 March 1964.

Deadman argues that there should be more parent participation in the life and affairs of the school because children need the backing of both parents and teachers, and schools need the interest of parents to force politicians to improve school conditions.

Index